# THE HOODED HAWK

*By the Same Author*

FRANÇOIS VILLON: *A Documented Study*
KING SPIDER
ON STRAW, AND OTHER CONCEITS
THE STUFFED OWL: *An Anthology of Bad Verse*
(with Charles Lee)
WELCOME TO ALL THIS
CHARLES OF EUROPE
A CHRISTMAS BOOK (with G. C. Heseltine)
THE NONSENSIBUS
RONSARD

JAMES BOSWELL

*Portrait by Reynolds.*

# THE
# HOODED HAWK

## OR

## The Case of Mr. Boswell

D. B. WYNDHAM LEWIS

LONGMANS, GREEN AND CO.

NEW YORK

1947

LONGMANS, GREEN AND CO., INC.
55 Fifth Avenue, New York 3

THE HOODED HAWK

Copyright • 1947
By D. B. Wyndham Lewis

FIRST EDITION

Printed in the United States of America
Van Rees Press • New York

TO

EDITH SITWELL,

FAVOURITE OF THE NINE

# CONTENTS

# INTRODUCTORY

Even before Colonel Ralph Isham of New York revealed a few years ago the secrets of the ebony cabinet of Auchinleck, no lover of Boswell's golden and imperishable masterpiece who had also studied his correspondence with his friend Temple could be unaware that he was what the French would call an *étourdi*, or Harley Street a borderline case: an eccentric; a scatterbrain; in the graphic folk-phrase, something of a crackpot. While his private papers amply confirm this impression, they show also that if Johnson's Boswell, like Luther and Swift, is a gift to the Freudians, who could hardly hesitate to label him a maladjusted introvert with unbalanced thyroid and pituitaries, his condition can be, and has been, grossly exaggerated. All his life Boswell was teetering on the verge of complete sanity; no madder, I suggest, than a thousand retired British colonels preoccupied today with the secret of the Pyramids and the Lost Anglo-Saxon Tribes of Israel, and infinitely more attractive. Moreover, his aspirations were noble. With all his vanity he lacked *hubris* and that rancid spiritual pride which is the doom of the dons. He yearned and struggled regularly for goodness. Like the wild poet Dafydd ap Gwilym in Llanbadarn parish church, he was regularly dismayed at finding himself, when the bell rang at the Elevation, with 'my face to some dainty wench and only the nape of my neck turned to the dear God.' Not without a curiously appropriate symbolism is his family crest, the hooded hawk, under the motto *Vraye Foy*. James Boswell is perpetually

1

attempting to soar into the empyrean, clogged by his tirings, and perpetually falling to earth again, baffled; and perpetually in his own imagination he is the passage-hawk in yarak, free of the air and 'plumed to the very point.'

That mental instability which is the dominant Boswell note is not necessarily a handicap, of course. Many academic phoenixes have extremely peculiar habits,[1] and semi-lunatics like Blake and Christopher Smart have endeared themselves to the English for all time. But in Boswell's case a touch of eccentricity took an alarming form which the world can never forgive. Other men of eminence may love wine to excess and run after women as indefatigably as he; other men of note may possess an absurd vanity and a devouring passion for the limelight. But either a sleepless discretion veils their lapses altogether from the public gaze, or—as in the case of a modern statesman found dancing an unsteady farruca in a London hotel cloakroom after a public dinner—the occasion is deemed private and the eyes of the world are tactfully averted. Alas, tact and discretion Boswell, like Peter Pan, never knew. His candour is appalling. There is no spark of malice in his nature, but, unlike the rest of us, he simply cannot keep his artless mouth shut. A world in which human figures swim grandly to and fro like icebergs, nine-tenths of their real feelings and reactions carefully submerged and invisible (or what becomes of the social fabric?) is hardly likely to overlook lapses from the code like Boswell's. The malign disapproval of censors who can overlook any sin but sincerity follows him round perpetually like a cold white spotlight.

Montaigne has said it, as many have remarked, for all mankind. 'Certes c'est un subject merveilleusement vain, divers, et ondoyant que l'homme; il est malaysé d'y fonder jugement constant et uniforme.'[2] Man is frivolous, complicated, changeful, and elusive as flowing water, and to draw a clear conclusion from him is difficult. Notwithstanding which immortal truth more arbiters than one have handled and judged James Boswell with great ease and annoyance.

Moral reprobation, a suit in which few decent British critics are weak, has in fact been this fellow's lot ever since he attracted

[1] Cf. E. F. Benson's acid memoir on the dons of Cambridge.
[2] *Essais*, i, i.

public notice. Everybody knows his unfortunate effect on my Lord Macaulay. The Himmler of the Whigs lashes himself into a quite violent and menacing passion over Boswell's frailties. 'Servile and impertinent, shallow and pedantic, a bigot and a sot, bloated with family pride, a talebearer, an eavesdropper, a common butt in the taverns of London'—the prisoner has practically everything hurled at him except the final shattering charge, 'un-English'. Carlyle, echoing some of Macaulay's moral wrath, adds with bare justice that Boswell has a heart of gold; though as Carlyle needs this to bolster up his Strong-Man-as-Hero whimsy his motive may be deemed a trifle suspect. Many of Boswell's own contemporaries, from Horace Walpole down to the minor playwright Holcroft, chant a contemptuous chorus of 'fool, blockhead, zany, lickspittle, buffoon.' Hume, half playfully, said he was mad, and an authority of the progressive 1930's has diagnosed his case as incurable and established once for all by heredity, a theory which is not only scientifically unsound but smacks vilely of materialist determinism, as if the unhappy Boswell were a dog.

None of his judges, if I may say so respectfully, explains clearly how this deboshed rake and lunatic managed to create, in virile comely English, in the years of his alleged collapse, at least two works which will give delight as long as the language endures, and reveal the literary artist on almost every page; and equally, no attempt seems to have been made to apportion a just amount of blame for his follies and backslidings to at least one obvious source. Even odder, I think, is a unanimous gentlemen's agreement to glide with uplifted eyebrow over one impulse of Boswell's which, by bringing him in contact with a long-established therapeutic system notorious for its consummate knowledge and treatment of every spiritual malady conceivable, might possibly have changed his entire life. Good taste no doubt dictates this attitude, which Mr. Podsnap would highly approve? Good taste can possibly be overdone. It will not defile these pages to any extent.

A warm affection for James Boswell—shared, one is glad to remember, by men of the stature of Paoli, Johnson, and Reynolds—is the excuse for reviving his case here. With no desire whatsoever to idealise or whitewash or explain him away, one

feels the prosecution has so far had things too much its own way.
Boswell, though not a bad man, is no edifying figure, certainly;
yet to sit under some of his censors makes one wonder whether
they themselves have no mark-book to show the dread brother
of Ole-Luk-Oie when he swings them on to his great galloping
horse. An elementary course in moral theology might (one feels)
have left some of them less easily liable to be surprised and
maddened by human weakness. It is consoling to think that the
bouncing Macaulay, for one, will have to explain himself at
Doomsday-Leet with the rest of us. If the company of James
Boswell was good enough, right to the end, for Burke, Malone,
and Langton, it was certainly good enough for him.

Few of Boswell's leading critics, apparently, have ever been
drunk. This disability no doubt makes them tend, when they
assume the pince-nez of the *juge d'instruction* and open Dossier
D, to lean more towards drama than reality. For example, the
shambling Zolaësque wretch we are invited to contemplate
slithering down the slope to boozy dissolution from 1777 onwards
is actually the Boswell to whom Johnson says contentedly at this
very period, 'Sir, I don't care though I sit all night with you',
and the Boswell who two years later is charming the Bishop of
Chester and the prim tea-tables of Lichfield with his agreeable
presence. How does this chime with the prosecution's case? And
what of the trip to Cornwall in 1792? And the dinner at Lambeth
Palace in 1794?

I suggest the truth is that though he was regularly tipsy,
Boswell was not what the late Mr. Don Marquis would hail as
an Old Soak. He stood up to the bottle no less and no more
successfully than distinguished fellow-topers in English literature
like Addison, Steele, and Lamb, who have managed to capture
the sternest critics' indulgence so successfully. With his superb
constitution he was never a candidate for a nursing home, and
between the bouts he was plainly fit for any company. *Distinguo*,
as St. Thomas Aquinas, greatest of modern philosophers, would
say. I think a man may be *ebrius*, and even *ebriolus*, yet not
necessarily *ebriosus*; a drinker, yet not a drunkard. And is Boswell
at his worst any more despicable than Pitt, whose excesses are
so leniently handled by all historians? Or Fox, of whom Lord
Rosebery merely remarks that his dissipation 'was hardly

paralleled in that dissipated age', and passes on without scolding? Boswell should have been a politician, perhaps.

Due regard, therefore, will be paid in the ensuing pages to the forces which helped to make James Boswell what he was, and equally to the good intentions he so often and so desperately displayed. It is a nuisance to have to hale Macaulay to the bar again, but Britannia's Lictor-in-Chief suffers one outstanding handicap in this connection, clearly revealed in one of his comments on Boswell's *Life*. Dr. Johnson relatively approved a certain Dr. Campbell, who always doffed his hat on passing a church, though he rarely entered one; which doffing showed (Johnson argued) that Campbell at least had good principles. This moves Macaulay to a hoot of mirth. 'Spain and Sicily must surely contain many pious robbers and well-principled assassins!' he cries. They do, or did a hundred and fifty years ago; and as Mr. Christopher Hollis has observed, it is difficult to imagine how these bad hats could have bettered themselves by turning atheist, or even Whig. Quaintly enough, Macaulay's grandfather had been rapped over the sconce by Dr. Johnson for precisely the same naivety. 'Sir,' boomed the Doctor at the Rev. Mr. McAulay in the Hebrides, 'are you so grossly ignorant of human nature as not to know that a man may be perfectly sincere in good principles, without having good practice?' Such innocence ran, apparently, in the Macaulay family, and perhaps the Doctor's correction was still rankling in the grandson's orgulous bosom when the Doctor's disciple came up for trial.

Boswell was to some extent, to say it again, a pathological case, and this is not a technical treatise. But apart from the keen pleasure (which every Johnsonian will admit and excuse) of writing about him and mingling thereby with old and dear friends and delightful company, and apart from the fact that a new book on or around Johnson and his circle should be written every ten years, and generally is, it is clear that there are facets of Boswell yet to be fully revealed, and a Diderot, or a Barbey d'Aurevilley, or a Proust would probably find his curious character as fascinating in its complexities as that of a Rameau, a Brummell, or a Charlus. There are times, indeed, when Boswell strangely recalls the entrancing Nephew of Rameau, without that hero's ineffable poise and irony. 'Vous savez que je suis un

ignorant, un sot, un fou, un impertinent...' What is this but the
essence of some of Boswell's asides to his friend Temple, despite
that buoyant complacency which enables him to dispute religion
with Voltaire and discuss Royal family matters with George III?
He conceals as little from Temple and his diaries as any Society
woman unbosoming herself to her favourite psycho-analyst. He is
at times almost equally frank about himself in his books, and I
suspect he enjoyed such parades, as Rousseau enjoyed his own
spiritual strip-tease performances.

The influence of the *Nouvelle Héloïse*—and even the *Confessions*, though he did not encounter these till 1792—on Boswell
might be worth estimating, perhaps. He had imbibed Rousseau-
ism at the fountain-head, and though he affects to call Rousseau
'the wild Philosopher' and takes Hume's side against him, he is
obviously fascinated and impressed, like half Europe. Apart from
latent paranoia, Rousseau and Boswell have more than one trait
in common. In the Rousseau who preached the moral responsi-
bilities of parenthood and packed off the fruits of his disgustful
amours (Burke) to a foundling-hospice there is a streak of pure
Boswell; I mean, of course, in the antinomy, not the act, for
Boswell loved his children. In the Boswell who would fly to his
inamorata from the arms of a drab, detail his lapse with 'all the
eloquence of a young barrister', and end a luxurious emotional
orgy by kissing her feet and being forgiven, there is an obvious
strain of vintage Rousseau. The vanity of both men was about
equal. In the matter of madness Rousseau's sombre persecution-
mania gives him the lead, naturally, for Boswell never ceased to
be a sociable and kindly person. But morally Boswell takes the
lead of the great Rousseau, for he knew good from evil.

In his narcissism, therefore, Boswell is to some extent a true
child of his age. All through the second half of the eighteenth
century, and beyond, sentimental Rousseauism permeates the air
with its sweetish, headachy aroma. Its attraction for the military
mind is especially striking. Not the *Contrat Social* but the
*Nouvelle Héloïse* was packed among that trunkload of works
on military science and Oriental politics which accompanied
Colonel Arthur Wellesley, afterwards Duke of Wellington, to
India in 1796. Not the *Contrat Social* but the *Nouvelle Héloïse*
was included in the slightly more showy literary baggage which

General Bonaparte took to Egypt with him two years later. Byron and Shelley picking roses at Clarens on their joint honeymoon with Claire and Mary in 1814, feeling reverently that these blooms were perhaps the progeny of those planted by Rousseau's Julie, demonstrate a late but still ardent flowering of this addiction. Shelley's adoration of Rousseau was fiery, and Byron's impulse to advertise his incest with Augusta Leigh to the initiate in *Manfred* and *The Bride of Abydos* worthy of the Philosopher himself. For this mystical longing for penance and expiation does not necessarily have the direct connexion with religion we see in the case of St. Augustine, or the types of Dostoievsky. The obscurest diarist who, like Pepys and Boswell, is completely frank in self-examination, demonstrates it to some extent. And since such diary-keeping, like Buchmanism and psycho-analysis, knows nothing of the discipline and reticence of the confessional, the rankest morbidity may lie behind the rather priggish satisfaction of its adepts; the same morbidity, the same muddled need for expiation, I think, which drives the unhappy rich to cultivate the society of poets, literary men, actors, clowns, the dregs of the populace, and implants in jaded women of fashion that desire to be humiliated and beaten by their protégés which is so familiar to psychiatrists. Where the narcissist, often an invalid, writes deliberately, like Amiel and Marie Bashkirtseff, for publication, this exhibitionism can painfully embarrass and bore the reader. It should be noted here and now in Boswell's favour that he wrote neither his letters to Temple nor his private papers for publication. One must be careful, therefore, not to magnify or distort his self-revelation. He cheerfully saw no objection to admitting more than once in print that he sometimes got drunk. He is extremely careful never to mention in print his other great obsession, confided strictly to Temple and to his diaries.

Whether the fashionable Rousseauism of his period had any direct influence on Boswell or otherwise, more palpable forces were at work from an early age on this whirligig and impressionable brain. From late adolescence onwards Boswell was the proud friend and more or less constant associate of three intellectuals and philosophers, *esprits forts* on the French model, painstaking enemies of Christ. What he calls their 'vain subtlety' undoubtedly had some effect on him, though nobody seems to have taken it seriously into account as yet. And even if the sophistries and negations of Hume and Dempster, which Boswell, no metaphysician, found difficult to answer (his stout attempt to get Hume, a little before his death, to admit the immortality of the soul shows that he was not entirely wax in their hands) secured no permanent hold, the more positive fascination of the brilliant and eminent John Wilkes, 'my classical friend, Mr. Wilkes', 'my gay friend', Mr. Wilkes of the Hellfire Club and the House of Commons, whose public record is so admirable and whose private life so vile, seems to me to have been monstrously ignored. Wilkes, one might say, is the Eighteenth Century as Rabelais is the Sixteenth and Aquinas the Thirteenth. Wilkes is the Primal Goat leering behind all that dainty flafla we love in Thackeray and Austin Dobson; a cynic whose genial, cultured, destructive charm strangely recalls that of Goethe's Mephistopheles, and whose smile Boswell never could resist. Nor could most people.

To defeat such influences was not easy. Boswell needed to frequent a strong prehensile intellect coupled with a calm and sweet and absolute sanctity, a Vincent McNabb, to cite a modern example. Like the rest of Europe, England was conspicuously short of such types in the eighteenth century. Johnson and Paoli were great and good men, but not saints. Wesley is habitually canonised by his admirers, yet one may be excused for doubting whether that vicious bigotry which earned Wesley at length what Boswell describes metaphorically as a 'hearty drubbing' from Father O'Leary qualifies him for total sanctity in the final test. One other possible candidate on the fringes of the Johnsonian circle, the Rev. 'Rock of Ages' Toplady, displayed almost the same spite against Wesley himself. There was nobody else of spiritual note in Boswell's orbit but Bennet Langton, a good man but a dull one. The angelic Bishop Challoner he never encountered, since Challoner was a hunted man most of his life. It was a bad age for the mentally unstable; as Bishop Butler said, the contemporary intelligentsia had one agreed topic for mirth and ridicule.

The intelligentsia never know much about the eternal verities; yet I think the epicureans of the eighteenth century have more excuse for nescience than any moderns, for they lived in and

animated a world of grace and dignity as dead today as Troy,
and admitting only one life, they knew the art of living it.

That gracious eighteenth-century world, so cruel to the unfortunate, so delightful to its favourites, was no doubt all
Thackeray called it, shrinking aghast from the revelations in
Hervey's memoirs; it was rouged and fawning and lying and
pushing and struggling and heartless and godless, and it lacked
most of the virtues which have since come in with industrial
capitalism and the late Liberal Party. Yet to hear some twittering
pedant of the twentieth century patronising it gives one a grue.
For if the eighteenth century lacked a great many things,
including that mass-produced brilliance of thought and expression which is the glory of its present heirs, it did not lack a
certain distinction of its own. Its privileged classes defended
themselves against the poor with laws of devilish savagery, but
its most odious politicians quoted Homer and Virgil in the House
of Commons as a matter of course. To be rich under the Georges
was to be disliked, as in every other age, yet what delicious com-
pensations the Georgian rich enjoyed in their brief uneasy
passage through this world! Their dignified pavane to that paradise reserved for them, despite themselves, by their State clergy,
who, like Pope's Dean, never mentioned Hell to ears polite, was
chimed away in Palladian mansions by the mellow comely clocks
of Tompion and Rimbault. Their delicate 'chaney' lived in
cabinets by Chippendale and their soberly elegant, apricot-calf-
bound books in tall cases carved and gilded by the school of Kent.
Their wine was sipped from the glass of Venice and Bristol, their
tea poured, sugared, and creamed from silverware signed by
Paul Lamerie. Their ceilings and coaches were painted by
Angelica Kauffmann and Cipriani. Their tradesmen's cards, engraved by Hogarth and Bartolozzi, are collectors' pieces today.
Their most wayward excesses in baroque and chinoiserie and
toyshop-Gothic bear the gracious stamp of the craftsman. The
age had poise and individuality and the *bel air,* and its courteous
smiling acquiescence in the caprice of such temperamental play-
things as women,

> Say, cruel *Iris,* pretty Rake,
> Dear mercenary Beauty . . .

or lapdogs, like Horace Walpole's Tonton, is an object-lesson to
its neurotic successors. Caliban, having banged the Adam
brothers' Adelphi into dust with huge iron balls (so stoutly did
those fine houses, where Garrick entertained and Nelson's Emma
posed, resist the Woolworth Age) may well pause a moment
and scratch himself thoughtfully before rejoining Big Business,
the usurers, and the inventors of the atomic bomb in the Song of
Progress.

With all the gracious comeliness of metropolitan high-life
mirrored in Walpole's letters has likewise vanished that prevailing resilience, toughness, and defiant gusto which enabled the
inhabitants of the inferno of misery on which the social structure
was based to extract a kind of desperate, ribald, rollicking savour
from their fate, whether the pox, the poorhouse, the pressgang
or the gallows. From public entertainments like Tyburn and
Bedlam especially the mob derived the deep sensual satisfaction
which League football and dog-racing yield it today. Tyburn's
appeal was perhaps the more democratic; it could fascinate a
supercilious dilettante like George Selwyn and a fashionable
artist like Reynolds as powerfully as the raggedest sneak-thief
from St. Giles's. Boswell's own lifelong relish for public hangings
is notorious. According to the textbooks this should have developed a sadistic streak in him, as it did in so many other habitués;
but although this taste for the macabre may have thickened his
recurring gloom it certainly did not diminish his natural kindliness or his pity for the unfortunate. I would personally link his
addiction to Tyburn with his equal addiction to *The Beggar's
Opera*, which spelt London to him. And London beglamourised
him all his life. Unlike Johnson, who loved the town in a different
way, Boswell remained the typical country cousin, perpetually
avid of metropolitan sights and shows and sensations and swayed
to the end of his days by that association of ideas—'London=
pleasure'—which had captured him in his twenties.

And it must be admitted on behalf of all provincial playboys
that eighteenth-century London was full of surprises, often
fascinating. If I were compelled to choose one single anecdote
containing the quintessential London of this century, I think my
choice would be the adventure of the gentleman who sat one
night playing picquet with the eminent sculptor Roubiliac, whose

masterpieces help to clutter up Westminster Abbey, at Old Slaughter's Coffee-house in St. Martin's Lane. Some time after midnight Roubiliac's friend discovered that he had forgotten the street-door key of his lodgings, whereupon the hospitable Roubiliac offered him a room for the night and they finished another bottle and the game. Retiring eventually and undressing, the guest, parting the bed-curtains, started back in panic at the sight of a black corpse stretched before him. He ran. He shouted. His host arrived. 'Oh, dear! My good fren', I beg your pardon! I did not remember Mary vas dare—poor Mary! she die yesterday wid de small-pock! Come, come, you must take part vid my bed—come—poor Mary vas my hos-maid for five-six year—come!' [1]

This bawdy and breathtaking Town I have ventured to etch as a background in some detail, in Boswell's behalf and defence. In the London he loved so passionately all the wickedness the Victorians drove underground flaunted itself openly, with a thousand jovial gestures, beckoning Mr. Boswell on. London is part of his existence, and even the Paris he visited, I think, needs a little similar attention if we are to see him there clearly, for he was a plastic creature, strongly affected by environment and circumstance. We need to view the sights he saw, the sounds he heard, the fiddles and the candle-light, the racket and the glitter and the stench. Fortunately there are a thousand ways of re-creating Boswell's London. I have drawn on Hogarth, Fielding, Smollett, Lady Mary Coke, Horace Walpole, Hervey's Memoirs, *Lives of the Most Remarkable Criminals*, etc., the Newgate Calendar, J. T. Smith's *Life of Joseph Nollekens, R.A.*, contemporary files of *The Gentleman's Magazine* and *The London Chronicle*, the archives of Drury Lane, and a dozen other obvious sources.

For the rest, I have principally used Boswell's *Life of Johnson*, the Corsican and Hebrides journals, the Temple Correspondence, Hawkins's *Life of Johnson*, Farington's Diaries (ed. Greig), the memoirs of Mrs. Thrale, Hannah More, Fanny Burney, Laetitia Hawkins, and Thomas Holcroft, and Murphy's *Essay on the Life and Genius of Samuel Johnson, LL.D.*, and I have, of course, browsed deeply on Lieut.-Colonel R. H. Isham's privately-pub-

---

[1] J. T. Smith, *Biographical Sketches, etc., of several Artists and Others, contemporary with Nollekens.* 1829.

lished edition, in eighteen handsome volumes, of *The Private Papers of James Boswell* (1932), edited by Geoffrey Scott and F. A. Pottle. This luxury of scholarship deserves an envious word. An enormous mass of original MS. entrusted by Boswell a little before his death to a much-prized ebony cabinet at Auchinleck, a Kincardine heirloom, was acquired by Colonel Isham in 1928 from the owner, James Boswell, Baron Talbot de Malahide, Boswell's great-great-grandson and reigning male descendant. To decipher and arrange this jumble, much of it in Boswell's most difficult scrawl or in abbreviated script, in faded ink, often on half-perished paper or mere scraps, was a considerable feat, involving immense labour. Superb as the result is, the collection is even then not quite complete, by no fault of the editors. For example, the Wilkes correspondence has vanished, and a bundle of manuscript notes pertaining, apparently, to the middle of the *Life* perished in or after transit from Auchinleck to Ireland, many years ago. As Boswell's intimate papers are occasionally, but not abnormally, lewd, and far less so than Pepys's, discreet censoring will enable them some day, no doubt, to be published in the ordinary way for the world's pleasure. They contain fascinating pieces like the daily journal of Boswell's German tour of 1764 and of his Cornish holiday in 1792, the entrancing interviews with Rousseau and Voltaire, a fair amount of Johnsoniana which he never used, a marvellous view of London and Scottish life, and a wealth of information about himself and his enormous acquaintance. To everyone fortunate enough to possess this very expensive and limited set the *Private Papers* must increase the enjoyment of the *Life* a thousandfold. My thanks are due to Colonel Isham for permission to draw on them for the purpose of this book.

Among modern authorities, the study of Boswell by Mr. C. E. Vulliamy (1932), from whose implacable conclusions I differ passionately, and Professor C. B. Tinker's *Young Boswell* are noteworthy. I have to thank the Recorder of Carlisle, Mr. Edward Wooll, K.C., and the Town Clerk for very kindly supplying me with information concerning Boswell's brief recordership of that city, 1788-90; Mr. H. V. Morton, for valuable topographical data; the Director of the National Portrait Gallery, for permission to reproduce the portrait of Boswell by Sir Joshua Reynolds.

The reader is smoothly urged to bear in mind that this book is but a sign-post to Boswell's *Life of Johnson*. It is hoped that if nothing more, it may add one or two to that large company whose copy of the *Life* stands ever at the bed-head, dogseared and shabby with handling. Which indeed was a very good reason for attempting it.

# Chapter One

---

# A BEDROOM IN
# GREAT PORTLAND STREET

1

STEPPING INTO HIS SOBERLY ELEGANT CHARIOT ON THE EVENING of May 18, 1795, outside a house in Great Portland Street, and rolling westward, Dr. Richard Warren, Physician to the King, could hardly help reflecting, as he smoothed his neat ruffles and nursed his goldheaded ebony cane, that the notable patient he had just quitted was more amenable *in extremis* than some.

It was four years since an unfortunate example of Dr. Samuel Johnson's characteristic 'bow-wow' manner on his dying bed, endured by Dr. Warren in person, had been printed for all the world to read in Mr. James Boswell's *Life* of the Doctor, which had been so successful. Over their claret some of Dr. Warren's less prosperous brethren of the Faculty doubtless discussed it still, with a certain relish.

'I hope, Sir, you are better?'

'No, Sir; you cannot conceive with what acceleration I advance towards death.'

As a member of the Literary Club and a man of broad culture, apart from his wealth and professional eminence, Dr. Warren, brooding afresh on this affront to his bedside manner, may have compared it in his mind to some of the ruder freedoms of Molière. It was too late, alas, to hope that this anecdote might be omitted from the forthcoming Third Edition. Mr. Boswell himself was now dying.

The Great Portland Street house, No. 122—in Boswell's day

No. 47—still exists as to its foundations, but Dr. Warren would recognise neither its interior nor its grimy red-brick Victorian frontage, with an engineering store occupying the whole ground-floor. The street no longer opens to the north on a rural prospect backed by the green hills and village windmills of Hampstead and Highgate, and it is difficult to realise, as one paces its greater length today, that a couple of weeks before this particular May evening of 1795 Dr. Warren's chariot was undoubtedly held up by a group of tousled milkmaids, brave with ribbons and wreaths and posies, dancing a rondo in the roadway to the tune of *Come, thou rosy dimpled Boy!* scraped by a blind fiddler, and followed by a capering and slightly drunk sweep dressed as Jack-in-the-Green, covered with shrubbery and jingling bells.[1] These artless tinklings and fiddlings, which so captivated the sculptor Nollekens, R.A., were not to enliven Great Portland Street on a May Day much longer. The shadow of the Industrial Revolution was on the horizon, though the last feeble vestiges of those Arcadian rompings with which the eighteenth-century London proletariat still welcomed in the month of Mary—its primal significance had of course been forgotten long since—were to linger late into the Victorian age. Labour celebrates May Day now with less charming rites, and is possibly no happier.

Mr. Boswell lay dying in his house in Great Portland Street. His bedchamber one may easily restore in imagination. The curtained mahogany four-poster, chairs, brass-handled tallboy, and chest of drawers, the Wilton carpet, the small pyramidal wash-hand-stand with its flowery china, the candlesticks of brass, plate, or silver, the prints on the walls, the gilt-framed mirror, even the wig-block in the alcove might be reassembled now from a dozen London repositories and sale-rooms. Boswell was suffering from a tumour on the bladder and, apparently, uraemia. Taken suddenly ill during his last evening with the Literary Club, five weeks previously, he had been conveyed home in a coach and put to bed. There was not much mystery about the roots of his distemper. 'I thank you sincerely for your friendly admonition on my frailty in indulging so much in wine', he had written a few months previously to his old clerical friend Temple. 'I *do*

---

[1] The (rebuilt) Green Man tavern by Portland Road Underground station perpetuates Jack-in-the-Green's memory in this particular district.

resolve *anew* to be upon my guard ... How miserably have I
yielded to it in various years!'

Temple and all his other friends had long lost count of the
number of times he had taken this vow in various forms over the
past thirty years. Boswell was always resolving not to drink so
much. His sociable temperament and the most sottish age in
English history were against him. By the 1760's panic-legislation
controlling the sale of poison to the poor had Hogarth's Gin Lane
('*Drunk for 1d., dead drunk for 2d., straw for nothing*') more or
less in hand; but a myriad ever-open taverns and the smoking
nightly punchbowls of a myriad clubs and other convivial and
patriotic assemblies did not notably discourage that sturdy
Nordic devotion to the Dive Bouteille illustrated at one end of
the social scale by the great Pitt's historic and nearly fatal
midnight highway frolic, 'his reason drown'd in Jenkinson's
champagne', with Dundas and Lord Chancellor Thurlow, and at
the other end by Thomas Turner, the Sussex village tradesman,
hallooing in a rustic orgy with 'the Parson of the Parish', being
hauled out of bed in the early morning for more potations by
the parson's wife and other revellers, and a week later, with the
same company, 'drinking like Horses, as the vulgar Phrase is ...
dancing and pulling Wigs, Caps, and Hats ... behaving more like
Mad People than they that profess the Name of Christians'.[1]
Midway between these two poles and a little below the Squire
Westerns, those mighty tosspots before the Lord, came the solid
bourgeoisie such as the 'decent people of Lichfield', whom
Johnson remembered as getting drunk regularly every night; a
habit which sobered down to once a week by the end of the
century. In what Dr. Young called 'Britain's aweful Senate' itself
you might find a Prime Minister or Foreign Secretary, full of
Bellamy's port, perhaps too drunk to rise, perhaps swaying gently
on his legs and outlining Government policy thickly to a glazed
and muzzy House. Even more than continuous over-eating, continuous boozing expanded the waistcoats and shortened the
lives, as Thackeray neatly put it, of the eighteenth-century
British. In Lord Rosebery's more stately phrase, speaking of
the corpulence of the House of Hanover, 'their danger lay in

[1] *The Diary of Thomas Turner of East Hoathly, Sussex* (1754-65); ed. by
F. M. Turner, London, 1925.

a full habit of body'. Boswell was only fifty-five when he died, and far too plump.

Since Johnson's death, though not on account of it, he had taken a little more steadily to the bottle. He was a disappointed man. His earliest and principal ambition, to ruffle it in the Parks and the fashionable coffee-houses in the scarlet-and-gold of His Majesty's Guards, he had relinquished under parental pressure in adolescence. The spectacular legal and political career he had promised himself at intervals ever since had fizzled out in boozy dreams. His reputation had defeated him at the Scottish Bar. He had not made any figure at the English Bar. As for a public career, his most strenuous attempts had failed to make Pitt and Dundas realise his importance to the country and the desirability of recognising it with the gift of a snug place. His one and only active patron, Lord Lonsdale, Dictator of the North, to whom he owed his brief Recordership of Carlisle, had not long since shattered any final hopes of a Parliamentary seat with insulting brutality and humiliated him in front of a couple of Lowther flunkeys; as is the lot of men who place their trust in the wayward and insolent great. Propped on his pillows and awaiting death, Boswell had little to fortify himself with now but the affection of his elder daughters, Veronica and Euphemia, and his two schoolboy sons, Alexander and James, the certainty, despite some of the critics, of having lately published an enduring masterpiece, and the last consolations of a religion he had discussed all his life, drunk and sober, but rarely practised. Unlike some of his critics, I am not inclined to raise a quizzical eyebrow over the assurance of a friend of Boswell's after his death that 'at the end prayer was his stay'. He had as good a right to the infinite mercy of God as Lord Macaulay himself.

It has been rightly pointed out by Mr. Vulliamy that Johnson's influence for good over Boswell can easily be exaggerated if based, as it usually is, on the assumption that they were practically inseparable during the greater part of their twenty-one years' friendship. The most casual study of the *Life* shows that apart from the fourteen weeks of the Hebrides tour they were together relatively little. I have not tried to count up the approximate total number of days they spent in each other's company. It would be an interesting experiment. More than six years when they never saw each other at all can be subtracted in a lump from that twenty-one to begin with, in three separate periods; probably another four or five could be added almost immediately. And Johnson's influence was often intermittent even when they were both in London. For this reason it is clearly a mistake to regard the years after Johnson's death as essentially the years of Boswell's decline and fall, as it has been called. He had been up and down more than once or twice before Johnson died. He was always climbing and slipping. Paoli as well as Johnson tried to steady him. His wife also did her best. It must have been like trying to grasp quicksilver. The unstable Boswell defied all discipline. To some extent, of course, Johnson was able to project his influence over him at long-distance, as their correspondence shows. It is plain that Johnson was his principal sheet-anchor, and that but for meeting Johnson he might rather sooner than later have disgraced himself for ever in some wild folly or sunk long since into that madness of melancholia, the fear of which often haunted him, as it did Swift, in black moments.

A bitter thought for a dying man. Yet the cloud over his departure need not have entirely excluded, from the world's standpoint, a ray or two of sunshine. The Biographer had created the Book. The celebrity-hunter had bagged other big fish than Johnson: Paoli and Hume and Voltaire and Wilkes and Rousseau, for example, and Sterne, and Mrs. Rudd, heroine of a famous Old Bailey case, and very nearly Frederick the Great, had the blue Scots bonnet Boswell flaunted so eagerly at Potsdam managed to hold that sergeant-major's attention from the drill-ground. The connoisseur of life and letters had been on terms of friendship with not only the most eminent Englishmen of his time, Johnson, Burke, Reynolds, Garrick, Burney, Goldsmith, but, judging by his diaries, half London.[1] For one bully like Lonsdale the man of the world had known a dozen patricians more genial—Lord Eglintoun, for example, who took him as a youth to the Jockey Club at Newmarket; Lord Mountstuart, his companion in Italy; the Duke of Montrose, at one of whose parties he got so royally drunk; Lord Errol; Lord Pembroke, who entertained him nobly at Wilton; even the great Argyle, despite his lady Duchess's

[1] The Index to the *Private Papers* contains some 6,500 names, numbers of them distinguished.

coldness. Among the flower of Scots elegance and nobility young Mr. Boswell had danced a minuet at Holyrood Palace on the Queen's Birthday, and had frequently been a guest since then in marble halls, amid the silver flambeaux, the powdered flunkeys, the feathers, the fiddles, and fal-lals; where only once, in the drawing-room of Miss Monckton, afterwards Countess of Cork, had he made a really notable exhibition of himself in the presence of a frigid, glittering assembly, for at Lord Falmouth's in 1792 his host was equally drunk. On the whole, viewed in 1795 down a long diminishing vista of polished floors and crystal chandeliers and Venetian mirrors, the strutting figure of James Boswell, Esquire, of Auchinleck made no inconspicuous or inelegant appearance. Though he enjoyed high-life, like most people, he was no more of a tuft-hunter than the majority of men in an age which greatly revered peers, allowed them to plead privilege when they collided with the laws of England, and protected their lowest menials from arrest. It is ridiculous to style any eighteenth-century man a snob for bending a flexible back before a title. Johnson himself addressed with respect the obscurest nobleman of the Irish Plantation. We may note in passing that this traditional halo round the peerage lingered well into the Victorian Age. Mr. Jawleyford in *Mr. Sponge's Sporting Tour* is a gentleman with a large and complicated crest and a pedigree as ancient as Lord Scamperdale's, but his obsequious attentions to that scrubheaded Mohock still mark the proper distance between a commoner and a peer of the realm. Boswell may have deferred to peers politely, as convention required, but he did not run after them to any extent. His marked predilection for the company of actors, indeed, was almost enough to show his social equals that he was slightly cracked, despite the way he perpetually flourished his descent from Robert Bruce and Boswell of Flodden Field, and his kinship with the Kincardines and the Sommelsdycks.

An animated life; a life he had largely relished, good times and bad. It may be that as he lay in Great Portland Street, staring at the tender May sky which makes London briefly enchanting, there was mixed with the comforting memory of good deeds— for he had that warm heart so few men have, as Carlyle rightly says, and he had always been generous; as a lawyer he had fought for the miserable, as a landlord he had cared for his people—a glimpse of one or two of those picaresque strolling players and theatre-men of his youth whose own 'animation and relish of existence' had so fascinated him, and who, one or two of them, were so oddly connected with the great event of his life. The shabby-genteel figure of Francis Gentleman, actor and ex-Army officer, may have lingered before his eyes especially. Gentleman, who dedicated a bad play to Boswell (for money) at Glasgow in his student days, had been the first to describe to him *de visu* the figure and manner of the celebrated Dictionary Johnson. The more respectable Mr. Thomas Sheridan, who lectured on elocution at Edinburgh and had been likewise captured by Boswell, had been the great man's guest, and was apt to flourish the fact. The equally respectable Mr. Thomas Davies, ex-actor and bookseller, to whom he owed his introduction to Johnson, loomed even larger. As he looked back across the years that consummate experience must surely have come back to the sick man in almost its first freshness, blotting out all the bagnio-orgies, the tavern-parties and their ensuing headaches, the lights and fiddles of Drury Lane and the Haymarket, the symposia at the Literary Club, the squalid embraces of the Juliets of a night, the confused bustle, music, talk, the multitudinous sights and sounds and emotions of the London he had loved. At least once again he must have seen the glass-door of the back-parlour of No. 8 Russell Street, Covent Garden, and glimpsed through it a shabby, rolling, grunting, pockmarked, tremendous figure steering its purblind way through the bookshop towards him, in the light of the late May afternoon.

'Look, my lord, it comes!'

Mr. Davies the bookseller's facetious cry was apt enough. Hamlet on the midnight battlements felt fewer tremors than the plump young Scot in the parlour, for all his snub-proof nerve. Thirty-two years ago, and pretty Mrs. Davies's graceful ex-actressy titter still clear in his ears! Her mirthful glance, her mob-cap and ribbons, the dusky, cosy, shabby little parlour with its haphazard piles of books, the prints on the walls, the cat asleep on the hearth, the tea-equipage and its slops on the small round table, the darned, worn chintz of the armchair, the sunlight slanting across the faded carpet and the dust-motes dancing in it, the kettle on the hob, the ticking of the eight-day clock, the obsequious forward dive of Davies at the sight of the opening shop-door . . .

'Sir, this is Mr. Boswell——'

(*'Don't tell where I come from!'*)

Too late. The roguish Davies must have his fun. It was an awkward time for Mr. Boswell's countrymen in London, with Lord Bute as Britain's late loathed Prime Minister and his favourites increasingly hooted. Not since James I's rawboned and predatory followers aroused the enmity of the London mob had Scotsmen been temporarily so unpopular. Johnson's own distaste for them was almost morbid.

'——from Scotland.'

'Mr. Johnson, I do indeed come from Scotland, but I cannot help it!'

Alas for young Mr. Boswell's light pleasantry, 'designed to soothe and conciliate him'. The first of many buffets from the lion's paw is imminent, and it stuns and dazes.

'That, Sir, I find, is what a great many of your countrymen cannot help.'

Thirty-two years ago.

Boswell died at two a.m. on May 19, 1795. A barely-decipherable L.C.C. tablet on the façade of No. 122 records the fact for the benefit of the automobile salesmen who throng busy Great Portland Street today.

## 2

The twenty-one-year friendship begun in 1763, the major event in Boswell's existence, must naturally bulk large in any survey of it. All his life up to 1763, one might say, he is preparing for the advent of Johnson; from 1784 to the end he is living more or less on his connection with Johnson, the glory of which has increased a thousandfold with the years. Time has reapportioned the fame of both in a striking way. How many of Boswell's devoutest readers today ever open the *Idler*, the *Rambler*, the *Lives of the Poets, Rasselas,* or any other volume of the Doctor's once-conquering prose? How many consult his admirable Dictionary? (It would repay perusal. It is packed with good things.)

The one-time Dictator of English Letters lives today only by his disciple's brilliance. One cannot help thinking that had Johnson been able to foresee this it might have affected their relationship considerably. The Doctor was subject, like the rest of us, to certain human failings and the noise would have been, one is tempted to think, quite abominable.

It seems to me that before attempting to survey the dappled career of Boswell one should examine his quiddity first of all; the thing that made him; the thing some would say he was predestined and born for: Johnson's patronage. Why did Johnson, who disliked the Scots on principle as a nation of liars and was never tired of gibing at them, pick out this one particular obscure chance-met young Scot, thirty-one years his junior, in the early summer of 1763 and bestow on him the most tireless of intimate affection? In 1763 Johnson was already a towering figure in contemporary letters. His greatest work was nearly all behind him. His pre-eminence as a moral and literary force had been recognised by a pension from the Crown, though he naturally had still some years to wait for due recognition from Oxford. Why should he have adopted Boswell as his *famulus* rather than any other of the respectful young men who surrounded him— Langton, say, or Beauclerk, or Murphy? I fancy Boswell supplies a great part of the answer himself in a letter to his faithful Temple from Newcastle-on-Tyne in 1775, on one of his return journeys north:

> . . . a very good journey. An agreeable young widow nursed me and supported my lame foot on her knee. *Am I not fortunate in having something about me that interests most people at first sight in my favour?*

He certainly had something. Voltaire and Rousseau alike discovered it. In the *Journey to the Western Islands,* twelve years after their meeting, Johnson extols it. Mr. Boswell's acuteness, gaiety, politeness, and 'inquisitiveness seconded by great activity' are awarded high marks. Mr. Boswell is sure of a reception wherever he goes. Mr. Boswell's gay frankness 'makes every body communicative'. He was in fact pre-eminently what his century called an agreeable rattle. He diverted Johnson, whose hypochondriac temperament needed constant recreation. His candour about himself and his weaknesses was attractive. He yearned for a guide. He was an ideal listener. And he venerated Johnson so fervently, to begin with, that the Doctor at length took refuge with the Thrales at Streatham for some time before admitting his disciple to his retreat. Undoubtedly the basis of Johnson's feeling was paternal. The kindest of men when not in a passion, he loved advising people, especially young people, and God knows Boswell gave him plenty of scope. Compared with the dull, amiable, indolent, stork-like Langton, or a wayward and expensive rake like Beauclerk, or a preoccupied man of the theatre like Murphy, Boswell was the perfect companion; attentive, vivacious, grateful for favours, impervious to noise and bullyings. And Johnson, as Davies accurately guessed that day, took a warm and instant fancy to him, though this was a habit of the Doctor's which did not invariably lead to long friendships. The case of the learned Abbé Roffette at Rouen is one example. Mrs. Thrale relates amusingly how the Abbé and the Doctor charmed each other at first sight and enjoyed a long Latin literary conversation, how the Abbé rose and embraced the Doctor in a transport, how Thrale, who was present, thought it only polite to invite the Abbé to Streatham to continue these delightful symposia, and how Johnson instantly turned on Thrale and rent him in pieces for inviting a man he knew nothing about; after which the Abbé took his leave, amid the Thrales' embarrassment, and was seen no more by any of them. Contact with Johnson was exactly like contact with a sociable, highly temperamental lion. You never knew when the purring would stop, for no apparent or conceivable reason, and a hideous mangling befall you. Boswell had the nerve and the stamina to endure, though there are grounds for believing that after some years of it the pleasure of being savaged by Johnson at intervals had somewhat waned.

The Doctor sincerely loved him. There could be no doubt of that, even if Johnson had not written it down so often. Whether Boswell loved the Doctor as sincerely has been disputed. It has even been suggested that exploitation was probably far more his real motive. Quite likely the curious fellow could not have analysed his sentiment for Johnson completely himself. There was certainly egotism in it; there was undoubtedly a flattered content at being the chosen confidant of a terrific celebrity and sharing the public attention he everywhere received; there was a genuine passion for Letters; there was the triumph over jealous and touchy rivals like Baretti and Goldsmith; there was the fact that the Doctor never bullied him without making up for it later by some extra kindness; and above all, I am convinced, there was that fine gold in Boswell's composition which Carlyle justly underlines. 'The man, after all, had an "open sense", an open, loving heart, which so few have. Where excellence existed, he was compelled to acknowledge it; was drawn towards it (let the old sulphur-brand of a Laird say what he liked); *could not but walk with it*—if not as superior, if not as equal, then as inferior and lackey: better so than not at all.' It is easy to dismiss this pronouncement as being merely a pompous way of describing a confirmed notoriety-hunter and celebrity-hound. In the case of Voltaire and Rousseau this opinion can be justified. In the case of Johnson and Paoli it is ignoble. The goodness and greatness of Johnson and the nobility of Paoli drew and magnetised one neither good nor great nor noble. Even in our own age the phenomenon has been witnessed. There were many who mourned the loss of Chesterton for the same reason.

Having established Boswell as *sympathique*, with certain gifts of keen, gay, polite, benevolent vivacity and volubility, which are sufficiently uncommon in England to give their possessor, though afterwards suspect, an initial advantage if making new acquaintances is his hobby, together with a reverence for true greatness, we practically conclude the list of his more obvious charms. He was far from beautiful. He was (if the maliciously entertaining John Thomas Smith, biographer of Nollekens, R.A., may be trusted) far from cleanly in his person, like his great mentor and vast numbers of other distinguished contemporaries. White ruffles enclosing a dirty neck are almost symbolic of the Age of Reason. And there were some of his acquaintance to whom his social gifts were by no means perceptible. He could assume, with certain members of the Johnsonian circle, a manner they greatly resented. For example, Sastres the Italian tutor, an obscure but excellent character to whom Johnson left five pounds in his will 'to be laid out in books of piety for his own use'. Sastres, who had evidently suffered from Boswell, so far forgot Christian charity as to describe him to Thomas Holcroft, the actor and dramatist, as 'a proud, pompous, and selfish blockhead'. Holcroft himself, though he never met Boswell, knew him well by sight. In his memoirs he too sets Boswell down, on this slender evidence, as a 'most solemn, pompous, and important coxcomb. His grave strut and elevated head, with a peculiar self-important set of his face, entirely corresponded with the character he unintentionally draws of himself in his writings'. It is clear that Boswell the polite rattle, the engaging three-bottle man, the frank, pleasant companion ever ready for a frisk, was a Boswell not known to all and sundry. Is it difficult to reconcile a certain aloof pomposity towards some—not all—inferiors with his humility in the presence of Johnson, the bankrupt provincial tradesman's son? With the invariable meekness with which he allowed Johnson to snub and humiliate him in public and in private? Carlyle still supplies a good answer, I think.

Occasionally Boswell's enemies become diverting in their dislike. There is an acid story about him in Holcroft's memoirs, told by Mauritius Lowe. Readers of the *Life* will recall that Lowe, a struggling but mediocre painter, was greatly distressed when the Royal Academy Hanging Committee of 1783 rejected— probably rightly, since Northcote, R.A., described it as 'execrable beyond belief'—a large canvas representing the last surviving giant of the Noachic Deluge standing in the sea and holding aloft his infant child, menaced by a famished lion crouching on the last remaining piece of dry ground. Lowe carried his despair to Johnson, who at once wrote warmly in his behalf to the no less kindly Reynolds, and this intercession, says Boswell, was too powerful to be resisted. It so happened that Boswell was present when Johnson handed Lowe the letter for Reynolds. When Lowe left the house he found Boswell, who had been hitherto unaware of his existence, dogging him into Bolt Court, wreathed in unaccustomed smiles. Lowe's own words to Holcroft give the ensuing comedy perfectly:

'How do you do, Mr. Lowe? I hope you are very well, Mr. Lowe. Pardon my freedom, Mr. Lowe, but I think I saw my dear friend, Dr. Johnson, writing a letter for you?'—'Yes, Sir'—'I hope you will not think me rude, but if it would not be too great a favour, you would infinitely oblige me if you would just let me have a sight of it. Every thing from that hand, you know, is so inestimable.'—'Sir, it is on my own private affairs, but'—'I would not pry into a person's affairs, Mr. Lowe, by any means. I am sure you would not accuse me of such a thing. Only if it were no particular secret——'—'Sir, you are welcome to read the letter.'—'I thank you, my dear Mr. Lowe, you are very obliging, I take it exceedingly kind' (*having read*). 'It is nothing, I believe, Mr. Lowe, that you would be ashamed of?'—'Certainly not.'— 'Why then, my dear Sir, if you would do me another favour, you would make the obligation eternal. If you would but step to Peele's Coffee-house with me, and just suffer me to take a copy of it, I would do any thing in my power to oblige you.'

I was overcome (said Lowe) by this sudden familiarity and condescension, accompanied with bows and grimaces. I had no power to refuse; we went to the coffee-house, my letter was presently transcribed, and as soon as he had put his document in his pocket, Mr. Boswell walked away, as erect and as proud as he was half an hour before, and I was ever afterward unnoticed. Nay, I am not certain (added he sarcastically) whether the Scotchman did not leave me, poor though he knew I was, to pay for my own dish of coffee.

From Bolt Court to Peele's on the corner of Fetter Lane—the modern public-house still keeps the old name—must have been less than ten minutes' walk through the normal Fleet Street traffic of the 1780's. Mr. Boswell probably thought ten minutes' continuous affability more than repaid a Bohemian nonentity and an exploiter of Johnson's kindness like Lowe. Most eighteenth-century men of his rank would have thought so, too. Fifty years later a creditor of Brummell's was to learn to his genuine surprise that a languid nod of recognition from the Beau, seated in the window of White's, had settled their little account for a few hundreds. But Brummell, stoic and wit, was merely being Brummellish for the benefit of his public, whereas Boswell's leaving Lowe to pay his own twopence at Peele's, if the sour Lowe recollected this rightly, may have been less due to closeness—Boswell, like many Scots, was notably generous—than to a feeling that one really must not spoil these people.

How often the more important personages he so ruthlessly dunned for copies of letters and other Johnsoniana snubbed and evaded him we do not know. Fortunately for us, he possessed that will of chilled steel for which the Scots are justly feared. It is necessary to remark in passing that authorities like Professor

Pottle tend to dismiss that familiar picture of his perpetually whipping out a notebook at the dinner-table as a legend promulgated chiefly by Mrs. Thrale, who so disliked him. Boswell performed this anti-social trick once at least at her house, but he was bred a gentleman, and there is no evidence this was a habit. On the other hand, he would certainly slide up closer to the Doctor in order not to miss anything. Since it must come sooner or later, I cannot forbear quoting here and now Fanny Burney's well-known and daintily malicious description of an occasion at Streatham when Boswell actually moved his chair from table and placed it behind Johnson's as the booming began. Miss Burney revels in the comic sequel:

His eyes goggled with eagerness; he leant his ear almost on the shoulder of the Doctor; and his mouth dropped open to catch every syllable that might be uttered; nay, he seemed not only to dread losing a word, but to be anxious not to miss a breathing. And there he remained until Johnson happened to turn and see him and shouted an ill-pleased 'What do you do there, Sir? Go to the table, Sir!'

Boswell did not mind this. Nor did he mind the sneers of Garrick and others at his self-chosen role of Johnson's stooge, to borrow the perfect word from American vaudeville. He drew out the great man not to please the company, but to add a little more to what he knew to be an imperishable monument long before his final manuscript reached Dilly's publishing-house in the Poultry. It was this consciousness of a mission, I believe, which gave Boswell that strutting, pursy self-complacency some of his contemporaries objected to. They might bask in the sunshine of Johnson's talk, but they could not preserve its precious essence for posterity, as events were to prove. Sir John Hawkins, the sanctimonious but musical attorney, Boswell's chief biographical rival, makes no attempt at it, though his *Life* of Johnson is not utterly despicable. Mrs. Thrale in her slapdash way succeeds occasionally, despite her bias and her inaccuracies. Only little Fanny Burney, with her demure sense of fun and her ear for music, can reproduce the Johnsonian cadences as unerringly, sometimes, as Boswell himself. For example, her report of a chat on Miss Carmichael, one of the needy pensioners on the bounty of that great compassionate bear:

*Mrs. Thrale*: But pray, Sir, who is the Poll you talk of?—she that you used to abet in her quarrels with Mrs. Williams, and call out, 'At her again, Poll! Never flinch, Poll!'

*Dr. Johnson*: Why, I took to Poll very well at first, but she won't do upon a nearer examination.

*Mrs. Thrale*: How came she among you, Sir?

*Dr. Johnson*: Why, I don't rightly remember, but we could spare her very well from us. Poll is a stupid slut. I had some hopes of her at first; but when I talked to her tightly and closely I could make nothing of her; she was wiggle-waggle, and I could never persuade her to be categorical.

Boswell could do no better and certainly no more amusingly. The Johnson Fanny knew was a more continuously playful old gentleman than Boswell's. Had she not later conceived the unfortunate idea of trying to write in Johnsonese, had she had Boswell's range and opportunities, Boswell might almost be taking second place just above Hawkins today.

It has often been suggested—chiefly for mischief, I think, by bored and idle dons—that Boswell created Johnson and that the unboswellised article is the only genuine one. How simple to refute this childish heresy from the Hebridean journal. Boswell's first attempt at reproducing Johnson's conversation. The Doctor read the greater part of Boswell's journal in manuscript during the tour. Can you see a man so proud of his talk, so jealous of its sinewy form, such a precisian for the Johnsonian idiom, letting anything be passed off as his own which was anyone else's? He read, smiled, and approved. *Ergo*, Boswell reported him in the Hebrides accurately. *Ergo*, I make bold to deduce, even without Sir Joshua Reynolds's assurance that 'every word might be depended on, as if given on oath', that Boswell always reported the Doctor accurately, to the very limit of human ability, having a scrupulosity on this point which does him honour as a literary artist. Nor was the task as difficult probably as one is sometimes liable to think. With his prehensile memory, his steely nerve, his abbreviated script, his familiarity with the Johnsonian rhythms, and his immense anxiety always to get the words down on paper before they were cold, Boswell could undoubtedly report the Doctor before long with almost entire fidelity, his groans in the Hebrides notwithstanding. Nor did devotion to other pleasures hamper him unduly in his task, as we know—or is that excessive? He left out quite enough. A life of Johnson by Boswell three times its present length would not be too long for some of us.

3

How many of Boswell's eminent friends of the past—there were not many left, he laments in 1792—visited Great Portland Street in his last illness is not recorded. Burke and Malone, Courtenay and Windham may have cheered him. Bennet Langton's presence would have been grateful, I think, for though a heavy man, his kindness and piety were real. But I am wondering chiefly if the dying Boswell, grasping desperately after spiritual things at the end, was ever perturbed and battered in his last hours by a visit from one of his oldest living friends, one whom, as I have said already, I believe to have been more actively responsible for some of his vagaries than anyone has yet admitted: John Wilkes, Esquire, late M.P. for Aylesbury and Middlesex, champion of liberty, ex-Lord Mayor of London, one-time darling of the nation, with admirers by the thousand in France and America.

When and where Boswell first met Wilkes is not known; almost certainly in 1760, and quite likely in a Covent Garden brothel. In the *Life* and elsewhere Boswell mentions his intimacy with this eminent man always with a flick of pride. 'The celebrated John Wilkes'. 'My gay friend'. 'My classical friend, Mr. Wilkes'. Several of Wilkes's printable jests are quoted in the *Life*, where Boswell also sets down, with some complacency, the significant fact that he nerved himself for his second encounter with Johnson (Tuesday, May 24, 1763) by enjoying 'the witty sallies of Messieurs Thornton, Wilkes, Churchill, and Lloyd'; three at least of the worst men in London, with whom he had spent a jovial morning. The degree of intimacy thus implied makes it more than ever likely that Wilkes and Boswell had met during Boswell's first visit to London. It was not an easy thing to be accepted by Wilkes and his clique; a bad circle, but a circle of wits who would not tolerate a bore. One may take it that quaint gaiety and good listening had triumphed once more. Wilkes and his friends liked Boswell very much.

In 1760 Wilkes was 35, fifteen years older than Boswell; a dutiful Government backbencher representing Aylesbury in the Commons, well-known about town as a wit, a debauchee, and a leading spirit in that 'Order of Monks of St. Francis', popularly known as the Hellfire Club, which defiled the converted remains of Medmenham Abbey, near Marlow-on-Thames, with its midnight orgies.[1]

Boswell does not mention the Hellfire Club, which need not imply that Wilkes never introduced him to the meetings of that select society. It has perhaps been over-rated as a nest of advanced wickedness. The most notable roysterers composing it were Sir Francis Dashwood, professional rake, dilettante, and militant atheist with a Continental reputation—while making the Grand Tour he had been expelled from the Papal States for outrageous conduct—and later Chancellor of the Exchequer; the dissolute Lord March, celebrated in years to come as 'Old Q', the Piccadilly satyr; the dull but laborious Lord Sandwich, later First Lord of the Admiralty, after whom the Sandwich Isles are named; the halfwit Lord Orford, Horace Walpole's nephew; the unfrocked clergyman, satiric poet, and all-round blackguard Charles ('Bruiser') Churchill, a very choice ruffian indeed; his faithful henchman Robert Lloyd, one-time usher at Westminster School; the rakehelly man-about-town Thomas Potter, son of a late Archbishop of Canterbury, who had introduced Wilkes to the lewdest fashionable circles of London, Bath, and Tunbridge Wells, and launched him into politics with introductions to Temple, Grenville, Pitt, and the leading London moneylenders; the raffish poet Paul Whitehead; and Wilkes himself.

To anyone acquainted with the scientific black magic practised at Versailles by the Guibourg-Montespan clique, the midnight gambols of the Hellfire Club and their odalisques will seem relatively as harmless, almost, as modern folkdancing. Primitive

[1] Not to be confused with the original Hellfire Club, founded by the Duke of Wharton in 1721 and suppressed the same year by Royal order. This club had branches in Edinburgh and Dublin, and represented, so to speak, the Low Church school of satanism.

and repetitive blasphemy, excessive tippling, and extravagant lechery were the staple of the 'Order's' devotions, spiced with that naive delight in dressing up as monks and nuns which, I am told, is familiar to students of technical treatises on sexual aberration, in a Reformed society especially.[1] The Medmenham frolics included an elaborate erotico-orgiastic ceremony in honour of Venus and another in honour of Satan. Each parodied in amateur fashion the ritual of the Mass, yet even the satanic ceremony was innocence itself compared with the authentic Black Mass. For this terrible rite the 'Order' lacked the two principal requisites, which were more difficult to find in eighteenth-century England than they are now.

It would not be unfair to sum up the proceedings of the Hellfire Club as the revels of smutty but simple-minded public schoolboys. Wilkes and Churchill supplied the culture (e.g. Wilkes's obscene Latin inscriptions adorning the Abbey walls, and Churchill's poem *Night*, of which the *Critical Review* remarked 'This Night like many others at this time of the year, is very long, cold, dark, and dirty'), and Wilkes, who had a brain and preferred his debauchery unhampered by elementary satanism, grew bored with the tomfoolery in due course. The comic story of his revolt is well known. Smuggling a large, angry, black baboon into the Abbey and equipping it with horns and hoofs, he released it from a chest at the climax of the choral service to the Devil, an apparition which stampeded the worshippers and nearly drove the dribbling Orford into one of his periodical fits of insanity. The 'Order' languished after that. Its 'prior', Dashwood, turned to politics, like Wilkes and Sandwich, and ended his life as a mild old gentleman with a taste for church-building, an inglorious collapse by all Medmenham standards.

Whether or not Boswell ever joined in the Hellfire Club's frolics—there is no diary for 1760, but he certainly would have enjoyed himself, given the chance, in such exalted company—the extent of Wilkes's recurring influence over his giddy mind is a factor to be considered, I feel. Boswell was possibly oftener in Wilkes's company than in Johnson's. In 1763 they were already

[1] Cf. the marked prevalence of monastic, cardinalate, and papal costume in all the London masquerades of this century.

intimate. In 1765-6 they were intermittent companions for some weeks on the Continent; in Rome, a rich field for Wilkes's wit, in Naples, that agreeable sink of iniquity, in Turin, and in Paris. In 1772 Boswell sat next to Alderman Wilkes at the Lord Mayor's banquet. He was one of Lord Mayor Wilkes's principal guests at the banquet of 1775. In 1776 he succeeded in a diplomatic feat which inspired one of the most exquisite conversation-pieces in the *Life*, the bringing of Wilkes and Johnson together at the Dillys' dinner-table; a dramatic spectacle, Vice and Virtue, his bad angel and his good, as it were, hobnobbing warily over the decanters. In 1781 he repeated this feat. In 1786 Wilkes helped him to celebrate his call to the English Bar. One of the last entries in his private journal, before it stopped for ever, is the record of a dinner-party at Wilkes's house in Grosvenor Square in March 1794. They dined together at least fifty or sixty times as recorded by Boswell, and doubtless much oftener, since his journal is not complete and Wilkes's letters to him, which on Boswell's own showing were highly prized, are lost.

To exaggerate Wilkes's hold over Boswell is of course easy and picturesque. I do not desire to suggest any vision of a demon king springing up in red fire at regular intervals through the trap-doors of Boswell's existence. I do suggest that the effect on Boswell over thirty-five years of this brilliant, seductive, and admired man, who could no more help being wittily offensive on the topic of the Christian faith than he could help breathing, was considerable, especially when the counter-influence of Johnson, and after him Paoli, was removed.

Not that Wilkes was by any means the devil incarnate George III called him. Like many bad men he was not without virtues. He lacked neither courage, honesty, generosity, nor a sardonic kindness, he was free from hypocrisy, and it is a commonplace to add that many an Alderman Gripe of the City who waddled regularly to Mattins and Evensong and spent his waking hours in usury, gluttony, and debauching his housemaids is a far more odious spectacle. Wilkes's lifelong devotion to his daughter Mary is another needful credit-entry. His public achievement is almost entirely praiseworthy, especially when one recollects that he was a spectator and a dilettante by inclination, and a demagogue despite himself; a demagogue, moreover, who never had any truck with the dogma of the Divinity of the Proletariat, as the Gordon rioters discovered to their cost. In the City and the House of Commons alike Wilkes fought for the political liberty of the subject and the liberty of the press, for what that is worth in practice; he fought indefatigably for justice to the American Colonies and electoral reform and better treatment for prisoners and a reform of the criminal code; he even supported a Bill to relieve Nonconformist ushers from compulsory subscription to the Anglican Articles. As City Chamberlain, a post he held from 1779 to his death, he saved London from the Gordon rioters, audited the Corporation accounts with strict probity, and took only the lawful perquisities and pickings of his office. As church-warden for the year 1759-60 of St. Margaret's, Westminster (he blandly claimed membership of the Establishment on more than one occasion) Wilkes was not so successful as at Medmenham, and was not even mentioned in the vestry's annual vote of thanks. No doubt this office was beyond even his powers.[1]

It was the private life of this professional pagan, his pleasures, his fixed attitude to the Christian religion, his flights of playful fancy which were as vile as his charm was overpowering. The great Chatham called him a 'wicked and agreeable fellow' and chuckled hugely over his obscene verses, though he turned on Wilkes later in the House to denounce him as 'a blasphemer of his God and a libeller of his King.' Gibbon, after dining in a militia mess with him in 1762, wrote in his journal: 'I scarcely ever met with a better companion; he has inexhaustible spirits, infinite wit and humour, and a great deal of knowledge; but a thorough profligate in principle as in practice, his life stained with every vice, and his conversation full of blasphemy and indecency.' 'Grossest bawdy', wrote the fastidious Walpole to George Montagu after Wilkes's visit to him in Paris three years

[1] To Wilkes in this pleasing incarnation attaches a riposte which is even to-day quoted as annihilating. A Catholic having good-humouredly asked him 'Where was your Church, Sir, before the Reformation?', Mr. Church-warden Wilkes replied with equal good-humour, 'Where was your face, Sir, before you washed it this morning?' The natural counter-retort, 'When you washed *your* face this morning, Sir, did you permanently remove nose, eyes, and ears?' did not occur to Wilkes's questioner, or perhaps this incident would not be so frequently quoted.

later. 'His conversation shows how little he has lived in good company.' Like other professional wits, Wilkes was often lured by his dæmon and by appreciative audiences into wilder excesses than he intended, no doubt. His raillery had, perhaps, a more than normal tinge of sadism. One of his admirers, Charles Johnston, remarks that Mr. Wilkes would sacrifice his dearest friend to a scurvy jest. It is a deplorable habit of the Samurai.

A man of Boswell's type was bound to be fascinated by a Lucifer of such overwhelming attraction, equipped with a perpetual gaiety and a high-spirited magic no woman could resist, despite that appalling squint which the Earlom portrait in chalk so gracefully minimises, and very few men; a magic acknowledged by even his bitter Royal enemy ('I have never before met so well-bred a Lord Mayor'), and by stout Samuel Johnson himself. 'Jack has great variety of talk,' the Doctor rumblingly admitted after meeting him in 1776; 'Jack is a scholar, Jack has the manners of a gentleman'. Yet we should remember that in Johnson's company Wilkes was on his most superfine behaviour. Johnson never met the essential Wilkes Boswell knew, the mocker whose brilliant extravagance made Voltaire look like a mild dissenting clergyman and Diderot his milder spouse. I still deem Wilkes to represent the Eighteenth Century at its most striking, the personification of that almost hysterical rebellion against the Incarnation which the Age of Reason, so called, developed to its zenith in the advanced drawing-rooms of Paris, boring and sickening even the neutral Horace Walpole.[1] '*Voltaire?*' said a scornful lady of fashion. '*Il est bigot! C'est un déiste!*'

So Boswell, facing death, may have been able to assure himself with relief that Wilkes at seventy was too preoccupied with his latest mistress, young Miss Sally Barry of Dean Street, Soho, to come from Grosvenor Square to crack a few genial

[1] Walpole's letters from Paris made more than one allusion to this, e.g. 'Good folks, they have no time to laugh. There is God and the King to be pulled down first, and men and women, one and all, are devoutly employed in the demolition.' (To Thomas Brand, October 19, 1765) 'The *savans*— I beg their pardon, the *philosophes*—are insupportable, superficial, overbearing, and fanatic; they preach incessantly, and their avowed doctrine is atheism. Don't wonder, therefore, if I should return a Jesuit!' (To the Hon. H. S. Conway, October 28)

seasonable jests on the Four Last Things, or to recall a few lines
from his filthy parody of the *Veni Creator*. Brushing away echoes
of that parody, like blowflies buzzing in his sick brain, Boswell
may have recollected from another great Mediaeval sequence,
suitable to his state, a verse which the great and good Johnson
had never been able to repeat without tears.

> Quaerens me sedisti lassus,
> Redemisti crucem passus,
> Tantus labor non sit cassus.

No doubt such speculations are what dons call 'otiose'. Yet I can
think of no good reason for suppressing the fact that if Boswell
lived like a fool, he apparently did not die like one.

## 4

There is one final thing to recall with sympathy about this
bed-chamber in Great Portland Street, as we linger on the
pavement outside listening to the last distant rumblings of Dr.
Warren's chariot-wheels conveying the King's Physician to the
bedside of some fashionable client in St. James's or Belgravia.
The room had been haunted—who knows how often, in these
last four years?—by a special kind of nightmare, now nearing
its end.

In a Tunbridge Wells Guide (1786) which lies before me
there is mentioned, among the nobility and gentry frequenting
this fashionable spa, a lately-deceased Mr. Dunmall, 'a very
handsome but (*sic*) profligate man, with a head of hair white
as snow'. Mr. Dunmall, who was born at the Creation and was
immortal, had once assured Lord Chesterfield that the Prophet
Jonah, with whom he had travelled in the whale's belly, was
'a great coward'. Apart from his immortality Mr. Dunmall was
advised on all matters by the Archangel Gabriel, and would
gallop of a morning to the Sussex Tavern by the Assembly Rooms
and cry to the landlord: 'Jack! I have received an order from
the Angel Gabriel to drink eighteen gills of white wine before
I get off my horse!'
This type of harmless lunatic—Johnson incidentally must have

*+ Because of me, tired unto death*
*Y'u have redeemed me on the cross*
*Set not such great labor be wasted*
*From Dies Irae (10th v.)*

met Mr. Dunmall on the Pantiles, if that well-known print
including the Doctor among the 'remarkable Characters at
Tunbridge Wells in 1748' is authentic—has been a common
object of the English landscape for some four hundred years,
and has founded more than one quaint sect. Shakespeare is
notoriously fascinated by the mad. It seems to me remarkable,
and possibly significant, that only one mental case gets into the
pages of an eager observer of humanity like Boswell, in an age
when Bedlam was a popular house of entertainment. He will
dwell readily on that hypochondria he shared with Johnson,
as he delighted to think, and on Dr. Cheyne's classic treatise
on it, *The English Malady*. He will bring up the topic of
melancholia, delusions, and even madness to discuss alone or
with Johnson more than once, betraying at least an intermittent
preoccupation. But he mentions none of the fantastics and
eccentrics, the talk of the town, who bob into so many
eighteenth-century letters and memoirs. Among them were
'Walking' Stewart, who went crazy over the polarization of moral
truth and earned a memorial essay of De Quincey's; the miserly
Joseph Nollekens, R.A., who clipped George III's nose with his
callipers and stole Academy Club nutmegs; 'Count' Combe,
author of *Dr. Syntax;* Horne Tooke, one of Wilkes's cronies;
Bampfylde Moore Carew, 'King of the Beggars'; the Hon. Henry
Cavendish, the hermit who established the chemical composition
of water, lived exclusively on mutton, and rarely opened his
mouth; Dr. George Fordyce, the three-bottle anatomist, member
of The Club and pillar of Dolly's Chop-house in Paternoster
Row; the Duchess of Newcastle, the Duchess of Queensberry,
and Lady Mary Wortley, the laughing-stock of the Florentines;
Lords George Gordon, Orford, Coleraine, Coke, and Petersham
(*the peerage was rich in lunatics*); the Millenarist prophet,
Brothers; Smart, the eminent engraver, who launched the
prophetess Joanna Southcott; Hannah Snell, the one-time 'Female
Grenadier' and actress, whose Wapping public-house was
famous; Ward, the celebrated miser, and a score more.

With these marched and tripped a crowd of minor eccentrics
to whom J. T. Smith, for one, testifies in his biography of
Nollekens. Boswell must have sniggered often over the stories
they inspired. Yet the only one mentioned in the *Life,* or, so far

as I know, elsewhere, is the very mild provincial Elwal, who had an Old Testament bee in his patriarchal beard and challenged George II to dispute with him, and I cannot help toying with the fancy that Boswell deliberately avoided mention of the more splendid crackpots of his time because he was secretly perturbed by his own giddiness and by fear of 'going off his rocker', to use another excellent folk-phrase, a little more often than his letters and journals in dark moods reveal. To this fear might be attributed, I am assured by a psychologist, many of his desperate plunges into debauchery. No doubt psychologists, who like alienists, are often madder than their patients, willingly exaggerate. But it is clear that like Swift, Boswell was a haunted man, at least at intervals, being no more cracked, God knows, than hundreds of his contemporaries, but, unlike them, being aware at times of the tiny dark speck in his brain, and terrified lest some day it might spread and overwhelm him. Bedlam he apparently visited only once, in Johnson's company. His calm and detached comment that 'there was nothing peculiarly remarkable about this day, but the contemplation of insanity was very affecting' may—who knows?—have concealed a thousand private terrors. I do not suggest that Boswell was ever in a prolonged sweat over his hypochondria, but the Temple correspondence alone reveals that he brooded over it inter-mittently; being also well aware, I think, that nothing would divert enemies like Gibbon and Horace Walpole more than the caricatures of 'the celebrated Mr. B-sw-LL', naked, wild-eyed, crowned with straw, and proclaiming himself Emperor of Corsica, which would infallibly flood the London print-shops a week after his removal.

The pages which follow will endeavour to bear this preoccupa-tion sufficiently in mind. The vindictive Macaulay had not read the Temple letters when he judged and condemned Boswell. They were discovered by pure accident in 1850 at Boulogne, of all places, having been sold in a lump as waste paper to a local tradesman; from which it is to be deduced that the heirs and executors of Temple's eldest daughter and amanuensis, who lived and died near Boulogne after her marriage, had no Johnsonian addictions. These letters might conceivably have tempered Macaulay's wrath with a little decent pity, though I am afraid

Colonel Isham's more recent discoveries would have inflamed him again to the trumpeting pitch of a Major Prophet. In any case Macaulay would have no sympathy at all with one early impulse which could conceivably have changed Boswell's life and saved him. Dr. Johnson was right about Whigs.

# Chapter Two

## SPRINGTIME OF A GAY DOG

### 1

JAMES BOSWELL, ELDEST SON OF ALEXANDER AND EUPHEMIA HIS wife, was born in Edinburgh, on October 29, 1740.

Both he and Johnson have sufficiently described the 'sullen dignity' of the ruined ancestral castle of Auchinleck, Ayrshire, where Boswell's grandfather reigned until Boswell was nine years old; the elegant Palladian manor adjoining the older house built partly, as Boswell regretted, from the stones of the ancient disused chapel of St. Vincent; the high ruin-crowned rock overlooking the river Lugar, the timbered rocks on the opposite bank, the 'pleasing brook' near the manor and its summerhouse. It was as 'romantick' a home as any eighteenth-century child could wish to be born in. Boswell's father, a judge of the Court of Session, bore an honorary title, in the Scots manner, taken from his estate. Lord Auchinleck is no inconsiderable figure, despite his homely features and the broad rustic brogue he constantly affected. Addicted in his youth to modish red heels and stockings, in 1740 he was an impressive personage in his great periwig: a scholar who had studied at Leyden, like David Balfour, but to more purpose; a friend of the Gronovii; a legal lion; a man of position and substance; a collator of Anacreon editions and the Greek lyrists; the owner of a library which was one of the finest in Scotland, possibly in Great Britain. Auchinleck moreover was skilled in classical gardening, ordered his estates admirably, and, as Johnson says, 'advanced the value of his lands with great tenderness to his tenants'. Of his descent from the Bruce and the Kincardines he was as proud as his son, and showed his

pedigree enscrolled on parchment with some complacency. His
wife, an Erskine of the Mar line, hovers dimly in the background
as what her son calls 'a woman of almost unexampled piety and
goodness', and makes no perceptible sign. In marrying a cousin
and bringing more inter-marriage into a family already tainted—
the marriage of Alexander Boswell's grandfather, the Earl of
Kincardine, to Veronica Sommelsdyck, of a noble Dutch house,
had begun it—the judge showed less than customary Scots
prudence, perhaps.[1]

James Boswell's childhood was happy enough. Lord Auchinleck though ponderous and irascible, was no *cafard*, as the red
heels perhaps indicate. He was even remarkable, his son tells
us, for humour—strictly Scottish and legal, it appears from
specimens quoted in *Boswelliana*—though he could ill brook any
affront to his dignity. A passionate Whig and Presbyterian,
despite his fondness for Anacreon, he imposed no Genevan
tyranny on his household. James and his two younger brothers,
John, a taciturn misty figure who became an Army officer, and
David, an agreeable, if dull, merchant in Spain, had as carefree
a childhood as most eighteenth-century children of their class.
One sees them descending the staircase of a morning, freshly
washed, or at least neatly combed, bowing gravely to their
parents in the breakfast-parlour. 'How do you do, Sir? How do
you do, Mamma? I hope you have enjoy'd a good night's repose';
at the same time—I quote from *The Young Gentleman and Lady's
Private Tutor*, 1770, by Mr. Towle, dancing-master, of Oxford—
having a special care 'not to make any kind of Faces, that is,
such as grinning, winking, or putting out the tongue and the
like', tricks which make a child despised by all. They had an
attractive enough playground in the rocks and woods and water
of Auchinleck, where Boswell told Johnson how he and David
once vowed boyishly to 'stand by the old castle of Auchinleck
with heart, purse, and sword'. Boys wore little swords then in
full fig, even if, like James Boswell, they never drew them in
later life.

As he grew older, it is clear that James spent a fair amount
of time in his father's library, where *The Gentleman's Magazine*,
*The Literary Magazine*, and *The Rambler* gave him his first

[1] See Appendix, *A Note on Heredity*.

gulps of Johnsonian prose. Whether he ever dipped much into the classics lining the library in their sober golden calf, parchment, and pigskin, or the sermon-volumes accompanying them, is doubtful. His Latin and Greek, like his theology, are never very advanced. Would he have developed into the passionate Johnsonian he became if the Judge's library had been less exclusive? A light mind had no great choice at Auchinleck, where no stage-plays or novels disfigured the shelves. It was perhaps just as well. On a Boswell nourished from childhood on Congreve and Wycherley and the lesser Restoration playboys, not omitting Mrs. Aphra Behn, a Johnson might have had no hold.

Into his childish world had stalked long since the sable-clad square-toed figure of the Rev. John Dunn, the parish minister, to whom Lord Auchinleck gave the family benefice in 1752. From Mr. Dunn James got his earliest tutoring. Before long (there is not much record of him at this time) he was sent to the private academy of James Mundell. Thence in due course he proceeded to the University, where he began on the rudiments of law, as his father had decided. Here he made two lifelong friends, one warm, one cool: William Johnson Temple, later Rector of Mamhead, Devon, and St. Gluvias, Cornwall, and grandfather of a celebrated Victorian Archbishop of Canterbury, and Henry Dundas, first Lord Melville, whose powerful political influence Boswell was never able to exploit in later life, hard as he tried; from which fact alone could be deduced a faculty of shrewd judgment in Dundas. As for Temple, a mild and monochrome personality, unfortunately wedded and a Whig to boot, his claim on posterity is the fact that he was Boswell's chosen confidant and only intimate correspondent most of his life, and to some extent one more mentor to that 'weak distemper'd soul', as the rake calls himself in moments of self-pity. Temple is the indispensable 'Charles, his friend' of the Boswellian comedy. Had he not existed it would have been necessary to invent him, perhaps.

Edinburgh in the 1750's had no great attractions to offer vivacious undergraduate youth fresh from paternal bonds. The nightly clubs, all boozy and some orgiastic, with which its more prosperous citizens mitigated their daylight Calvinist decorum, were not open to everybody. There were the taverns, of course, and there were the women on the streets. To both delights James Boswell was already not averse, and he was often in no nimble state to dodge, as he stumbled home to his lodgings through those cobbled, dark, and stinking streets, the unsavoury cascades from upper windows ('Gardy-loo!') which were so celebrated a feature of eighteenth-century Edinburgh's night-life. But from his first published letter to Temple, dated July 29, 1758, we perceive a worthier pastime already exciting him. He has begun to feel the love of literature and to chase his first celebrity.

Some days ago I was introduced to your friend Mr. Hume; he is a most discreet, affable man as ever I met with, and has really a great deal of learning, and a choice collection of books ... We talk a great deal of genius, fine language, improving our style, &c., but I am afraid solid learning is much wore out. Mr. Hume, I think, is a very proper person for a young man to cultivate an acquaintance with ... I own myself obliged to you, dear Sir, for procuring me the pleasure of his acquaintance.

A strange introduction from a candidate for Orders, one cannot help feeling, broadminded as so many eighteenth-century clergymen were. Hume, now a man of 45, had already demonstrated in print that the only thing we can really know is the existence of our own ideas, which themselves are pure illusion. These and other attractive negations and an agreeable manner made Hume the chouchou of the atheist fashionables of Paris when he was secretary to Lord Hertford at the British Embassy between 1763 and 1766, despite his thick Scots brogue and what Lady Mary Coke called his 'violent stomach' at table, unbecoming a philosopher. 'No lady's toilette was complete without Hume's attendance', noted Lord Charlemont. 'At the Opera his broad unmeaning face was usually seen *entre deux jolis minois*.' Hume's affable and authoritative conversation must very soon have dissolved not a few half-held beliefs implanted in his new young friend by a pious Presbyterian mother, for Boswell, no metaphysician, no theologian, yet perpetually itching to discuss religion, was not in a position to say, as Johnson could say, that 'everything Hume has advanced against Christianity had passed through my mind long before he wrote.' If Hume did not succeed in destroying the vague faith of Boswell entirely before Paoli and Johnson appeared, we may take it that in the presence of such a distinguished sceptic the silver trumpets of the Resurrection sounded very faint and far-off indeed, and the Decalogue an obsolete platitude; though even had he succumbed it would be doing Hume's dazzled young friend an injustice to apply to him at any time what Johnson said of Foote, that he was an atheist 'as a dog is an atheist', having never thought about the matter.

Hume and his doctrines were not preoccupying Boswell to any extent at this moment. I continue from the same letter:

You know I gave you a hint in my last of the continuance of my passion for Miss W——t. I assure you I am excessively fond of her.

To identify Miss W——t would seem indelicate. She is (writes Boswell, who drinks tea with her) extremely pretty. She is affable, she dances, sings, plays on several instruments, reads the best authors, and has a 'just regard for true piety and religion' and a fortune of thirty thousand pounds; just the partner for his soul eighteen-year-old Boswell is seeking. However, after this mention Miss W——t is no more heard of; the first of a series of beauties to capture and retain, for a moment or two, this butterfly heart. For Boswell is as capable of virtuous love as of desire for any passing drab of the town, and both passions can flourish in him simultaneously.

There is another interesting passage in this letter. Boswell tells Temple his father has kindly promised to take him on the Northern Circuit. This could be hardly as agreeable as Edinburgh taverns and Hume's conversation and paying court to Miss W——t over the tea-table. It meant a fair amount of travelling in postchaises over bad roads; of mediocre cheer in uncomfortable inns; of prosy law-talk over indifferent claret at mess; of droning and dozing in stuffy, smelly courts. But to Boswell it also turned out to mean the conversation of Lord Hailes, that distinguished lawyer, who accompanied them, and it was Hailes who first made tangible to him the actual living presence of Johnson in London and established in his mind that 'kind of mysterious veneration' with which he figured to himself 'a state of solemn elevated abstraction, in which I supposed him [Johnson] to live in the immense metropolis.' Thus did Sir David

Dalrymple, Lord Hailes, prepare the way for the *Life* to come.

Back in Edinburgh at the end of 1758, Boswell began scribbling, in his spare time,[1] for the magazines and associating with the theatre and its players. An old Drury Lane actor named Love with whom he took elocution-lessons gave him, unwittingly, one more shove towards distant fame by advising him to keep 'an exact Journal' of his daily doings; and pretty disreputable some of the entries were to be. In 1759 he sponsored a vexing comedy stolen anonymously from Corneille by Lady Houston and called *The Coquette, or The Gallants in the Closet*, which was hooted off on its third night. Only the prologue and the production were Boswell's (and the money his father's), but for some time he bore the entire blame for this play. The actresses engaged do not figure in his letters to Temple. They can hardly have escaped young Mr. Boswell's attention. One connects them in imagination somehow with the blowsy harridans in Hogarth's *Actresses Dressing in a Barn*, but they must have been of a higher rank in their profession, or professions, since the theatre at Edinburgh was patronised by the nobility and gentry. We may remember that Johnson himself fell in love in his youth with an actress who played in *Hob in the Well* at Lichfield. Not all the youth and good looks of the stage could stay in London when there were only two or three theatres to employ it.

It may have been these dramatic experiments which decided Lord Auchinleck in 1759 to transfer his son to the more decorous University of Glasgow, where in November we find him attending the lectures on moral philosophy and rhetoric of the famous Adam Smith; Smith of *The Wealth of Nations*, the Smith of whom the attractive story (Sir Walter Scott tells it, I believe) of a first and last meeting with Dr. Johnson resolves itself, after a row over the nature of Hume's deathbed, into two pregnant valedictory lines.

> 'Sir, you lie.'
> 'Sir, you are the son of a whore.'

---

[1] 'From nine to ten I attend the law-class; from ten to eleven study at home, and from one to two attend a class on Roman Antiquities; the afternoon and evening I always spend in study. I never walk except on Saturdays.' (Letter to Temple, December 16, 1758)

After which, according to the story—which some pragmatists, alas, denounce as unauthentic—the two intellectual lions turned sharply on their heels and stalked away from each other. Johnson's own version to Boswell is simply: 'Sir, I was once in company with Smith, and we did not take to each other.' It would have been asking too much, even for Boswell, to inquire too closely into that farewell scene, possibly.

While imbibing moral philosophy at the fount of Adam Smith Boswell kept up his lighter interests. In 1760 the actor Francis Gentleman, as has been mentioned already, accepted a few guineas from him for the dedication of Southern's *Oronooko*. The publicly-recited compliment was probably worth to Boswell whatever it cost, but it may have raised a bushy eyebrow at Auchinleck.

> But when with honest Pleasure she [1] can find
> Sense, Taste, Religion, and Good-Nature join'd,
> There gladly will she raise her feeble Voice,
> Nor fear to tell that BOSWELL is her Choice.

Undesirable notoriety enough for a young lawyer of birth. A worse kind was to befall him almost immediately. To the consternation of all his respectable acquaintance Boswell, in some freakish quirk, connected possibly with his raffish stage friends, began attending the 'Romish chapel' in the Saltmarket, and evinced every intention of becoming a Papist.

## 2

It is a curious episode, dismissed hitherto by decent commentators in half a dozen words as a rather scandalous youthful prank, or even—in the case of a dour Scots Whig surveying Boswell in the 1890's—an indication of mental disorder; which seems a somewhat severe judgment on the religion of Aquinas, Pascal, Descartes, and Mendel and the final solution of the problems of Bergson. And it occurs to one that any step needing considerable courage and changing a man's entire existence and fortunes overnight surely demands a moment or two of examination, distasteful as the topic may be to the progressive mind.

[1] The Muse.

There exists a rococo piece of whimsy by the Presbyterian gossip John Ramsay of Ochtertyre, the original of Jonathan Oldbuck in *The Antiquary,* to the effect that Boswell not only turned Papist with the express intention of entering the priesthood, but prepared himself for this vocation by eloping to London with an actress, as Papists do in such circumstances; from which imbroglio Boswell's father rescued him. The one grain of fact in this fantasy is Boswell's bare statement to Rousseau in 1765 that he did, in fact, become a Catholic for a brief space at this period. What Boswell meant by this we cannot tell. Conversion to the Catholic Church entails, over and beyond the spiritual metamorphosis involved, certain formalities whereby the convert seals and proclaims his faith; essential instruction beforehand, a simple ceremony of reception to follow. It seems doubtful whether Boswell ever went to this length, judging by his frequent questions to Johnson on points of Catholic belief. Possibly, like Gibbon and Wilde and others, he did not think instruction necessary. His prompting was undoubtedly emotional and romantic, with no firm basis of reasoning, and as such would have faded away like measles, even if Lord Auchinleck had not swiftly intervened.

But even if his decision lasted only a month or two it rendered Boswell liable to certain practical and highly unpleasant sanctions. Its implications were far more serious to him, materially speaking, than merely being debarred in practice if not in theory like any modern English-speaking Catholic from the Presidency of the United States and the Lord Chancellorship of Great Britain, with a few minor disabilities here and there. If publicly admitted or discovered, his act spelt at least professional suicide, apart from the immediate vengeance of the thunderbrowed old Presbyterian Whig at home. Some of the penalties incurred seem interesting enough to be worth a glance in passing, for they are often ignored by tactful British historians.[1] Yet they may return in the New Utopia, who knows?

Neither in Scotland nor in England at this moment were the whole of the Penal Laws being applied in all their scientific savagery, as formerly, and in Ireland. Troops of His Majesty's

---

[1] E.g. the two sumptuous volumes of *Johnson's England* (Oxford Univ. Press, 1933) do not mention the Penal Laws at all.

dragoons were not now employed by the Government, as in George I's reign, to swoop on Catholics secretly assembled for Mass, disperse the congregation, seize the priest, loot the altar, and ransack the district for lists of Papists; nor, in England or in Scotland, unless somebody informed on him, would Mr. Boswell be forbidden to wear the sword of his rank, or compelled to dismount and sell for five pounds any horse he happened to be riding if a passing Protestant took a fancy to it. Nevertheless under a useful Act (1722) of George I, which had already wrung some £100,000 out of the Catholics of Great Britain, Mr. Boswell would still be liable as a Papist to regular double taxation and, if necessary, confiscation of his estate. He would also find himself forbidden to inherit property, deprived of his parliamentary vote, forbidden to educate his children anywhere in the United Kingdom, debarred from a naval, military, political, or Civil Service career and from two of the three learned professions,[1] and prohibited to a large extent from practising his religion, unless he lived in London, where diplomatic privilege and foreign charity kept the Catholic Embassy chapels—eight in number, headed by the Bavarian and Sardinian Chapels, and decreasing towards the end of the century to five— open to the public.[2]

Here and there in the country, chiefly in the North, Boswell might fulfil his religious obligations in the rare and widely-scattered private chapels of those of the old English Catholic families, Howards, Welds, Talbots, Hornyolds, Leyburns and others, whose defiant courage and endurance in the darkest days of the Terror and onwards will undoubtedly outweigh, at Doomsday-Leet, their normal follies and weaknesses. In London, again, if he chose to run the risk, Boswell could disguise himself as an Irish labourer and sit hunched over a pint-pot in the still-existent, though rebuilt, long first-floor room of the Ship

[1] Medicine, the exception, was not completely what is called in Trade Union circles a 'closed shop'.

[2] The 'Romish chapel' at Glasgow frequented by Boswell and destroyed in the anti-Catholic riots of 1780 was merely a room in a poor private house, with no legal existence. A few English towns had a similar 'chapel'; its existence was mostly semi-secret and always at the informer's mercy. There were one or two licensed chapels, as at Morfields and Bath; all destroyed in 1780.

Inn, Lincoln's Inn Fields, amid a gathering of the very poorest, awaiting the moment when the watchers at door and windows gave the 'all clear' signal and the room could be hastily prepared for the Mass. After the Last Gospel he, his fellow-worshippers, and above all the officiating priest, in whom saying Mass was a crime punishable by life-imprisonment, banishment, or death, would be, as an illegal assembly, at the mercy of any common informer or police-spy in their midst; for example, a Mr. Payne, who derived a comfortable and regular income from the Government in this way.[1]

Apart from all these harassings Boswell, barred automatically, as we have noted, from a commission in the Army, his real ambition, would have been equally unable to follow the law, his second choice, except—and this only in England, and by accident, and naturally the department was overcrowded—by practising obscurely 'under the Bar' as a conveyancer in chambers. Owing to some oversight in the Penal Code the usual oath against the Blessed Sacrament was not demanded of lawyers in this branch, who were not called to the Bar, and in consequence it became in time almost a Catholic preserve. In Scotland a papistical Mr. Boswell, prohibited from practising at all, would be ostracised with great thoroughness.

A bleak outlook for the new convert. No doubt in a rational moment young Mr. Boswell, in whom courage, physical or moral, was not frequently conspicuous, had counted the cost, even before his father intervened.

Gibbon *père* packed his wayward undergraduate son off to Switzerland for a Calvinist rest-cure. Lord Auchinleck's emergency plan to rescue his own heir from the Scarlet Woman took a somewhat peculiar form. Early in March 1760 James visited London for the first time, fell heavily under London's spell, under the auspices of Mr. Samuel Derrick, Beau Nash's successor as Master of Ceremonies at Bath, and was especially dazzled by the dashing elegance of the Guards. Having apparently agreed

---

[1] A partial Relief Act in 1778 abolished the penalty of life-imprisonment for Catholic bishops and priests, with the £ 100 reward paid on conviction to informers, and allowed Catholics to inherit their own land on certain conditions. The Act was followed by violent anti-Catholic rioting and destruction in Scotland and England alike.

to consider a commission in the Brigade, which would mean permanent immersion in Babylonian follies, Auchinleck begged Lord Hailes to ask Prebendary Jortin of St. Paul's to give the prodigal a course of religious instruction; a singular proposal from one to whom Prelacy and Popery were much the same thing. However, the Anglican *via media* did not, at the time, appeal particularly to James Boswell. Dr. Jortin wrote to Hailes in due course, rather acidly, that 'your young Gentleman' called once at his house in his absence, made another appointment by letter, did not keep it, and had since not been seen or heard of. Lord Hailes's young gentleman was, in fact, plunging vigorously between March and May into the gay life with his mentor Derrick, and had no time to waste on theology or apologetics. In due course, as we shall see, Boswell will acquire sufficient conviction ('though not clear', he will explain to Johnson, 'as to every point considered to be orthodox') to attend church in Johnson's company with sincere if fitful devotion, and even to take the Anglican Sacrament.

He is not, I think, to be despised unduly for waywardness in religious practice, which matches all his other waverings. He might, after all, like Gibbon, have recovered from his brief attack of Roman fever to become one of Christianity's most vicious slanderers. Boswell's own reaction, one gathers from the available evidence, was merely to regard his Catholic interlude as an experience to be suppressed. He never discussed it with Johnson, even when Johnson gave another convert (and a clergyman at that) generous praise for 'conscientious regard to principle', and exclaimed fervently 'God bless him!' Nowhere does Boswell hint, either in the *Life* or any of his minor writings, or in any existing letter, at his own case, nor does he exhibit any sympathy with the persecuted Catholics whose lot he had once thought of sharing.[1] When Johnson denounces the British Government's 'barbarous debilitating policy' designed to stamp out the Mass in Ireland, Boswell reports it but has nothing to say. At the same time something of his brief experience seems to have lingered. It renders his Corsican book, for example, notably free from insular grimaces when he describes, and joins in, the Cor-

[1] One instance, a footnote in the *Hebrides Journal* criticising Wesley's bigotry, excepted.

sicans' devotions and mingles with their monks and clergy. And
evidently nostalgia was mixed with memory. His questions to
Johnson on points of Catholic dogma are numerous, even if the
Doctor's answers are occasionally, but by no means often, ill-
informed, vague, or testy. In Germany, Italy, and France Boswell
frequently attends Mass and haunts the churches with, he says,
sincere happiness, and he goes to Mass often in London, at one
or other of the Embassy chapels, till the end of his life. His relations with any priest he meets, and almost invariably debates
with, are courteous and pleasant, and one of his principal ports
of call during his brief stay in Paris in 1766 will be the Scots
College, which would seem to old Auchinleck one of the gates
of Hell.

However, the experience of 1759 did not 'take', as doctors say
of inoculation, and was not, accurately speaking, a conversion at
all, since it involved no change of heart. For Boswell the world
did not 'turn over and come upright', and he was not to know
that 'spouting Well of Joy within' which Paoli knew. I think we
should still have had a masterpiece of biography from him, with
certain differences. With a similar profound and indestructible
philosophy behind him, he might have become an English
Montaigne. His clarified mind would have indulged in none of
the spiritual bumblings and bombinations *in vacuo* we find here
and there in his pages. He would have talked about religion
infinitely less and no doubt practised it more. And I think he
would have enjoyed the same intimacy with Johnson, who had
a marked, if fluctuating, tenderness for the faith of his fathers
and a warm friendship for more Catholics than Paoli and Dr.
Nugent of the Literary Club, and extended cordial esteem to
priests like Dr. Hussey, senior chaplain to the Spanish Embassy,
and the learned Père Boscovitch, S.J.

Apart from all else, Boswell might have afforded us passing
glimpses of an almost unknown eighteenth-century London
which would greatly have enriched his book: the London, so to
speak, of the Catacombs, of Government spies and police informers, of hidden doors and whispered passwords, of heroism
and treachery, of arrest and escape, a London underworld in
which a grave, taciturn citizen in sober broadcloth lighting his
long clay pipe in a Strand coffee-house with three distinct

gestures might be a bishop of the Universal Church appointing a secret time and place for Confirmation behind locked doors; being liable thereby to appear a week later at Old Bailey, charged, like Bishop James Talbot of the London District in 1771, with 'unlawfully exercising the functions of a popish priest', and issuing thence, if convicted, to prison or exile. Dickens essayed, not too unsuccessfully, to capture something of the atmosphere of the Penal days in *Barnaby Rudge,* from the outside. No one has described it from the inside as Boswell might have done.

However, he changed his mind, and, as Johnson used to growl with such admirable finality *'there's an end on't'.*

Meanwhile that entrancing Guards commission had bloomed and, apparently, faded from Boswell's sight almost as quickly as the Catholic religion. I have called it 'his real ambition' because soldiering is the only profession for which he ever expresed any personal choice. During this three months' initiation into London life the thrasonic effulgence of the Life Guards prancing in and out of the Mall and St. James's Park had impressed him so deeply, as we have already noted, that it is not impossible that Lord Auchinleck in his perturbation seized gladly on this fancy and used it as bait to bring the gomeral James to reason. After Boswell's unwilling return to Edinburgh in May 1760 his father took him to see Archibald Duke of Argyle, one of Marlborough's veterans, who dismissed the suggestion with such bluff alacrity that he may well have been prompted beforehand. 'My lord, I like your son. This boy must not be shot at for three-and-six a day'; which indeed was far from James Boswell's intention. He had, as he informed his countrymen in 1785 in that eccentric *Letter to the People of Scotland on the Present State of the Nation,* 'no high heroick blood'. His view of the military life is indicated with candour in a wail to Temple in 1761:

A young fellow whose happiness was always centred in London, who had at least got there, and had begun to taste its delights—getting into the Guards, being about Court, enjoying the happiness of the *beau monde* and the company of men of genius, in short everything he could wish—consider this poor fellow hauled away to the town of Edinburgh (etc., etc.).

From which we may gather that Boswell's conception of the profession of arms was military, but not warlike. In 1761 the Seven Years' War with France and Austria had still two more years to run. The tide had turned in 1759, after a long sequence of failure and defeat, in favour of Great Britain and her ally Prussia, though a few more set-backs were to come. The British were still vociferously celebrating that glorious year of Minden, Quebec, Quiberon, Guadeloupe, and the foundation of the Indian Empire in an immensely popular song Garrick had written and introduced into *Harlequin's Invasion* at Drury Lane at the end of 1759.

> Come, cheer up, my Lads! 'tis to Glory we stear,
> To add something more to this wonderful Year . . .

with its rousing chorus, defying the Mounseer and his invading flat-bottoms:

> Heart-of-Oak are our Ships,
> Heart-of-Oak are our Men,
> We always are ready,
> Steady! Boys! Steady!
> We'll fight and we'll conquer again and again!

One may guess therefore, not unfairly, that in 1760-1 Ensign Boswell, a devil of a buck about town in his new regimentals, would deem the war to be practically over and would be content to leave any further victories to the Line; and that any rumours in the St. James's chocolate-houses pointing to his being himself involved in any unpleasantness abroad would mean a £2,000 commission for sale or exchange.

For Mr. Boswell, as he so readily agreed himself, was not a man of wrath. In an age of hastily-drawn swords and swiftly-cocked pistols he never fought a duel—on principle, as he says himself—though at least four times on the verge of one: once in Berlin, when an indiscreet remark offended a French officer; once in London, after his remarks in the *Hebrides Journal* on the parsimony of Sir Alexander Macdonald of Sleat had infuriated that chieftain; [1] once, years later, in Edinburgh, over a law-case; and once, finally, at Barnet in 1790, when his brutal patron Lord Lonsdale threatened to put a bullet in his belly. And though he loved scarlet, for some reason unknown he scorned a commission in Pitt's Militia or Home Guard, though the uniform was agreeably gaudy and Wilkes, Gibbon, and Langton all wore it. [2]

Boswell did not take Argyle's pooh-poohing greatly to heart. It did not, after all, mean the end of his soldierly ambitions, still less the golden London dream he had been enjoying so thoroughly. He had had, to use the consecrated phrase, a wonderful time. His new friend Samuel Derrick, 'my first tutor in the ways of London', to whom he had been introduced by the actor Francis Gentleman, had shown him 'the Town in all its variety of departments, both literary and sportive'. It is amusing to find Johnson later advising him to put 'the particulars' of this experience in writing. A nice bawdy epic it would have made, I imagine.

## 3

See them picking their way delicately one fine April morning of 1760 over the filthy paving of the Strand towards a waiting hackney-coach, the dapper Master-Elect of Ceremonies of Bath and his eager young Scottish friend.

A neat, brisk, amiable little butterfly is Mr. Samuel Derrick, ex-actor, minor poet and playwright, Beau Nash's successor in 1761. Johnson had a condescending kindness for him, and in *Humphrey Clinker* a few years later Miss Lydia Melford from Wales awards him a glowing testimonial after his official visit as M.C. to Mr. Bramble's Bath lodgings. 'A pretty little gentleman, so sweet, so fine, so civil, and polite, that in our country he might pass for the Prince of Wales'; the prototype, in fact ('Welcome to Ba—ath, Sir') of Mr. Angelo Cyrus Bantam.

[1] Macdonald wrote him a letter of violent abuse which compelled Boswell to call him out, after learning from his friend John Courtenay, M.P., how to handle a pistol; his trepidation was due, he says, to thoughts of his wife and children. Macdonald fortunately wrote again and obviated a duel. Colonel Isham reproduces Boswell's formal note requesting the pleasure of Sir Alexander's company in Hyde Park. The writing is quite firm.

[2] Wilkes, a major in the Buckinghamshire Militia, wore the uniform constantly till he exchanged it for the uniform of City Chamberlain. Gibbon was an efficient musketry officer, like Langton.

I see dainty Mr. Derrick, frizzed, powdered, perfumed, queued, and cocked-hatted, stepping point-device in the high-waisted cutaway coat of coloured velvet for which, round about 1750, all the beaux had discarded the stiffly-flared, full-skirt brocade frock of an earlier fashion. His flowery gold-laced waistcoat, black satin knee-breeches, lace jabot and wrist bands, clocked silk stockings, speckless silver-buckled shoes, amber-topped malacca cane, dress-rapier, quizzing-glass, and snuff-box are all exquisitely modish. By his side young Mr. Boswell, attired in the more sober fancy of his Edinburgh tailor, cannot help looking provincial, though even now inclined to be a little pursy and consequential, and developing a strut. Mr. Boswell's role, like that of the adaptable country cousin in *The London Spy* fifty years before, and of Jerry Hawthorn in the Regency after him, is 'for to admire and for to see', as Mr. Derrick's fluting voice and gracefully-waved cane point out the smartest and latest, from the reigning Society toasts in the Mall to the Jacobite heads of the '45 rotting on Temple Bar, to view which spy-glasses are available at a halfpenny a peep.

It was still the brutal, enchanting London of Gay and Addison, with its brightly-coloured and, in high winds, lethal forest of heavy, creaking signs, a few years hence to be dismantled by Act of Parliament, with those rows of street-posts which will give place to raised pavements. Many of the signs where as elaborate and decorative as those in Addison's pages. J. T. ('Nollekens') Smith remembered with regret seeing outside a broker's shop a full-length portrait of Shakespeare, painted by Clarkson, richly framed in gilt and swung from a magnificent confection in wrought-iron, which had hung for many years right across the Piazza end of Little Russell Street, Covent Garden, outside the Shakespeare Tavern. It had cost some £200 and was one of the sights of London, and as there was no South Kensington Museum it was allowed to perish. More beauty was brought to the streets by the noblemen's coaches, gilded and painted and wonderfully baroque with their carved Neptunes and mermaids, Cupids and cornucopias, panels by Cipriani and gaily-liveried footmen; as Sir Osbert Sitwell has remarked, 'it is impossible to exaggerate the loveliness added to everyday life by the spectacle of them.' Or, one might almost add, to exaggerate the noise of them. Their great iron-tyred wheels and the hooves of their horses banging over stone flags added to the already formidable din of the hackney-coaches, waggons, drays, and other vehicles, the cracking whips and the screaming drivers. To swell the symphony itinerant musicians scraped and blared, hawkers and ballad-singers bawled, church bells and clocks chimed and rang at regular intervals, the handbells and horns of watchmen and postboys and newsboys clanged and brayed, beggars of every description whined, and every street-trader had a cry, often melodious (see Smith), generally ear-piercing. Hogarth has captured so much of the furious racket of London in his time that it almost deafens one to look at some of his prints. Those who tried to escape it by travelling the river way— and the river traffic was considerable, affording the contemplation of such masses of noble and graceful shipping as we do not see today—did not get off scot-free. From *The London Spy* we note that in the 1700's citizens of spirit using the Thames made it a point of honour to bespatter each other, when within hailing-distance, with the loudest and foulest possible abuse. The custom still existed. Dr. Johnson's shattering riposte to a rude waterman is undoubtedly one of the finest ever heard on London River. 'Sir, your wife, under the pretence of keeping a bawdy-house, is a receiver of stolen goods.' Few amateurs could compete with the Doctor in water-music, as in any other sphere.

A rare and fairly noisy print by Boitard called *The Covent Garden Morning Frolick*, dated 1747,[1] exhibits perfectly the kind of London young Mr. Boswell wanted to see. Amid a cheering, jeering mob a sedan carried by two surly chairmen is staggering over the slimy cobbles. Inside it, fast asleep, is the well-known Covent Garden toast Miss Betty Careless. Perched drunkenly on the roof is 'mad Captain Montague'; escorting it, flourishing an artichoke, is Captain Marcellus Laroon, that excellent artist; and a third notorious character of the Garden named Little Cazey, afterwards transported, heads the procession with a link, side by side with another ragamuffin playing a hurdy-gurdy. 'Charming Betty Careless', whose name is scrawled on the

---

[1] *Catalogue of Prints and Drawings, British Museum (Vol. III, Political and Personal Satires No. 2887). See* frontispiece.

banister in the Bedlam scene of *The Rake's Progress*, died in the poorhouse, like most town-ladies of her time, notably excluding Moll King, the eminent Covent Garden brothel-keeper, who retired from business to build a row of cottages at Haverstock Hill and die in respectability. The frolic depicted by Boitard was certainly not the last of its kind Covent Garden was to witness, and nobody could enjoy such muzzy gambols more than James Boswell, though Derrick may have warned him incidentally that the moods of the London mob were unpredictable. It might easily have welcomed Miss Careless and her escort, for example, with half-bricks, dead dogs, broken bottles, and miscellaneous offal. Its aim was accurate, owing to much pillory practice, and its target sometimes died under its playful attentions.

To see the savage humours of the London mob, as ferocious and famous as its Parisian opposite-number, but less eerily disciplined, at their best, Mr. Derrick would naturally carry Mr. Boswell to Tyburn, for there was no interesting pillory-performance at the moment, so far as I can discover, and no woman was being burned at the stake for coining or husband-murder, a recurring public diversion up to 1790. From *The Gentleman's Magazine* and other sources I gather that Tyburn was not at its best at this moment, either. Four robbers were hanged on Monday, March 28, but though the criminal hero of the decade, mad Earl Ferrers, was sentenced by his peers in Westminster Hall on April 18 for shooting his steward, the actual hanging at Tyburn, by a silken rope, of this nobleman in his wedding-finery did not take place till May 5, so that Boswell probably missed it. In which case Mr. Derrick doubtless apologised for the poor entertainment at Tyburn Fair, where even a highwayman of the vulgarest sort would have been welcome; still more so a product of the great public schools. These foundations, not as yet a close corporation as nowadays, are represented in the Tyburn records by at least two Old Etonians, an Old Westminster, and a gentleman of no named school who seems to me to bear all the obvious stigmata of the Wykehamist. This Macheath in real life, a Mr. John Turner, hanged in 1727, worked the High Toby on the Great West Road, and never held up the Bath coach without winning encomiums from his victims for 'great Gentleness and Good-Manners, putting

is Hat into the Coach and taking what Money they thought
it to give him, nay, sometimes returning a Part of that, if the
Dress or Aspect of the Person gave him Room to suspect that
their Wants were as great as his. From this extraordinary
Conduct he obtained the name of *Civil John*, by which he was
very well known to the Stage-Coachmen'. I quote the reluctantly-
admiring prose of the Grub Street gentlemen in inky ruffles who
compiled the Newgate Calendar's earlier companion-volume,
*Lives of the Most Remarkable Criminals, etc.* Public-school men
still took to the highway now and again in the 1760's, doubtless,
but apparently with more luck.

All gentlemen of the road and other interesting Tyburn clients
were escorted by the mob with joke and song all the way from
Newgate, cheered or pelted all the way. The great triangular
gallows, Deadly Nevergreen, the Three-Legged Mare, which
could take twenty-four at one operation, had been erected in
1571 for Catholics exclusively.[1] The last of the long procession of
London martyrs had been hanged, cut down, and disembowelled
alive some eighty years before Boswell's visit, though he missed
by only six years the last disembowelling of all, that of the
Jacobite agent, Dr. Archibald Cameron, who died as gallantly as
the martyrs. Walpole tells Sir Horace Mann: 'His only concern
seemed to be at the ignominy of Tyburn; he was not disturbed
at the dresser for his body, or at the fire to burn his bowels.'
Walpole adds with a shrug of contempt that in his anxiety to
get a better view of the final ceremony, the clergyman attending
Dr. Cameron let down the top of the landau he was sitting
in.[2]

It will easily be gathered that when the hangman no longer
had the specialist by his side with the knives and the brazier,
Tyburn's entertainment-value became materially reduced. There
could be little complaint as to quantity. Walpole calls Tyburn

[1] The site marked with metal studs in the roadway at Marble Arch is
approximately exact.
[2] It is to be noted that the Government's vindictiveness in punishing a
man of Cameron's admirable character with such savagery, eight years after
the '45, shocked even the Eighteenth Century. Smollett notes that some
of the crowd round the gallows, 'though not very subject to tender
emotions', shed tears, and that Cameron was regarded even by many
Hanoverian Whigs as a victim.

a shambles. Johnson had chanted sombrely in *London, a Poem,* in 1738:

> Scarce can our Fields, such Crouds at *Tyburn* die,
> With Hemp the Gallows and the Fleet supply.

There was still no shortage in the 1760's. The quality of the show was, however, variable. Hundreds of Tyburn's clients lacked what the modern theatre business calls 'box-office appeal', and not a few were so poor-spirited as to be swung off in a state of penitence, though on a lucky day you might view some dashing highwayman and fop like Sixteen-String Jack Rann, or a public idol like Jack Sheppard, delighting his admirers with a gracefully dignified exit, or some stout hot-tempered virago like Mrs. Hannah Dagoe causing howls of mirth by fighting the hangman and knocking him off the scaffold. It may be—I have often suspected it—that when disembowelling ceased, the slow triumphal procession from Newgate became far more amusing than the Tyburn ceremony, which was often an anticlimax, despite those free fights for the bodies between friends of the deceased and emissaries of the surgeons, which shocked Samuel Richardson even more than the oaths and jests exchanged between the condemned and the crowd. I think the favoured occupants of the grand-stand, where now the big cinema stands on the corner of Oxford Street and the Edgeware Road, may often have judged the entertainment hardly worth the trouble. But it satisfied the ruck of the spectators, including the gin-and-gingerbread men, and especially those fearful gangs of child-savages from the rookeries of St. Giles's and Clare Market, Strand doomed from birth to abandonment and starvation, and at length, almost inevitably, to playing the leading part in the public show they now revelled in. These children's every prospect in life ended in a transportation-ship or a gallows, they mostly slept on the bulks in the streets (where Johnson with aching heart would often press a penny into a small grimy paw as he passed) or under chance archways, and no hand was lifted to save them by a country justly famed for care and skill in breeding sheep and cattle. The existence of such children is perhaps, with the tremendous negro slave-trade, which so enriched the pious citizens of Bristol, the blackest of all the stains on this age.

Boswell's lifelong enjoyment of public executions I have already mentioned. His first experience of Tyburn Fair most likely introduced him unawares to several members of the cast of *The Beggar's Opera* mingling with the crowd—Filch and Jenny Diver, for example—and picking his pocket with the greatest ease. There is a real Jenny Diver, alias Mary Young, in the Newgate Calendar; a more vivacious and enterprising character than Gay's. She invented, for example, a pair of false arms, enabling her to steal gold watches and jewellery with impunity at church, lived in style on the proceeds when transported to Virginia, and for some time after her return, until its inevitable sequel at Tyburn, was one of the most efficient and popular toasts of the underworld. From her Gay may have taken the name, which seems to have become a professional honorific, borne by more than one lady after her. By day nobody in a London crowd was safe from Miss Diver and her colleagues. By night, under the sparse and winking oil-lamps, the underworld took more vigorous action. Emerging suddenly from some dark court or twisting alley, sinister figures with drawn blades would surround the foot-passenger even in main thoroughfares; Dr. Johnson, held up once by four bravoes thus, held them at bay till the watch arrived. Linkmen conveying a gentleman home in a fog might knock him out and rob him. Wooden-legged beggars claiming to be veterans of Butcher Cumberland or Hawke or Vernon might whip off a limb and do the same. A hook-and-line dangled from an upper window, or a small boy concealed in a basket on a passing porter's head, might spirit away his hat and wig for ever (a good wig cost anything up to £20). A passer-by's knife might dexterously strip off his gold or silver greatcoat-buttons. In the vicinity of the Parks a particularly odious form of blackmail flourished, then as today. After dark it was better to keep off the streets of London unless you were in a coach—though a coach might be held up, still more a sedan, as the Earl of Scarborough discovered in the 1730's near St. James's, Piccadilly, and Horace Walpole discovered twenty years later, when a highwayman robbed him in Hyde Park [1]—or with

[1] Another of Walpole's experiences: 'I was sitting in my own dining-room (in Arlington Street) on Sunday night, the clock had not struck eleven, when I heard a loud cry of "Stop thief!" A highwayman had attacked a

a well-armed party. Boswell, no swordsman, soon grasped this,
I imagine.

4

Apart from such incidental risks, the night-life to which the
amiable Derrick introduced him was attractive enough to please
more critical neophytes than Mr. Boswell of Auchinleck. A good
dinner would be its natural foundation. The Strand has long
since lost that double festal line of red-curtained tavern windows
glowing like rubies through the murk and fog, eloquent of good
fires and candlelight and comfort, with bursts of laughter and
song—men were allowed to sing in London taverns then—issuing
from them, and a sudden gush of agreeable odours from opening
doors. One dined round about four and supped at a late hour,
and all-night parties were frequent. The fare at a good tavern
was less of a jumble than those dinners at private houses which
to a modern eye seem disconcerting and even barbarous. Not
everybody clamoured constantly, like Dr. Johnson, for veal-pie
with plums, pork boiled to rags, and salt buttock of beef, and not
every dropsy-patient would make a hearty dinner of 'a French
duck-pie and a pheasant' a fortnight before his death; [1] nor did
everybody indulge in the Doctor's cannibal tricks of taking
lobster-sauce with his plum-pudding and pouring melted butter
into hot chocolate and capillaire into port. But even the great
world had peculiar dietetic notions. Returning one night in the
1760's from Lady Blandford's, Lady Mary Coke records in her
diary, with disapproval, a dinner of 'a great round of boil'd Beef,
little mutton-pyes, beans & Bacon, Mackerel without fennel-
sauce. The second Course, a neck of Lamb, a gooseberry-pye,
& two other little things, not Meat'. Even this menu is less curious
than some of the complicated imitation-French cookery the Beau
Monde currently indulged in; and the recurrence of a sauce of
melted butter and flour as a 'dressing' for all vegetables in-
discriminately strikes a sinister note. But in the taverns, at least,

---

post-chaise in Piccadilly, within fifty yards of this house; the fellow was
pursued, rode over the watchman, almost killed him, and escaped.' (Letter
to Sir Horace Mann, September 20, 1750.)
[1] Hawkins, *Life of Samuel Johnson, LL.D.*

you could get a plain and wholesome dinner, and there was no need to hurry over your wine at the cry of an alcoholic host.

Issuing from their Strand tavern towards seven or eight p.m., with a couple of bottles of burgundy or port apiece under their belt and the night before them (we may assume that on this occasion they are not going to the play beforehand), the steps of Mr. Derrick and Mr. Boswell would naturally turn towards Covent Garden, the Palais-Royal of London, where the choicest wickedness of the town was concentrated. Since the nobility and gentry moved west early in the century Covent Garden had become a nest of brothels, dives, gaming-houses, taverns, coffee-houses, supper-clubs and bagnios; brothels like the famous house of the late Moll King, widow of the Old Etonian who founded the business, bagnios like the celebrated Turk's Head, advertised in the fourth plate of *Marriage à la Mode*, and 'Mr. Lovejoy's Bagnio', mentioned by the *London Chronicle* as a casualty in the Covent Garden fire of 1769; a name which seems to me to argue a certain waggery in the pimping world of the period.[1]

Close by Mr. Lovejoy's under the Piazzas was Mr. Rigg's Hummums, a more elaborate thermal establishment where Mr. Derrick and Mr. Boswell might bathe, rest, refresh themselves, and meditate on the night's pleasures, to the clinking of the Mattins-bell of St. Paul's, Covent Garden, having their wigs combed and freshly powdered meanwhile by Mr. Carroll, the adjacent perruquier. To the Hummums attaches the strange ghost-story, related in the *Life*, of Dr. Johnson's rakehelly cousin, the Rev. Cornelius ('Parson') Ford, hero of the *Midnight Conversation* print of Hogarth, whose pencil has caught the roaring, sweating divine in mid-bacchanal. The Hummums service included Turkish, perfumed, and herbal baths, cupping, sweating, massage, and a wine-cellar; one of its specialities, since luxury is essentially conservative, like vice, may still have been the 'Crown

[1] The Oxford Dictionary defines a bagnio as 'a bathing-house (not now in England); Oriental prison; brothel.' In 18th century London it combined the amenities of a night-club, a house of assignation, a brothel, and a bath-house. Another celebrated one was the Bell Bagnio, under the window of which the sculptor Roubillac was buried in 1762, in the churchyard of St. Martin's-in-the-Fields. The Bell advertised 'good Attendance and neat Wines.'

Bath Extraordinary, enrich'd with *Essences* and *Sweet-Herbs'*, which the 'very fine Lady of the Town' orders in that graceless anecdote in *The London Spy*. Apart from these regular pleasure-resorts, many of the taverns in the Strand and Covent Garden district possessed *cabinets particuliers;* [1] for example, the Three Tuns in Chandos Street, where the Honble. J–– F–– (the Newgate Calendar tactfully suppresses his name) was stabbed at 2 a.m. by a Miss Sally Salisbury, who was entertaining him there over a bottle of Frontiniac; for which act of petulance, seeing she did not kill the gentleman, she was with extraordinary leniency merely fined £100 and sent to Newgate to die of gaol-fever.

Pacing the dismal rotten-fruit-stinking remains of Covent Garden in 1946 one finds it a severe effort to summon up its privacious past. From a drawing of the Piazzas in the 1790's by Thomas Sandby, R.A., it would seem that this fine covered promenade has shrunk considerably not only in extent but size since the last rakes and mopsies quitted it. Even St. Paul's church, though it closely resembles the St. Paul's of *The Covent Garden Morning Frolick,* is different. Inigo Jones's original building was burned down in 1795, and the great clock over the Tuscan portico, with its motto *Sic Transit Gloria Mundi* and the chimes by which so many sinners had set their watches, was not replaced on the new front. None of the tall old houses of the Garden Boswell knew survives. One of them, No. 4 Tavistock Row, on the south side, was to have an especial interest for him. Here for many years lived Miss Reay, principal mistress of the Earl of Sandwich, First Lord of the Admiralty, mother of nine of his children and victim of the Rev. Francis Hackman, who shot her dead on the night of April 7, 1779, outside the portico of Convent Garden Theatre; a case of frantic unrequited passion which fascinated Boswell so mightily that he rode, according to a story which has been disputed, in the coach to Tyburn with Mr. Hackman and the attendant clergyman. From Moll King's famous coffee-house and brothel, opposite, the nightly uproar may have quickened the eager steps of himself and Mr. Derrick more than once.

[1] Some fifty of these were 'flash houses', the recognised headquarters of thieves and pickpockets, well known to Bow Street.

We may glance in due course at the more decorous evening amusement to be enjoyed at places like Ranelagh and Vauxhall. Whether Boswell got into one of the more exclusive gambling clubs like White's, the Cocoa-Tree, or Boodle's I cannot say. Lord Eglintoun, with whom he seems to have stayed part of his time, may have taken him into one of these, purely as a spectator, for Eglintoun, who was keeping half an eye on Auchinleck's son, by request, took him down to Newmarket during this visit and introduced him to—though he never put him up for—the Jockey Club, where Boswell entertained the simple-minded racing men vastly with his schoolboy high spirits and gift of doggerel. Play at the great London clubs was appallingly high, and if Boswell ever lost money in any of them he would surely have mentioned it to Temple.

He was certainly fond of a throw. He admits to Temple in 1768 during a fresh outbreak that a few years before 'I had the rage of gaming', that he lost more money than he could afford, and that Sheridan the younger lent him enough to pay his debts, on a promise not to play again for three years. There were plenty of gaming-houses in London, of course, apart from the gilded clubs. Had Boswell ever played with the dukes we should have heard about it.

And of course the theatres...

Drury Lane would be a triple-starred advance-entry in any country cousin's engagement-book. Doors opened at 5.30 p.m., and the play, of anything up to five acts, with prologue and epilogue, began at 6.30, followed by a two-act farce. If Derrick and Boswell had reserved a box in advance, for which purpose the Drury Lane management entreated persons of quality to send their footmen to the theatre a little after five, they could dine at their leisure beforehand. If they chose the pit, it meant a crowded wait and very often a scrimmage.

Inside the vast, dim, cavernous theatre, lined on either side by three tiers of boxes over an enormous pit, with three galleries facing the stage, the orchestra beguiled the time before curtain-rise with three selections, called the First, Second, and Third Musick. The curtain rose on what to a modern eye, pampered by brilliant electrical devices and Schwabe-Hasait installations, would seem almost what Dr. Johnson would call 'inspissated twilight'. On a large stage lit by half a dozen chandeliers and a row of oil-footlights it must have been barely possible to distinguish the players' features from any great distance, which I think explains all the ranting and stamping and raving of the Old School, a style eschewed by the profession nowadays as 'ham'.

In 1755 the anonymous author of a celebrated pamphlet, *Reflections upon Theatrical Expression*, had striven to interest the players in a more subtle management of their limbs and features, and especially of the feet and legs:

> In *Astonishment* and *Surprize* arising from *Terror*, the *left Leg* is drawn back to some distance from the other; under the same Affection of the Mind, but resulting from an *unhop'd-for Meeting* with a beloved Object, the *right Leg* is advanced to some distance before the left. *Impatience* and *Regret* at being detected in some iniquitous Design may be heightened by shuffling of the *Feet* without moving from the *Spot*.

Certainly Garrick, on his return from his Continental tour in 1765, full of fresh ideas, including the abolition of the view-obstructing stage chandeliers in favour of concealed wing-lights, altered and improved his own style considerably, and, as Tom Davies remarks, dropped the 'claptrap'. Perhaps the new lighting helped.

By the beginning of this year, 1760, the glory of Garrick's fifteen-year reign as monarch of the London stage was waning a trifle. At 43 he was a little jaded; his mobile, quizzical features were beginning to show that professional wear-and-tear on which Johnson later commented; he was temporarily tired of fighting his leading ladies; he badly needed that rest from an exhausting routine he was wise enough to take four years later. In March 1760, moreover, his first beautiful, temperamental leading lady and mistress, Margaret Woffington, died in retirement. Garrick cannot but have been remembering with melancholy their splendid joint conquest of the town all those years ago and their stormy loves, even if he were not wearing at that moment the diamond shoebuckles she had given him, and which, always economical though notably generous, he had found himself unable to part with when the affair ended in the late 1740's and all presents were returned.

But whatever his weariness and trials and regrets, he was still a great actor, with sixteen more years of supremacy as a public idol before him, and drawing the usual full houses, on an average. A rather spiteful story, repeated by Knight, that one night about this time Garrick and Mrs. Cibber played to a house of five pounds is dismissed by the best authorities as absurd, as indeed it must be. Even the uproar of 1755, when swords clashed and blood was spilt in the pit of Drury Lane over the celebrated Noverre Ballet from Paris, whose visit had coincided unfortunately with the threat of war against France and who were hooted off the stage as lousy French papists—Noverre was a Swiss Protestant—and spies, after which the audience partially wrecked the theatre and did some £4,000-worth of damage, while Garrick dithered behind the scenes, had not materially affected the box-office. Since a scene would probably never have occurred in the days when Garrick could control a restive house by the lift of an eyebrow, Prospero was feeling too tired, perhaps, to cope with Caliban at this moment. His authority would return before long.

He kept unflaggingly at work, meanwhile. Drury Lane between March and May 1760 had plenty to offer young Mr. Boswell. Four or five nights a week at least Garrick made a personal appearance in the main piece, whether by Shakespeare, Ben Jonson, Congreve, Otway, Vanbrugh, or Rowe. I note from the Drury Lane archives that he played Hamlet, Romeo, and Shylock at this moment but left Falstaff, Richard III, and Macbeth to his talented leading man, Barry, and others; an indication, I deduce, that he was reducing his more strenuous roles—in old age Mrs. Siddons spoke of his 'terrible energy' as Richard—and conserving his powers for the tremendous Lear with which he was to electrify the town a few months hence, and was possibly rehearsing already. Modern actors playing Lear make up with a long white beard and aim at representing an approximate age of 195. Garrick's Lear, beardless, wore a white wig, high-heeled diamond-buckled shoes, and a short velvet ermine-trimmed cloak. Garrick's Romeo wore the rich clothes of a contemporary St. James's beau, like Garrick's Hotspur, who

sported a Ramillies wig, and Garrick's Macbeth wore the full-
dress uniform and sword of a Hanoverian officer against a background of pseudo-Scottish chieftains. His leading ladies wore
hoops whatever they were playing. The Eighteenth Century did
not think this odd.

How often Boswell and Derrick sat on the hard backless
box-seats or pit-benches of Drury Lane, and quizzed the fair
occupants of the boxes, and bought oranges from the orange-girls,
and heard the fiddles tuning, and dodged the peel from the
galleries, and watched the footlights slowly come aglow between
March and May in this year is not known. More than once, I
think. They must surely have been present on the night of April
11, when Derrick's and Johnson's friend Thomas Davies, shortly
to be driven from the stage into the book-trade by a brutal line
in Churchill's *Rosciad,* had a benefit-night and played Horatio in
Rowe's *Fair Penitent,* to which succeeded *The Upholsterer,* a
farce by Johnson's witty young friend Arthur Murphy. Another
evening's programme clearly to Boswell's taste is that of April
18, *Love for Love* followed by Macklin's farce *Love à la Mode,*
with the aged comedian-author playing the lead. I doubt also
if he would miss a spectacular Garrick performance like
Thomson's *Tancred and Sigismunda* on March 3, or the benefit-
night, March 22, of the star comedian Palmer, who played in
Townley's *High Life Below Stairs* after the curtain had fallen on
Verona. A month earlier we might have placed Mr. Boswell at
'the Lane' with absolute certainty, vociferously applauding a
five-act tragedy, *The Siege of Aquileia,* by his friend and fellow-
country man the Rev. John Home, whose tragedies should be
read by anyone curious to gauge the staying-power of the
eighteenth-century London audience. But runs were short in
those days, and Home's poorish piece had come off before
Boswell's arrival. The undated story he tells of his sitting in
Drury Lane pit in his youth with the Rev. Hugh Blair and
ravishing a crowded house, during the intervals, with a lifelike
imitation of a lowing cow, plainly belongs to this first visit.

At Covent Garden the ageing Rich was producing musical
drama and native opera, with a revival or two of Gay's masterpiece. Boswell was just a few months too early in 1760 for two
outstanding Covent Garden landmarks, Arne's *Artaxerxes* and

Bickerstaff's *Love in a Village*, but he may have sat, with difficulty, through Hawkesworth's *Zimri*. The only other London theatres licensed by the Crown were the King's Theatre, Haymarket, sacred to Italian Opera and the dilettanti, and 'the Little Theatre in the Haymarket', a small comedy-house made fashionable by those satiric sketches of Foote's which might have lived longer had they been less topical. One of Foote's current productions, *The Minor*, inspired a tiresome Boswellian pamphlet on his return to Edinburgh. The rough-and-tumble seasonal booths of Bartholomew Fair, now in dishonourable decline, where horseplay like *The French Flogg'd* kept up the John Bull spirit, would hardly attract him or Derrick, I think.

If it was music and dazzle combined with the company of the Beau Monde at elbow-rubbing quarters that Mr. Boswell desired during this short stay, Derrick may have been able to satisfy this need before he left London. The pleasure-gardens of London opened in May and closed in August, so Boswell could quite well have fallen this month, like Lord Chesterfield and Horace Walpole, and even Dr. Johnson, under the enchantment of fashionable Ranelagh, adjoining Chelsea Hospital; parading with half the Peerage round and round the vast and glittering Rotunda ('blind asses in an olive-mill', said crusty Dr. Smollett), cooling himself amid mazy sylvan walks where all the birds 'attuned their note to ears polite', admiring the lake and the Chinese Pagoda, and supping elegantly and expensively in one of the two tiers of supper-boxes, while the great organ, the string orchestra, and some artist like the eminent tenor Beard, or Parry the harpist, produced those quavery *fioriture* so admired by the age. Vauxhall, older and now slightly less modish, offered much the same attractions. The still less fashionable but very popular Marylebone Gardens, where Dr. Johnson incited a famous public revolt against Torré's non-operative fireworks one showery summer evening in George Steevens's company, had a Grand Walk amid tall trees and a charming music-pavilion and orchestra, mounted on pillars. The celebrated King of Pick-pockets, George Barrington, operated there. On the authority of *The Beggar's Opera*, Marylebone was also an off-duty haunt of Macheath and his High Toby friends, but what public resort in London was not? No doubt young Mr. Boswell mistook more than one ruffling swell-mobsman for a man of quality, and may even have been fooled, in the classic eighteenth-century manner, by the usual town mopsy or waiting-woman in borrowed plumage, to the air of 'Water parted', or the minuet in *Ariadne*. It is interesting to think that old tunes like these, played at the eighteenth-century pitch by fiddlers long dead, were last heard by living ears in the early 1900's, when those two sedate Oxford ladies had that eerie, fascinating adventure at Versailles.

5

The list of the town's pleasures in early 1760 is by no means exhausted. We may glance briefly at a few that remain while Mr. Derrick and Mr. Boswell finish taking their throbbing heads for a morning walk in the Mall, along the double avenue of limes and elms, and turn into one of the Pall Mall chocolate-houses, the Star and Garter or the Old Smyrna, for a dish of coffee and a glance at the *London Chronicle* or the *Public Advertizer*. Perhaps they have just seen, as they paced past Horse Guards Parade, a soldier flogged into insensibility, and viewed and admired some reigning toast, Lady Waldegrave, Lady Coventry, or the eccentric and slovenly Duchess of Devonshire taking the air. They have seen Rosamond's Pond by Bocage Walk, now covered by Wellington Barracks, and the Canal, and the water-fowl, and the carp, and the cows and deer browsing the grass, and Buckingham House, a mansion one-third its present size, not yet a Royal residence.

Their Pall Mall chocolate-house would be full of 'smoke and stratagem', tattle and perfume. The modish gentleman in peach-and-silver, in loud transports over the excellence of the new play at Drury Lane, would quite likely be on the payroll of Mr. Garrick, to whom none of the arts of publicity, including the *claque*, was a secret. If they decided later to take a hackney-coach to one of the outlying pleasure-resorts with which London was ringed, they had an embarrassing choice, since every suburban tavern of any pretensions had its gardens and its games, skittles and bowls especially.

At Sadler's Wells and Bagnigge Wells in Clerkenwell, at the World's End and the Bun House in Chelsea, at the White

Conduit House in Islington, Boswell could contemplate the middle class taking its pleasure, the 'greasy cits', the corpulent City tradesmen, many of them rich enough to buy the place, with their wives and daughters, drinking tea, eating cheesecakes, listening to the fiddles, watching the ropedancers. Even at these sober resorts exciting things might occasionally happen. It was at Bagnigge Wells in the 1770's that Sixteen-String Jack Rann the highwayman appeared one Sunday night in a fine scarlet coat with tamboured waistcoat, white silk stockings, and gold-laced hat, fully armed, drunk, boastful, posturing like a film-star, and creating such trouble that a party of young sparks bundled him ignominiously out of the window. There was more risky amusement to be sought, with proper precaution, among the merry blackguards of Hockley-in-the-Hole, where bare-fisted gladiators half-murdered each other nightly in the boxing-ring, and female pugilists (fists to be clenched over half a crown, by order, to prevent gouging and scratching) were a special attraction, and wrestling, cudgel-play, dog-fights, cock-fights, bull and badger-baiting, and every kind of relaxation brought together all the thugs, thieves, sharpers, pimps, crimps, bullies, blacklegs, and highwaymen in town, with their doxies, apart from patrons of manly British sport like Frederick, Prince of Wales. 'You should go to *Hockley-in-the-Hole* and to *Marybone*, Child, to learn Valour', says waggish Mrs. Peachum to Filch, referring not so much to Marylebone Gardens as to the taverns and gaming-houses fringing it. Nothing remains of the wicked glory or the dens of Hockley, which is now called Back Hill, Clerkenwell, the hub of London's highly respectable and industrious Italian quarter.

If Mr. Derrick's young friend enjoyed the spectacle of low life, further interesting experiences awaited them among the brawling sailors and their women in the pot-houses of Stepney and Ratcliffe Highway and Wapping, where the bones of pirates clanked and twirled in their chains at high-water mark. By daylight these places were relatively safe for tourists, it appears from *The London Spy*. More accessible and less risky to the spectator were the purlieus of May Fair, where duck could be hunted by hired spaniels on ponds behind the taverns, or the Long Fields behind Montagu House in Bloomsbury, now covered by the vast pile of the British Museum, where the scum of St. Giles's indulged in dog-fights and tipcat and cricket and other disreputable games, especially on Sundays and despite the magistrates and the Press Gang.

From all their expeditions the natty guide and his eager pupil would return in their hackney-coach, I think, weary but quite ready again, after a rest, a bottle, and a change of attire, for the evening amusements of the fashionable end of the town; the taverns, the theatres, the bagnios, and the brothels. If Boswell felt inclined to repose his mind for an hour or so before dressing with a little light reading, the current issue of *The Gentleman's Magazine* would most naturally supply it. The March number for this year contains a Survey of Thurot's recent naval expedition to Ireland, a Review of an Enquiry into the Beauties of Painting, a Table of the Duration of Life, *Ortogrul* (an Eastern Tale), and articles on the Militia Act, the Certainty of a Future State, and Frauds Practised by Farmers in the Payment of Tithe, together with the Story of a Lady in Derbyshire (who found her husband embracing her maid), the Idea of an English Academy, Governor Lyttleton's Treaty with the Cherokee Indians in 1739, the Minutes of Lieut.-Gen. Lord George Sackville's recent court-martial for refusing to obey an order of Prince Ferdinand of Brunswick at Minden, many book-reviews, and a section of light verse, notably an ode *On a Piece of Diacolon Plaster being Dropt before a Lady, folded like a Billet-Doux*.

Which will remind us that we seem to have overlooked the literary attractions Boswell mentions as part of his initiation into town life. These would include, no doubt, some dawdling round the more celebrated bookshops, Dodsley's at the Tully's Head in Pall Mall, Andrew Millar's and Tonson's in the Strand, Dodd's at Temple Bar, Osborne's in Gray's Inn; together, perhaps, with a bottle or two among the wits and bookmen and Templars at the Old Grecian in Devereux Court, Strand, the ghost of which still wanly flourishes, and an evening or two at Old Slaughter's in St. Martin's Lane, the Café Royal of the period. Though Johnson, his presumed lodestar, was to be seen any night at the Mitre or some other favourite Fleet Street tavern, and could easily be called on, Boswell seems to have made no effort to hold Derrick to his promise to present him. He explains himself that he came to suspect that Derrick had promised more than he could perform. More likely the gay dog had temporarily postponed Johnson and Derrick deemed it for the best. As for his remark to Temple about 'the company of men of genius', it appears from a recently-discovered letter to Eglintoun that Boswell called on Sterne in his lodgings in Pall Mall at least once during this stay. Sterne was the fashionable novelist of the moment and held a daily levee. Nothing came of their meeting, and doubtless Johnson's gargantuan contempt for 'the man Sterne' explains Boswell's lack of interest in him afterwards. It seems possible that Derrick introduced him to Goldsmith, his countryman, during this visit. He certainly met Tom Davies; possibly the younger Sheridan, and quite likely as I have suggested before, the fascinating Wilkes.

So passed, more or less, three months of sheer intoxication, in more senses than one, and it was time to book a reluctant seat in the Glasgow coach at its Holborn starting-place.

6

Edinburgh was naturally a provincial hole to the recent man-about-town, and the last letter to Temple (May 1, 1761) I have quoted exhales all the disgust of a Rivarol exiled to Hamburg, though not so wittily. After that sigh for the Guards and the Court and the Beau Monde, Boswell runs on:

Consider this poor fellow hauled away to the town of Edinburgh, obliged to conform to every Scotch custom, or be laughed at—'Will you hae some jeel! [1] Oh fie! Oh fie!'—his flighty imagination quite cramped, and he obliged to study Corpus Juris Civilis, and live in his father's strict family; is there any wonder, Sir, that the unlucky dog should be somewhat fretful?

The jolly Mohocks of the Jockey Club are in his mind as he compares himself to a Newmarket courser yoked to a dungcart,

[1] 'Jeel', I am informed by a learned Scots antiquary, was merely jelly. But the polite called it 'conserve'.

and in his fretful boredom he is inclined to be testy with Temple on a personal matter.

Your insinuation about my being indelicate in the choice of my female friends, I must own, surprises me a good deal. Pray, what is the meaning of it?

Here the judicious editor (1856) of the Letters, Mr. Philip Francis of the Middle Temple, leaves a blank, explaining that it is not at all desirable to follow Boswell into particulars of conduct here described and extenuated. Given Boswell's temperament, it is hardly worth while trying to conjecture what light on the Edinburgh underworld Mr. Francis suppressed. The peevish mood lifts very soon and Boswell is once more active and cheerful, scribbling and publishing a doughy facetious three-penny pamphlet on Foote's recent performance in *The Minor*, and an *Elegy on the Death of an Amiable Young Lady*, price sixpence, and starting a correspondence with Andrew Erskine, the Earl of Kellie's son, a captain in the 71st Foot, which is full of bad verse and flighty prose, often no worse than some of Horace Walpole's or Lamb's. The first letter gives sufficient indication of the style:

Auchinleck, August 25th, 1761.
Dear Erskine,
No ceremony, I beseech you! Give me your hand. How is my honest Captain Andrew? How goes it with the elegant, gentle Lady A——? The lovely sighing Lady Jane——? And how, oh, how does that glorious luminary Lady B—— do? You see I retain my usual volatility. The Boswells, you know, came over from Normandy with William the Conqueror; and some of us possess the spirit of our ancestors, the French. I do, for one. A pleasant spirit it is. *Vive la bagatelle!* . . .

Rather heavy frisking, and more authorities than Madame de Sévigné would raise an eyebrow, doubtless, at the young gentleman's claim to *esprit*. The note of the Erskine correspondence is fun of a rather vexatious kind. That itch for self-expression which had already inspired letters to Temple and verse for *The Scots Magazine* was increasing; not so Boswell's judgment, which badly needed a Johnson to chasten and direct it. He wrote a deal of trash at this time, notably a comic song in his own praise sung

by himself at the Soapers' Club, one of those nocturnal Edinburgh assemblies, already alluded to, where indefatigable Scots
rollicking was essential. It is not worth quoting, though he was
sufficiently proud of it to print it in an anthology called *Poems
by Scotch Gentlemen* in 1762.

What Lord Auchinleck and his weighty, snuffy legal friends
thought of such performances is not known. Such scribblings
show Boswell as a boozy kind of buffoon enough, yet he was
never entirely that. In his private papers there is the diary of a
round of country-house visits he paid with Erskine, called
*Journal of My Harvest Jaunt*, 1762, which shows him in a much
more attractive light: a rattle, perhaps, but not a clown; a gay,
polite, and welcome guest, with those off-moments of solemn
ambitious reflection he indulges in all his life. Moreover he was
moving at present in the most exclusive Edinburgh circles and
was a member of the Select Society, a club of gentlemen where
the native brogue was tabu. On the Queen's Birthday he was
seen, a festive but decorous figure, at the Holyrood Ball. 'I
exhibited my existence in a minuet', he reports to Erskine, 'and
as I was dressed in a full chocolate suit and wore my most solemn
countenance, I looked, as you used to tell me, like the fifth act
of a deep tragedy.' Gravity could not last long. A little later he
published—with Dodsley, of all people—his silliest effort so far,
a long, rambling, facetious poem called *The Cub at Newmarket*,
revealing how the fast men of the Jockey Club had laughed at
him in 1760. The Duke of York, to whom Boswell with characteristic aplomb dedicated this piece of drivel, was graciously
pleased to approve it. The *Monthly Review* dismissed it as 'scarce
intelligible'.

The Erskine Correspondence came out in book-form in April,
1763, at three-and-sixpence, full calf, with Boswell's name on a
title-page for the first time. 'Light and airy', said the *Monthly
Review* kindly. 'They are pretty fellows in Literature, and must
not be roughly handled.' The painstaking froth between these
covers is typical early Boswell. A self-portrait in a letter of
December 17, 1761, shows his best prentice or pre-Johnson
manner; the *Ode to Tragedy* in question he had published
anonymously, dedicated roguishly to himself, in that year, with
some thirty other poems, all bad.

The author of the *Ode to Tragedy* is a most excellent man; he is of an ancient family in the West of Scotland, upon which he values himself not a little. At his nativity there appeared omens of his future greatness; his parts are bright, and his education has been good; he has travelled in postchaises miles without number; he is fond of seeing the world; he eats of every good dish, especially apple-pie; he drinks old Hock; he has a very fine temper; he is somewhat of a humorist, and a little tinctured with pride; he has a good, manly countenance, and he owns himself to be amorous; he has infinite vivacity, yet is observed at times to have a melancholy cast; he is rather fat than lean, rather short than tall, rather young than old, his shoes are neatly made, and he never wears spectacles. The length of his walking-stick is not yet ascertained . . .

There might have been much more of this schoolboy stuff to raise Edinburgh's eyebrows, but lo and look ye! Who is this trim cavalier riding through Glasgow on November 15, 1762, dressed in 'cocked hat, brown wig, brown coat made in the Court fashion, red vest, corduroy small-clothes, and long military boots', with a servant on horseback behind him? Who but James Boswell, Esq., of Auchinleck, on his way to the London coach, with a letter to the Duke of Queensberry in his pocket and hopes of that Guards commission flaming high in his heart once more. How he had got his father's consent does not appear in the records. Possibly Auchinleck had come to the reluctant conclusion that since James was determined to make an exhibition of himself, he might as well do it in London, where he was unknown. James had already whooped joyously to Erskine:

My fondness for the Guards must appear very strange to you, who have a rooted antipathy at the glare of scarlet. But I must inform you that there is a city called London, for which I have as violent affection as the most romantic lover for his mistress . . .

So here he was again among the gay lights and the painted ladies, occupying his friend Temple's chambers in Farrar's Buildings, Inner Temple Lane, during Temple's residence at Trinity Hall, Cambridge, and plunging feverishly anew into the metropolitan whirl. Nothing except an invitation or two ever came of that letter to Lord Queensberry, who may, like Argyle, have had some private arrangement with Auchinleck about it, though ten minutes' interview with this curious candidate for a commission would have convinced the least sophisticated Guards colonel, I take it, that Mr. Boswell was hardly Heaven's surprise-gift to the Brigade. Once again the set-back does not seem to have worried Boswell particularly. We may not uncharitably assume that he was to some extent repeating the amusement-programme he had gone through with Derrick, with Wilkes or one of his satellites for a companion. But this time he was deter-mined to track down Johnson and annex him. Why he did not do so before March 1763 he explains, to some extent, in the *Life*: 'When I returned to London, at the end of 1762, to my surprise and regret I found an irreconcilable difference had taken place between Johnson and Sheridan.'

It was Sheridan—old Mr. Thomas Sheridan—who had assured Boswell at Edinburgh in 1761 that he should certainly meet 'the Sage' at his, Sheridan's, house in London in due course. Since then Sheridan had been given a Government pension, Johnson rather meanly resented it, and a hasty, contemptuous remark parted them for ever. Boswell's second string, as we have noted already, was Thomas Davies, the ex-actor-bookseller of Covent Garden, with whom Johnson regularly drank tea, and to whom Derrick had providentially introduced Boswell before retiring to his new duties in Bath. To haunt Mr. Davies's cosy back-parlour at intervals, therefore, was not only to rest a racking hangover and to roll a lacklustre but fascinated eye at Davies's extremely pretty and alas, virtuous ex-actress wife, but to be ready at any moment to make, so to speak, the kill. There were false alarms. Mrs. Davies set out the extra teacup for the Doctor in vain more than once, and her opinion on the plain, plump young Scot who sat and sat, so frankly using her house for his own purposes and drinking her best Bohea at half a guinea a pound, might have been interesting, like her comments on Boswell's statements in the *Life* that he was 'more than once invited' to do so. But whether his eagerness to meet Johnson was constant, as he says, or intermittent, as seems more likely, Boswell certainly was there when Johnson at last bethought him of a dish of tea at the Davieses'.

That day, that memorable day, was Monday, May 16, 1763.

# Chapter Three

# BIRTH OF A DISCIPLE

## 1

To attempt to compete with James Boswell in describing that meeting with Johnson would be so absurd that anyone tracing his career is placed in a mild quandary. Which is better, to quote Boswell's own words, which are in the *Life* and in their context for anyone to read, or to summarise and pass on with an apologetic grimace towards the master's work? I seize gladly on an obvious way out of the first of these difficulties, at least, by quoting Murphy's less well-known account of this celebrated occasion, at which he was present, though Boswell denies it hotly in a long footnote.

Arthur Murphy, himself in due course to write a pleasing *Essay on the Life and Genius of Samuel Johnson, LL.D.*, was a young Irishman of talent whom Johnson 'very much loved', in Boswell's words, and who might well have taken Boswell's place. Wit, playwright, man of letters, ex-pupil of the Jesuits of St. Omer, many of whose teachings he had gracefully discarded on coming to London, friend of Mrs. Thrale, he lounges elegantly in the Johnsonian background, one amused and quizzical eye, so to speak, on the ebullient Boswell. His version of the meeting of May 16 wears a subtle grin.

Upon another occasion this writer went with him [Johnson] into the shop of Davies, the bookseller, in Russell Street, Covent Garden. Davies came running to him almost out of breath with joy. 'The Scots gentleman is come, Sir; his principal wish is to see you; he is now in the back-parlour.'

'Well, well, I'll see the gentleman', said Johnson.

He walked towards the room. Mr. Boswell was the person. This writer followed with no small curiosity.

'I find', said Mr. Boswell, 'that I am come to London at a bad time, when great popular prejudice has gone forth against us North Britons; but when I am talking to you I am talking to a large and liberal mind, and you know that I cannot help coming from Scotland.'

'Sir', said Johnson, 'no more can the rest of your countrymen.'

A neater version of Johnson's riposte, perhaps, than the official or Boswellian one. But nobody could give the rest of the scene with more candour or vividness than Boswell. We see him fidgeting on the edge of his chair as the great man sits and turns composedly to talk to Davies. We see the erect ears, the popping eyes as Boswell hangs on every word, moistening his lips, swallowing, dying to cut into the conversation and distinguish himself, like Mr. Kipps in the Imperial Grand.

At last the longed-for, the fatal moment arrives. Johnson growls to Davies, 'What do you think of Garrick? He has refused me an order for the play for Miss Williams, because he knows that the house will be full and that an order would be worth three shillings.'

This is surely Mr. Boswell's cue. One can almost hear his shrill, excited pipe.

'Oh, Sir, I cannot think Mr. Garrick would grudge such a trifle to you!'

A fearful pause, and the lightning strikes from the cloud.

'Sir (said he with a stern look) I have known David Garrick longer than you have done; and I know no right you have to talk to me on the subject.'

*Hic finis rapto,* one might think. Boswell himself admits that 'had not my ardour been uncommonly strong, and my resolution uncommonly persevering', he might have accepted defeat and never dared to encounter Jove again. Fortunately for us, he swallowed his mortification, stayed, recovered his nerve, managed to put out 'an observation now and then, which he received very civilly', and retired from the presence bloody but unbowed, the kindly Davies assuring him that 'I can see he likes you very well.'

A week elapsed before Boswell, having taken counsel of Davies, and fortified by the 'witty sallies' of Wilkes and his

cronies, visited Johnson in his lair on the first floor of No. 1
Inner Temple Lane. He found the lion amenable and courteous,
holding a levee. Boswell's pen-picture is precious.

It must be confessed that his apartment, and furniture, and morning
dress were sufficiently uncouth. His brown suit of cloaths looked very
rusty; he had on a little old shrivelled unpowdered wig, which was too
small for his head; his shirt-neck and knees of his breeches were loose;
his black worsted stockings ill drawn up; and he had a pair of un-
buckled shoes by way of slippers. But all these slovenly particularities
were forgotten the moment that he began to talk.

Admirable reporting, yet not so brilliant as Boswell's description, earlier in the *Life*, of the first impact of Johnson on
Langton:

From perusing his writings, he (Langton) fancied he should see a
decent, well-drest, in short, a remarkably decorous philosopher. Instead
of which, down from his bedchamber, about noon, came, as newly
risen, a huge uncouth figure, with a little dark wig which scarcely
covered his head, and his clothes hanging loose about him. But his
conversation was so rich, so animated, and so forcible (etc., etc.).

Anyone who denies that Boswell was a conscious literary artist
should roll the cadences beginning 'Instead of which . . .' round
his tongue a few times. One can almost count the stairs creaking
one by one under that huge deliberate foot, and feel the youthful,
nervous visitor's heart bumping as he eyes the door.

The séance of May 24 settled everything. As Johnson's other
visitors rose to go Boswell rose too, was kindly prevented, resumed his seat, said the right thing this time ('It is benevolent
to allow me to hear you'), received a mellow reply ('Sir, I am
obliged to any man who visits me'), and on rising finally to go
was pressed—actually pressed—to stay longer, which he did.
And at length Boswell left Inner Temple Lane walking on air,
having extracted a promise from the Sage to visit him one day at
his lodgings.

On June 13 he called at Inner Temple Lane again, to make
certain, and this time all doubt was removed.

He again shook me by the hand at parting, and asked me why I
did not come oftener to him. Trusting I was now in his good graces,

I answered that he had not given me much encouragement, and reminded him of the check I had received from him at our first interview. 'Poh, poh!' (said he, with a complacent smile) 'never mind these things. Come to me as often as you can. I shall be glad to see you.'

The Doctor, in modern idiom, was in the bag. He had even agreed to a tête-à-tête supper at the Mitre tavern in Fleet Street in the near future. It would be only natural for the new disciple to prepare himself for such an event by keeping strictly sober and leading a more decorous life. It is therefore no surprise to find Boswell explaining gaily that being so occupied ('shall I call it?—or so dissipated') by the amusements of London, he did not see Johnson again for nearly a fortnight, and then by pure accident, in an eating-house in the Butcher Row, Strand, where now the Law Courts stand.

2

Bad news travelled fast enough even in those days, when an express postchaise-journey between London and Auchinleck took all but three days—'64 hours and a quarter', Boswell once timed it. Six months after his son's arrival in London Lord Auchinleck, who had undoubtedly been informed by a well-wisher of the kind of life James was leading, took him firmly in hand. 'I have had a long letter from my father', Boswell writes to Temple on July 15, 'full of affection and good counsel. Honest man! He is now very happy'.

The playboy had just agreed, after a threat to disinherit him if he did not, to the plan for his future his father had drawn up. The Guards mirage had finally faded. The Law had taken its place. Boswell was to leave London forthwith for Utrecht, with an allowance of £240 a year, to sit under 'an excellent Civilian in that University' and to pursue his legal studies, and Lord Auchinleck, like other people, had taken James Boswell's pledge for future good behaviour. 'He insists on having my solemn promise', continues the letter to Temple, 'that I will persist in the scheme on which he is so earnestly bent . . . I think I may promise this much: that I shall from this time study propriety of conduct, and to be a man of knowledge and conduct, as far as I can.'

There is some more about his eventually assuming the gown of the Faculty of Advocates and becoming a 'gentleman of business with a view to my getting into Parliament.' A career with not such an attractive costume as the Guards', alas; yet a dashing young Counsellor Silvertongue in a modish wig and well-cut gown may draw admiring crowds, of women especially, and a Member of Parliament has, or had, a certain glamour and prestige, apart from perquisites. Boswell already saw himself, it is plain, in the black-and-gold of a Lord Chancellor, and was happy again.

Meanwhile the promised supper at the Mitre in Fleet Street had fanned his trepidant respect for Johnson into a hot glow of affection and veneration. In the *Life* he remembers it with a thrill:

We had a good supper, and port wine ... The orthodox high-church sound of the MITRE—the figure and manner of the celebrated SAMUEL JOHNSON,—the extraordinary power and precision of his conversation, and the pride arising from finding myself admitted as his companion, produced a variety of sensations, and a pleasing elevation of mind beyond what I had ever before experienced.

Impossible to recapture the Mitre atmosphere in modern London. It evaporated with the Mitre itself, on whose site Hoare's Bank now stands. In a London tavern of this quality, we may reflect again, firelight and candlelight, sanded floor and red-curtained windows, mellow oaken furniture and panelling, white-aproned waiters and good fare blended in an aura of solid cheer which did not vanish completely, according to Disraeli, till the 1850's. At the Mitre there was no haste. Boswell and Johnson got there at 9 p.m. and sat till between one and two in the morning, eating a leisurely supper, finishing a couple of bottles of port, stretching their legs and having their talk out, like civilised beings. Nearly five hours of pure rational pleasure. No modern London restaurateur would endure it, even if the police allowed him.

Their talk drifted from literary matters to religion, the first of many discussions of its kind. Boswell admitted 'a certain degree of infidelity', as well he might, seeing his intimacy with Jack Wilkes and some of the Medmenham gang, which he took care not to mention. He was perfectly sincere in his impulse towards religious truth. It was impossible to be in Johnson's company and not to feel Christianity towering over you like Gibraltar. As the big, homely, pockmarked face, every scar and pit and depression in it thrown into strong relief by the candle-flame, like a map of the Moon, twitched and grimaced and frowned and beamed and rumbled opposite him, Boswell pardonably revered the Doctor as an oracle and a saint. The talk veered to ghosts, to Goldsmith, to Mallet's last play, to the estate of Auchinleck, and to Boswell's forthcoming journey abroad, which, if extended to 'perambulate Spain', Johnson suggested, to the young man's elation, might make a book.

They met next on July 1, at the Mitre, Goldsmith supping with them. Boswell had apparently met Goldsmith some time before. He does not say how or where; possibly, as we have conjectured, with Derrick. His attitude towards the jealous Goldsmith is always slightly supercilious. Goldsmith's childish but temporary triumph at this moment over Boswell as an 'esoterick' disciple, much deeper in Johnson's intimacy and admitted to drink tea late at night in Johnson's house with old Mrs. Williams, undoubtedly rankled a trifle. The contrast between Goldsmith's homely face and figure and the gay clothes he loved was not unamusing, like most of Goldsmith's oddities; Boswell, duly recording a few of them, is never chary of recognising the genius of a man he never cared for. In 1763, at the age of 34, Goldsmith had not yet written his comedies and was not yet able to indulge his sartorial passion to any extent; the famous 'bloom-colour'd' coat, the blue velvet, the silver-grey tamboured waistcoat, the steel-hilted dress sword, inlaid with gold, and the other finery for which honest Mr. Filby of the Harrow, Water Lane, and other tradesmen were never to get their money, were still below the horizon.

The night's conversation is in the *Life*, what amount of it Boswell managed to remember. He apologises himself for the relative imperfection of his early reporting. He has not yet become 'strongly impregnated with the Johnsonian æther'; but this gift will come soon, is indeed coming already. On Wednesday, July 6, Johnson was to sup with him at his Downing Street lodgings, but as Boswell had given his landlord notice for rude-

ness the night before, when he had had company, they supped
at the Mitre instead with Goldsmith, Thomas Davies, an Irish
friend of his, and a Scotch clergyman, Mr. Ogilvie. Johnson was
in playful mood on the subject of retaliating on the uncivil
landlord:

> Sir, you may quarter two Life-guardsmen upon him; or you may
> send the greatest scoundrel you can find into your apartments; or
> you may say that you want to make some experiments in natural
> philosophy, and may burn a large quantity of assafœtida in his house.

It is by no means unlikely that the 'greatest scoundrel you can
find' had actually been among Boswell's guests in Downing Street
that night. His landlord's version of an encounter with, say,
Churchill or Lloyd, roaring drunk, on Boswell's staircase would
be interesting. We may mark meanwhile how Boswell is already
able to capture and set down the typical Johnson remark, the
kind no other man would utter. His harvest will rapidly increase
in size and splendour. I do not propose to set myself, now or
henceforth, the task of choosing, amid such bewildering richness,
typical Johnsonisms to quote in these pages. They are all, in
their context, in the *Life*, to which this book is but a signpost.

Let us skip a few peevish Boswellian complaints, to Temple
and others at this time, of moods of languor, melancholy, and
indifference to all pursuits. On July 20 he asked Johnson to
dinner at his chambers to meet his uncle, Dr. John Boswell, 'an
elegant scholar and physician', and his admired friend George
Dempster, M.P. for Forfar. Dempster's vague and rootless
scepticism displeased Johnson extremely, and Boswell's impressionable mind swung over at once. On July 23 he writes to
Lord Hailes:

> *Entre nous* of Dempster—Johnson had seen a pupil of Hume and
> Rousseau, totally unsettled as to principles. I had infinite satisfaction
> in hearing solid truth confuting vain subtlety ... I must own to you
> that I have for some time past been in a miserable unsettled way, and
> been connected with people of shallow parts, tho' agreeably viva-
> cious ... I thank God I have got acquainted with Mr. Johnson. He
> has assisted me to obtain peace of mind. He has assisted me to become
> a *rational* Christian. I hope I shall ever remain so ... When I am
> abroad I shall studiously preserve my good principles ... When I

return from abroad I hope I may easily drop loose acquaintance. One mind can hardly support itself against many. But when we are with good men, whose opinions agree with ours, we are the more firmly fixed.

At last, we cry, the good has conquered. Two days later, informing Temple that he has received his letters of introduction to the Count of Nassau, Mynheer Gronovius, and other notabilities at Utrecht and Leyden, Boswell adds:

Mr. Wilkes is gone to France . . . I told him I was to be at Utrecht next winter; he said 'If you will write to me in George Street, I will send you the detail of this country'; this was very obliging . . . but I don't know if it would be proper to keep up a correspondence with a gentleman in his present capacity. It was a great honour to me, his offering it; I must be proud; advise me fully about it.

It might be easy to drop Churchill and Lloyd and Thornton and one or two more of Wilkes's satellites. It was not going to be so easy to drop the Devil Wilkes himself, as Boswell seems to be realising. John Wilkes, M.P., was now making a noise in the world and was bathed in that dazzle of notoriety Boswell always craved and envied. Blistering attacks in *The North Briton* on Prime Minister Bute, and hardly-veiled insults to the Queen, his alleged paramour, had culminated (April 1763) in the famous No. 45 of that journal, in which Wilkes described references to Prussia in a recent King's Speech as 'an infamous fallacy'. The Government seized the opportunity they had been waiting for. Wilkes was arrested for seditious libel on a general warrant and sent to the Tower, to be released a week later, on appeal, by the Lord Chief Justice. Having upheld the rights of the subject, made the Government look blundering fools, and become overnight, despite himself, the hero of the mob ('Wilkes and Liberty!'— the vengeful pencil of his enemy Hogarth fixes his grin for ever), Wilkes at once sued the Government for unlawful arrest.[1] But the Government had another card to play. A privately-printed copy of a poem by Wilkes called *An Essay on Woman* had come into their hands by bribery and was read aloud to a stupored House of Lords by Wilkes's old playmate of the Hellfire Club,

[1] Four years later he was awarded £4,000 damages, and the general warrant was dead.

Lord Sandwich. Apart from containing criminal libels on two prelates and a peer, the *Essay* is sufficiently described by the Lords' resolution denouncing it: 'a most scandalous, obscene, and impious libel, a gross profanation of many parts of the Holy Scriptures, and a most wicked and blasphemous attempt to ridicule and vilify the Person of our Most Blessed Saviour.'[1] A prosecution was imminent, and this spelt ruin to Wilkes, who depended largely on the Nonconformist vote.

Having annihilated 'Jemmy Twitcher' Sandwich with one of the most brilliant repartees in existence——

'I am convinced, Mr. Wilkes, that you will die either of a pox or on the gallows.'
'That, my lord, depends on whether I embrace your mistress or your principles,'

——and having been wounded in a pistol-duel in Hyde Park with an M.P. named Martin, Wilkes retired to Paris to visit his beloved daughter Polly, whom he was educating there, to send the Speaker medical certificates to the effect that he was unable to travel to England owing to his injury, and to await his formal expulsion from the House, which the Government engineered by January 1764, and the ensuing sentence of outlawry, following his failure to return and stand his trial. Meanwhile he had been received with open arms as a martyr for Liberty and Atheism by Baron d'Holbach, an old acquaintance, Diderot, Helvetius, d'Alembert, and the whole *philosophe* gang; and by the time his outlawry was declared in November, he was as great a pet, *pro tem.*, of the advanced Parisian drawing-rooms as Rousseau had been. To cast off a public character like Wilkes, who, though at this moment under a cloud, had powerful friends and was obviously only biding his time, was not going to be so easy, or politic, as Boswell had seemed to anticipate.

However, Wilkes was now across the Channel, and Johnson in London was able to exert his influence unchallenged; and Boswell clung to him desperately. He was with Johnson constantly all this month, and the indolent great man's surprising

[1] As a work of art the *Essay*, which is dedicated to Fanny Murray, a well-known harlot, has no merit whatsoever. It is a parody of Pope's *Essay on Man*, with footnotes alleged to be the work of Bishop Warburton.

offer to come down and see his young friend off at Harwich filled his grateful cup.

In the *Life* he has described a golden day together at Greenwich and the ensuing supper at the Turk's Head tavern in the Strand, their intimate discussion of his future, Johnson's 'animating blaze' of eloquence on that subject. Boswell was safe, happy and proud. Even a brief unfortunate moment at the same tavern on their final evening together a little later, when he roused Johnson's quick temper by an indiscreet remark about Convocation, could not spoil his large content. On August 5 they took coach together, spent the night at Colchester, got to Harwich next day at about three, dined, said a prayer together in the parish church, and walked down to the beach, where they 'embraced and parted with tenderness'. When the Helvoetsluys packet stood out to sea Boswell from the deck could long descry his good angel in the distance.

I kept my eyes upon him for a considerable time, while he remained rolling his majestick frame in his usual manner; and at last I perceived him walk back into the town, and he disappeared.

If only he could have felt like this always!

# Chapter Four

---

# GRAND TOUR

## 1

*'Elégant comme Céladon,
Agile comme Scaramouche ...'*

ABSENTLY GAZING AFTER A PLUMP, YOUTHFUL, COCKED-HATTED figure in flowered silk and a furred greatcoat tripping jauntily along the prim Oude and Nieuve Gracht of Utrecht on his way to a rout at the Countess of Nassau's one clear, cold, winter afternoon of 1763, I remind myself sympathetically, before following M. Boswell d'Auchinleck (such is the gentleman's style on the Continent) round the corner, to allow this absurd Casanova of the streets and the servants' hall due credit for living a completely decent life for the next twelve months. It undoubtedly meant a struggle. He was honestly determined to fulfil all his promises to his father and to Johnson. In his private papers there is a wonderful 'Inviolable Plan', drawn up by himself for this purpose, to be consulted every morning regularly at breakfast-time. The Plan, a monologue delivered to Boswell by his Better Self, giving himself instructions and encouragement for proper living, might appear faintly comic to some; to me it stands for an effort strongly tinged with heroism.

The more heroic, perhaps, because he at once found Utrecht intolerably dull. A 'plaintive and desponding' cry to Johnson on this theme shortly after his arrival got no reply, for Johnson despised such complaints. But very soon afterwards Johnson wrote him a long, warm-hearted letter, his letters of introduction began to work, and he cheered up. Conscientiously sitting at the appointed hours under Mynheer Trotz, Professor of Civil Law, with whom we find him in due course vowing everlasting friendship over 'a glass of cordial Malaga', he began in his leisure to go into society.[1] His noble kinsmen the Sommelsdycks at the Hague received him kindly. The Countess of Nassau introduced him into fashionable circles. There were soon frequent routs and parties, full of 'beautiful and amiable ladies', with whom he began falling in love. At one of these assemblies he met Isabella, daughter of Count van Tuyll, the Zelide—how evocative of a novel of the period by Voltaire or Crébillon *fils!*—of his dreams for a long time to come. Zelide, something of a bluestocking, something of a flirt, was gay, charming, and completely virtuous. It was therefore necessary for M. Boswell d'Auchinleck to ask her hand in matrimony, but she greeted this suggestion with silvery laughter, evoking thereby a long and unsuccessful letter to the Count her father and a didactic Boswellian sequence imploring her to be rational and less fond of pleasure. 'Believe me', writes Zelide's aspirant, 'God does not intend that we should have much pleasure in this world ... My notions of God's benevolence are grand and extensive. I puzzle myself not with texts here and texts there ... I worship my Creator and I fear no evil ... Pray make a firm resolution never to think of metaphysicks.' The tone is moral but not severe, like that of a letter recently advising Temple on his (Temple's) younger brother's future. 'I am glad he goes down to Cambridge. His going thither removes him from the dissipation and vice which idleness is apt to drive a young man to, in a metropolis.' The boon-companion of Wilkes enjoys giving advice, now and at all times.

Meanwhile, amid all the gentle dissipation of Dutch routs and parties and the delicious agony of being in love with a frivol like Zelide, Boswell is filling his notebooks under Mynheer Trotz and behaving perfectly. But the old restlessness conquers before the year is out. Utrecht is stagnation. Utrecht is death. He must travel and see the world. In July 1764 we find him, in his flowered silk suit, at Berlin, having travelled there with the

[1]Trotz (Christian-Heinrich), a German, lectured apparently in Latin. Whether Boswell attended his public lectures is not clear.

curious old ex-Jacobite, George, Earl Marischal, that crony of
Frederick the Great's who liked to live in Prussia, and his Turkish
mistress.

From the hideous little Prussian capital among its sandy wastes
Boswell wrote to his father explaining the urgent necessity of
extending his travels. This letter he showed to the British
Minister in Berlin, Sir Andrew Mitchell, an old friend of
Auchinleck's, who apparently approved, and gave him some
introductions meanwhile; and Boswell, having mixed a little in
Berlin society and viewed, with deep reverence, Frederick the
Great inspecting his grenadiers on the Potsdam parade-ground,
proceeded to visit the sights of Hanover and Brunswick while
awaiting his father's reply. On returning to Berlin in August he
found Mitchell away in Spa. A diplomatic letter from Boswell
to the Minister on August 28 shows that the reply from
Auchinleck was no sugar-plum, and that another from his father
had just followed it.

. . . He continues of opinion that travelling is of very little use and
may do a great deal of harm . . . I esteem and love my father, and I
am determined to do what is in my power to make him easy and
happy; but you will allow that I may endeavour to make him happy
and at the same time not to be too hard on myself.

After an envious reference to his father's strength of character,
he reveals to the Minister that he himself has a melancholy
disposition, and is apt to escape from 'the gloom of dark specula-
tion' into amusement, perhaps into folly. His intention then
begins to emerge.

My father seems much against my going to Italy, but gives me leave
to go from there [Utrecht, where the judge had directed him back]
and pass some months in Paris.

If his Excellency raised no astonished eyebrow at this, he
must have been a dour and non-committal Scot indeed. Guid
save and keep us—Italy! This loon, this featherbrain expects
his longsuffering father to allow him to rampage round Italy,
that hotbed of vice and Popery! Round Rome itself, maybe,—
the Lair of the Beast, as old Allan Ramsay called it? Yes, here it
is, egad, in black and white.

I own that the words of the Apostle Paul, 'I must see Rome', are strongly borne in on my mind . . . I am no libertine, and have a moral certainty of suffering no harm in Italy; I can also assure you that I shall be as moderate as possible in my expenses.

Boswell ends by begging his Excellency, as a friend of the family, to write and convince his father that to ask for 'my year and a reasonable sum' is not outrageous. His intention, he adds, is to go on from Berlin to Mannheim, and thence to Geneva, 'the point from which I may steer either to Italy or France. I shall see Voltaire; I shall also see Switzerland, and Rousseau.'

The Minister's chilling advice from Spa in reply to this rigmarole was to obey his father's wishes. But it was Auchinleck who, surprisingly, gave way a post or two later. Despair? Helplessness? Grim resignation? He gave his growling and reluctant consent, at any rate, enabling Boswell to write kindly to the Minister: 'I forgive you . . . for I say just the same to young people when I advise.'

So hey for the road.

2

Light-hearted and unselfconscious as a Viennese operetta is the journal of Boswell's tour, with credentials from Marischal, of some half-dozen of the little lumpish North German courts. They charmed M. Boswell d'Auchinleck in their overgilt baroque and he patronised them in high good humour, Brunswick and Hanover, Dresden and Saxe-Gotha, Mannheim and Baden-Durlach, chatting in schoolboy French and worse German with Serene Highnesses and Transparencies and Excellencies, high chamberlains, diplomats, ecclesiastics and soldiers and thoroughly enjoying himself. He was diverted by the absurd pomp and wooden-soldier formalism of these rustic Versailles, and he was especially charmed with Baden-Durlach, where he struck up a friendship with the Margrave and his Margravine, who had pretensions to culture, corresponded with them for a time, and all but got himself decorated with a star and ribbon. ('Le Chevalier Boswell'—how delightful that would have sounded!)

At Wittenberg he wrote to Johnson from the tomb of the mild Melanchthon, but on second thoughts kept his letter in cold-storage a dozen years, fearing it might seem 'superstitious and romantick.' During his progress he broke his vow of chastity, inevitably but economically. Towards the end of December 1764 he is in Neuchâtel, composing with great care a self-introductory letter to Jean-Jacques Rousseau. He had one in his pocket already from Marischal, who had been Governor of Neuchâtel and was Rousseau's friend; but he needed something more striking.

Rousseau was at this moment an invalid, living at Motiers in the Val de Travers, sixteen miles from Neuchâtel. The extraordinary—'besotted', is perhaps the word—infatuation of the highest French nobility for the ex-lackey who chiefly brought about their downfall, the extraordinary adulation showered on this brilliant paranoiac by admirers of the rank of the Prince de Ligne, the Prince de Conti, and Mme. de Luxembourg was still unabated, and was indeed to endure long after his death, when Marie-Antoinette and many of the Blood-Royal of France were among the trippers to the tomb at Ermenonville. Rousseau's persecution-mania had not yet developed.

Boswell's letter was in French, and typical. Extracts:

I am an ancient Scots gentleman. You know my rank. I am twenty-four years old. You know my age. I present myself, Sir, as a man of singular merit, a man with a feeling heart, a spirit keen yet melancholy . . . Oh dear Saint-Preux! Enlightened Mentor! Eloquent and amiable Rousseau! My presentiment tells me a friendship of the noblest kind will be born to-day. I find myself in serious and delicate circumstances, upon which I ardently desire the advice of the Author of *La Nouvelle Héloïse!* . . . Have confidence in your singular visitor. You will not repent it . . . I await your reply with impatience. —BOSWELL.

The sombre and suspicious Genevese fell for this, as we say nowadays, at once. A message reached Boswell's inn saying M Rousseau would receive him, though he begged that the visit might be brief, as he was not well. Arraying himself in gold laced scarlet coat and waistcoat and buckskin breeches, with a gold-laced hat and a greatcoat of green camlet trimmed with fur M. Boswell d'Auchinleck accordingly presented himself a Motiers on December 3, and was admitted into the presence by the watchful Thérèse Levasseur, the great man's mistress, house-keeper, and bodyguard.

The interviews between these two unbalanced characters—Boswell managed to get past the Levasseur three times in the first week, and twice in the week following, each time, save once, for a very brief stay—are one of the chief delights of the Private Papers. Rousseau, a 'dark, genteel man' with soulful dark eyes, wore the Armenian dress and nightcap he so oddly affected and spoke 'rapidly and forcibly'. Behind him, for Boswell had probably taken the precaution of looking up *La Nouvelle Héloïse* again, though he does not say so, loomed the shadowy figures of Julie and St. Preux swooning in the Alpine moonlight at Meillerie, with virtuous peasants in tears all round, and behind them, perhaps, the Noble Savage, ten feet high and beaming a fraternal message of love to all mankind. Rousseau succumbed to the Boswell spell instantly. They talked of parenthood, virtue, feudalism, Corsica, women, cats, dogs, democracy, the Simple Life, education, and a dozen more things. Rousseau was charming and unaffected, though (he explained) disgusted at that period with all mankind. As Boswell rose to go his host remarked again that he was unwell, but he could give M. Boswell a quarter of an hour the next afternoon. On his final visit, by which time he had clapped Rousseau on the shoulder at least once, Boswell was out in the kitchen before long, helping Mlle. Levasseur to prepare the frugal meal to which he had invited himself. After supper Rousseau unbent delightfully, sang to his beloved dog and cat in a sweet voice, and made them do their tricks together. At their parting he embraced M. Boswell and kissed him, saying he had much enjoyed his 'simple malice'. Boswell had unbosomed himself to the Philosopher without stint, and had given him a sketch of his life and a packet of Zelide's letters, begging for a critical estimate of her character. And of course he had led the talk to religion, urgently but firmly compelling the *Vicaire Savoyard* to bare his soul. O nights and feasts of the gods! It was delightful. It was ecstatic. It was an orgy of sensibility, and Boswell reeled away from the Philosopher's door, with the Philosopher's kisses on his cheek, in a trance of happiness; a friend—an unbosom friend would be more accurate—of the Cynosure of Europe.

The prickly, sickly Rousseau's reception of the bubbling young Scot was undoubtedly extraordinary. One key to his amiability is the possibility that he assumed Boswell to be a Highlander, a native of the mountains, from which, as every student of the Rousseau gospel is aware, derive the moral virtues. A little later he would be seeing in Boswell one of the persecutors with whom the entire world was crawling, but now he seems to have been as helpless and friendly as a kitten. And perhaps he recognised and warmed to a brother-madman.

With Rousseau's scalp in the bag, Boswell turned at once on an even more distinguished prey. By Christmas Eve he was in Geneva, preparing to call on Voltaire.

In 1765 the Patriarch of Ferney, the Emperor of French Literature, Frederick of Prussia's 'weasel', the god of every *esprit fort* in Europe and America, was in his seventy-second year; ill, emaciated, almost toothless, and strongly resembling a long-nosed, dried-up monkey, but mentally as vigorous and combative as ever, and darting the same famous mocking fire from those dancing, piercing, preternaturally brilliant black eyes. On his considerable estate four miles from Geneva, and on French soil, Voltaire lived in some style with several footmen and a niece-housekeeper, Mme. Denis, receiving distinguished visitors from everywhere, pouring out a vast correspondence and a stream of pamphlets, poems, and squibs, and still denying right and left that he had been exiled.[1] He was still an ardent believer in Progress, from which illusion all his irony could not save him, and he was still talking and writing a good deal about Liberty, though he had perforce long since abandoned that notable pastime of working to have people he disliked thrown into prison on a *lettre de cachet*, from critics like Fréron down to a one-time Parisian landlady whom he actually denounced to the police for blasphemy. This comic Voltairian trait, worthy of some ignoble (or Catholic) character in *Candide*, is illustrated in the well-known selection from the Archives of the Bastille published by Ravaisson, containing several shrill applications from the Apostle of Liberty to the Lieutenant of Police. The spinsterly venom with which the great man demands, for example, the tracking-

[1] E.g. a furious letter to the *London Chronicle* in 1761, attacking Lord Lyttleton for asserting this.

down and punishment of some half-starved hack who had printed
a bad poem under his, Voltaire's, name in 1744 is most diverting.
His admirers dilate quite rightly on Voltaire's activities, still
continuing in 1765, in the Calas affair and other fights for justice.
The evidence of the Bastille archives should likewise not be
overlooked, I think, by lovers of realism and ironic comedy.
*Il avait réellement,* remarks Funck-Brentano, *un génie de policier.*

There exists, alas, no verbatim account of the Ferney interviews in Boswell's papers. He wrote one, very carefully, but it
has vanished. Fortunately he poured out his triumph in a long,
hurraying letter to Temple, in which all the salient features are
included. Arriving at Geneva on Monday, December 24, he
assumed his ceremonial attire and called the same afternoon
at Ferney, to find a small intimate house-party assembled, one
of the guests being the Chevalier de Boufflers, whose painting
and *vers de société* were so admired. A more remarkable guest
was the venerable Jesuit, Père Adan, Voltaire's favourite chess-
partner, who was greatly esteemed by him, said Mass for him,
and was never without hopes of seeing this eminent prodigal
return to the Fold.

Boswell found Voltaire in a nightgown covered by a blue frieze
greatcoat, crowned with his usual nightcap. His reception was
polite, but not enthusiastic. Humped in a chair, his gimlet eyes
on his visitor, Voltaire seems not to have fallen at once, like
Rousseau, under the spell, and his fixed grin ('Monsieur, you see
a dying man') masked obvious boredom. Boswell took a rather
crestfallen leave before long, and on returning to his hotel in
Geneva—the city gates closed at 5 p.m.—thought long and hard.
He was not yet beaten. Next day he concocted a rattling letter
in his best French and in his best Erskine vein, begging gaily to
be allowed the honour of a night under Voltaire's sacred roof,
and despatched it to the all-powerful Mme. Denis. Voltaire read
this effusion and grinned. Here, evidently, was an *original.* To
Mr. Boswell's inn, on the 27th, came the reply in Voltaire's own
hand, inviting him to dine and stay.

Hastening accordingly to Ferney, flushed and excited, Boswell
was left alone in the drawing-room for a time to talk to his host
while the company went to dinner. Here follows the grand scene,
outlined to Temple, which must have read verbatim quite ex-

quisitely. Finding the old gentleman in high spirits, full of wit and humour, singing scraps of English ballads, swearing in English like a fishwife, now lavishly praising the British Constitution, now flying off into extravagant sallies of fun and nonsense, Boswell was emboldened, as one might have guessed, to steer him before long on to his favourite topic. Fantastic comedy ensued, for Voltaire was at the top of his mischievous mood and asked nothing better. Ringing for a Bible, he had it placed between him and his young guest, open. Hammer-and-tongs they went at it then, the desiccated old mummy with the dancing, fiery, black eyes and the snapping, bony fingers and the shrill, derisive cackle, the plump, heated young Scot sweating and orating a few inches away. For a time it seemed as if Boswell were saving Christianity for the world; then the diabolic old gentleman snatched it from him and began ripping it to pieces and throwing it away. Louder and louder grew the conflict. Voltaire screeched like a parrot and danced in fury. Boswell mopped his brow and stuck to him doggedly. All at once the old gentleman collapsed backwards in his chair with closed eyes. Dead? Swooning? Playing 'possum? Boswell watched him anxiously. At length Voltaire came to the surface. The Scot was ready for him.

'Well, Sir, as to personal immortality——'

No. No more monkey-tricks from Voltaire. The old gentleman had had enough. This terrible Scot, this *original,* was too much for him. Utterly shattered, he admitted under final pressure the existence of a Supreme Being. *Oui, oui.* Also a need to resemble the Author of Goodness? *Oui, oui. C'est ça.* And the immortality of the Soul? *Peut-être. Peut-être.*

Mr. Boswell rose with glittering eyes and was taken into the dining-room. Next day Voltaire was too ill and exhausted to appear in the drawing-room before dinner. The evening passed quietly *en famille,* and on retiring to his luxurious room Boswell sent a footman for a copy of one of his host's best plays, *Mahomet,* and read it through before going to bed. On the day following they had only half an hour's innocuous talk, Voltaire being still indisposed. With cordial and flattering thanks Boswell took his leave soon afterwards. We may surmise the old gentleman heaved a sigh of gratitude to the Supreme Being *de sa façon* as he heard his guest's chaise rumble away down the road to

Geneva and rang for the sedative chessboard. Yet he too had been fascinated. Colonel Isham reproduces in photostat a playful note, in Voltaire's neat, beautiful handwriting and in English, addressed to Boswell from Ferney about a fortnight after his departure, rallying his obsession with 'that pretty thing call'd Soul. I do protest you, I know nothing about it . . .'

By this time Boswell had crossed the Alps.

### 3

We who enter Italy by train, like fools or fish, we who are shot ignominiously into Lombardy through a long hole in the mountains, what do we know of the delights of travel as the Eighteenth Century knew it?

Everybody is familiar with Horace Walpole's shuddering account of crossing the Alps in the normal way with Gray in the winter of 1739. It is worth quoting again, perhaps, for what it leaves out.

At the foot of Mont Cenis we were obliged to quit our chaise, which was taken all to pieces and loaded on mules; and we were carried in low arm-chairs on poles . . . When we came to the top, behold the snows fallen! and such quantities, and conducted by such heavy clouds that hung glouting, that I thought we could never have waded through them. The descent is two leagues, but steep and rough as O——'s father's face . . . But the dexterity and nimbleness of the mountaineers are inconceivable; they run with you down steeps and frozen precipices where no man, as men are now, could possibly walk. We had twelve men and nine mules to carry us, our servants, and baggage, and were above five hours in this agreeable jaunt!

Boswell, who did not cross in such pomp, is therefore less to be excused than the *frileux* and old-maidish Walpole for telling us nothing about the portent, the wonder which greets every traveller from the north about halfway down the southern descent; that ghost of the suggestion of an adumbration of a soft, warm, gracious, faintly-perfumed breeze just stirring the icy mist and stealing tiptoe and touching his cheek and vanishing again in a whisper—*Italia!* The first Ausonian Zephyr, the first message from the olive-groves and the sunlight miles below, the first greeting from the radiant Mother of fruits and men. No

railway traveller can hope for it. Nor does Boswell mention it.
Perhaps he was feeling too nervous at the time to notice Italy's
welcome. Reluctantly quitting his chaise, he crossed the Mont
Cenis in the same kind of 'low arm-chair on poles' as Horace
Walpole, but with no retinue. I am informed by my friend Mr.
Arnold Lunn, from whom no Alpine secrets past or present are
hidden, that this Alps-Machine, as Boswell calls it, was the
customary *chaise à porteurs* of the period, consisting of two long,
strong, parallel poles, braced, with twisted cords stretched tightly
across them, an armchair-seat, and a foot-rest. Six brawny peasants
carried Boswell over the pass in this contrivance. The snow was
some six foot deep in places, and the scenery was 'horribly grand'.
On reaching the first hamlet of the plain Boswell heard Mass and
dined with the priest, who reminded him somewhat of Dr.
Johnson, except in conversation.

Romantic as he is, one could hardly expect to find Boswell
surveying the Italy of 1765 through the eyes of one to whom a
glimpse of

> ... the Venetian lady
> Who had seemed to glide to some intrigue in her red shoes,
> Her domino, her panniered skirt copied from Longhi,[1]

would be deliciously evocative of a fragrant, faded dream-
world, of the crystal melodies of Scarlatti and Cimarosa, the
comedies of Goldoni, the ballet of *The Good-Humoured Ladies*.
Red heels, dominos, and panniers spelt nothing nostalgic to him,
naturally, and Browning's line on Galuppi, with its perpetual tiny
thrill to a modern ear:

> While you sate and played toccatas stately at the clavichord ...

would convey no magic. Galuppi, who succeeded Handel as
music-director at Covent Garden in the 1740's, would himself
have shrugged gratified but puzzled shoulders at any such suggestion, being unable to conceive of a future age in which his
own amiable music and daily costume would symbolise graces
lost for ever.

So Boswell came down to the plains of Lombardy and to
Turin, where he put up at the sign of the *Bonne Femme* and

---

[1] Yeats, *On a Dying Lady*.

a night later at the Opera, caught sight of Wilkes in a box. To see a man 'whom I have so often thought of since I left England' gave him a 'romantick agitation'. Wilkes had left Paris towards the end of October 1764, for Boulogne, to meet his old hench-man Charles Churchill, who, with one or two other friends, had come to cheer him with promises of financial support and some 'obliging messages' from Lord Temple. Within one riotous week Churchill caught typhus. A few days later he ended his lewd and bellicose life in Wilkes's arms, at the age of 33. Deeply grieved, and deeply in debt, Wilkes resolved to follow his current mistress over the Alps and to economise, if possible, in Italy for a space. He had been keeping her for some time, very expensively, in a house in the Rue Neuve-des-Bons-Enfants, near the Palais-Royal; she was a tempestuous, extravagant, fascinating neurotic, an ex-dancer at the Venice Opera, named Gertrude Corradini. Joining her at Bologna, Wilkes drifted with her in due course to Milan and Florence, where he met Thrale, Johnson's friend, and Lord Beauchamp, and was well enter-tained. In Carnival Week, 1765, he and the Corradini were in Rome, where Wilkes made the acquaintance of Johann-Joachim Winckelmann, the Pompeian archaeologist, aesthete, Hellenist, and future idol of Goethe. His present stay in Turin was to be brief, for the Corradini had taken a villa at Vomero, just outside Naples, where Wilkes and she were to live in idyllic seclusion with her mother and uncle.

Wilkes in Turin! Here was a delightful surprise for Boswell, who was longing to pour into a discerning ear his late triumphs at Motiers and Ferney. He dashed off a note next morning in-viting his gay friend to 'a feast of most excellent wine and choice conversation'. Wilkes, excusing himself, informed him of Churchill's recent death. There is no reason for believing this melancholy to be assumed or exaggerated. Wilkes had been extremely fond of Churchill; they had collaborated at Med-menham and on *The North Briton*, and enjoyed many other pleasures in common. Wilkes, moreover, esteemed Churchill's verse highly, and was at this moment contemplating a collected edition, apart from honouring the dead poet's memory with an antique porphyry urn, engraved with an epitaph in 'the close style of the Ancients', which had been presented to him by

Winckelmann.[1] Despite all this, a flippant return-note from Boswell about Churchill's having 'bounced into the regions below' did not offend. Wilkes was staying only three days more in Turin, but they met before he left, as Boswell records in that demure memoir of his own life he composed years later for *The European Magazine*.

Nor was it a circumstance of small moment that he met at Turin, Rome, and Naples, the celebrated John Wilkes, Esq., with whom he had always maintained an acquaintance upon the most liberal terms, and with whom he enjoyed many classical scenes with peculiar relish.[2]

Which must have afforded Wilkes a chuckle in his retirement, remembering some of the classical scenes he and his young friend undoubtedly enjoyed in Italy together; particularly, I surmise, those to be viewed 'behind the shutter' in Naples, a seaport with a long tradition. Not that Boswell indulged himself exclusively in such amusements. He had, even so early, the gift of making interesting and vital acquaintance. After Wilkes's departure from Turin, for example, he had met John Turberville Needham, Fellow of the Royal Society and friend of Buffon, whose name, like that of his fellow-scientist, the electrician Gordon, does not appear in modern scientific works, since he was a priest, but who turned out nevertheless to be a fount of good talk. During one of those long discussions on religion which Boswell always loved, a remark by Needham to the effect that the Catholic religion as a general system is as capable of proof as the Newtonian philosophy impressed him greatly. Having noted it later in his diary, he felt, I am certain, that this must be looked into immediately. Meanwhile that pair of trim ankles and flashing eyes across the street might be worth following.

But from this standpoint, judging by his Italian diary, which breaks off at January 30, he was the victim of illusion. The Italian ladies laughed at and dismissed him, and his only successes, as usual, were the easiest, whose embraces so often

---

[1] Wilkes placed this urn years later in the garden of his villa at Sandown, Isle of Wight, on a hollow pedestal holding bottles of port.

[2] The brief, fragmentary foreign diary of Wilkes in the British Museum does not mention Boswell, being concerned with the Corradini affair almost exclusively.

filled him with ensuing terror. And before long his moods of languor and depression, increased by pitiless blue skies, increased. Then the company of Wilkes at supper would be a boon, and Boswell's brooding would vanish in gales of laughter and mighty potations.

If Wilkes was in form at Naples, where he and Boswell apparently climbed Vesuvius, it is not difficult to surmise that Rome inspired his gayest verve. The Capital of Christendom, swarming with priests, monks, missionaries, nuns, seminarists, and pilgrims of all nations, with the enormous target of the Vatican looming behind, would inspire an infinity of dirty pleasantries; for apart from the slightly irritated amusement the intelligentsia normally finds in contemplating the Catholic Church, the advanced thought of the Eighteenth Century was well aware that the thing was 'quite exploded', as Horace Walpole said, and due to vanish for ever in the imminent Great Rosy Dawn of universal enlightenment announced by Voltaire and the prophets. Aretino reincarnate in wig and ruffles, Mr. Wilkes must have seemed, laughing at the English Coffee-House. Young Mr. Boswell in convulsions of mirth. Even the uncomprehending waiters grinning at the merry mad Inglese. One of the chief preoccupations of Clement XIII's pontificate, which may have been engaging him even now in his Vatican study, was the common gossip of the Roman coffee-houses and would be naturally meat and drink to Mr. Wilkes. The principal politicians of Europe—always the politicians, Disraeli remarks in *Endymion,* never the people—were passing through one of their recurring phases of Jesuitophobia and were urging the Holy See to suppress the Society altogether. A fruitful topic for Wilkesian satire; nor did he fail to strike answering sparks from his companion, as Boswell later boasted.

When Wilkes and I sat together, each glass of wine produced a flash of wit, like gunpowder thrown into the fire—Puff! puff!

I grieve to think they missed an ideal third, for the purposes of Boswell's journal, by just four years. In 1769 young Francisco Goya arrived in Rome from Madrid with pencils and portfolio and proceeded almost immediately for a wager to climb the façade of St. Peter's to the lantern of the Dome; a hair-raising feat which much diverted the Romans, yet not so spectacular or amusing, in a Wilkesian sense, as Goya's later attempt to break, with sketchbook and at midnight, into a convent of enclosed nuns, for which act of sacrilege he escaped a death-sentence only by the activity of the Spanish Ambassador. Wilkes and Boswell would have enjoyed the pranks of the headstrong Aragonese. They do not seem to have encountered anyone interesting at the English Coffee-House. Barry and Nollekens, both future Royal Academicians and both fantastics in their way, were frequenting it about this time; but Barry was a moody and unpleasant type—one practical joke he is said to have played on Nollekens in Rome has a sadistic tinge which might have amused Wilkes [1]—and the miserly Nollekens was preoccupied exclusively with botching and faking antiques for the London market.

In due course Boswell became bored and restless again. In May 1765 he wrote from Rome to Rousseau, reminding him of a promised letter of introduction to Pasquale Paoli, the Corsican general who was winning the admiration of all Europe by his attempt to free Corsica from the Genoese yoke; adding that he, Boswell, was determined to go to Corsica in any event. Soon after this, and most likely at the English Coffee-House (since no British visitor to Rome over two centuries trusted any other) twenty-one-year-old Lord Mountstuart, Bute's eldest son, who was making the Grand Tour, met and took such a fancy to Wilkes's vivacious young friend that after loafing with Boswell in Rome for a time Mountstuart took him on a tour of Venetia and Tuscany.

A vagabondage in such company was an agreeable diversion, nerving Boswell to ignore a sequence of letters from Auchinleck ordering him home. During this time he ran, with or without Mountstuart, constantly after women, at Venice, Mantua, and elsewhere, with his usual qualified success; and it is plain that

[1] Nollekens used to tell the story. One night, leaving the English Coffee-House, Barry exchanged his gold-laced hat for Nollekens's plain and shabby one. Next morning, when Barry returned the hat and demanded his own, Nollekens asked for an explanation. 'Why, to tell you the truth, my dear Joey, I fully expected assassination last night, and I was to have been known by my laced hat.' It seems an improbable story, for Nollekens remained Barry's lifelong friend, but Barry was notorious for his irritating habits.

he periodically sickened of his stupid existence and longed for
the company of Johnson, to whom he had written once or twice
without getting a reply. He reveals this longing at the end of
a jaunty letter from Venice to his other mentor.

O John Wilkes, thou gay, learned, and ingenious private gentleman,
thou thoughtless infidel, good without principle and wicked without
malevolence, let *Johnson* teach thee the road to rational virtue and
noble felicity!

Wilkes must have grinned, tossing this precious effusion aside.
He was himself about to leave Italy, or perhaps had already
gone. The *ménage* at Naples had broken up in the June of that
summer. During Wilkes's absence on a visit at Ischia the Corradini, whose relations were urging her to press for a settlement
of £2,000, quitted the villa for Bologna, taking with her a little
portable property and leaving an invitation to Wilkes to follow.
But her lover, sacrificing passion to public spirit—the Whigs were
in power again—took ship in due course to Toulon, paid a visit
to the Grande Chartreuse, where his effusively polite inscription
in the visitors' book may still, I believe, be inspected in the
archives of that great monastery, and went on to visit the 'divine
old man' at Ferney. Arriving in Paris at length on October 4,
Wilkes announced that he was shortly going as British Minister
to Constantinople; but two days later, according to Horace
Walpole, who was also in Paris, visiting his 'blind old fairy', Mme.
du Deffand, he changed his tune and talked of returning to
England for good, 'if he can make his peace'.[1] This project also
fell through, for the time being.

Rousseau's reply, enclosing the letter of introduction Boswell
had asked for, reached him at length at Florence. After some
ineffective dalliance with 'an angelick charmer' at Siena, Boswell
arrived at Leghorn, the port for Corsica, at the beginning of
October. Lord Mountstuart's parting gift to him was a copy of
the English Bible.

[1] Walpole adds: 'I thought by the manner in which this was mentioned
to me, that the person meant to sound me,' but Walpole did not respond.
(Letter to the Hon. H. S. Conway, October 6, 1765). Wilkes at this moment
was desperately bored with exile and very short of money. Later he made
one or two flying trips to London, but returned disappointed.

4

Why *The Journal of a Tour to Corsica*, & *Memoirs of Pascal Paoli*, published in February 1768, is not better known I cannot imagine. It is an entirely delightful little book; gay, amusing, high-spirited, well-bred, unpretentious, full of gobbets of shrewd observation and surprising good sense, and refreshingly devoid of the conventional sneers found in insular books of travel. Boswell had the advantage over most of the travelling British of his age, and others, of some acquaintance with the religion of the majority of Christians; nor did he feel any Protestant obligation to keep his hat on in the presence of the Mother of God.

After recovering from the first shock of those dark un-English faces, so frequently unshaven, Boswell began instantly to enjoy himself, and the Corsicans reciprocated with kindness and hospitality. They were, as often before, in revolt against their overlord, the Republic of Genoa, but had this time nearly driven the Genoese from the island. Calling on French aid by treaty, Genoa had handed over certain Corsican towns to French garrisons under the command of the Comte de Marboeuf. The French made no offensive move, according to policy, and seem to have aroused no enmity. The forty-year-old Corsican leader, General Pasquale Paoli, is one of the historic figures; a Christian Garibaldi, a champion worthy of being set not far from Kosciusko and Sobieski. Tall, strong, dignified, cultivated, devout, with a 'manly and noble carriage' and the courteous ease of a gentleman, Paoli impressed Johnson a little later no less thoroughly than Boswell, whose loud enthusiasm for Corsican liberty is by no means all self-advertisement, as the Whigs allege.

General Paoli's first impressions of his vivacious visitor, related to Fanny Burney years later in his own English, are amusing:

He came to my country and he fetched me some letter of recommending him. But I was of the belief that he might be an imposter, and I supposed in my mind that he was an espy; for I look away from him and in a moment I look to him again, and I behold his tablets. Oh, he was to the work of writing down all I say. Indeed I was angry! But soon I discover he was no imposter and no espy, and I only find I was myself the monster he had come to discern. Oh, a very good man; I love him indeed; so cheerful! So gay! So pleasant!

The old Boswell technique, we observe. He had sailed from Leghorn, with his Swiss servant, in a Tuscan wine-barque. The sea was dead calm and the passage to Centuri took two days, Boswell singing the evening *Ave Maria* with the other passengers and finding it 'pleasing to enter into the spirit of their religion'. They landed just before dusk, and Boswell at once struck up-country with guides through the aromatic *maquis* for the estate of a Signor Antonetti at Morfiglia, a mile inland. Fierce faces looming suddenly over guns from covert in the twilight fright-ened him somewhat, though his party was armed to the teeth. He had been warned by a British naval officer—one can hear the sharp-bitten words and see the cold blue eyes—that the natives were barbarians and that he would be running 'the risque of my life.' But he got safely to Antonetti's, and was courteously re-ceived. Next day, Sunday, he went to Mass with the family, heard a village sermon containing 'some good practical advice', and moved on to the house of Signor Damiano Tomasi at Pino, with another letter of introduction, struggling along a steep and narrow rock-path overhanging the sea. His charm conquered the Tomasis at once. Like Goldsmith's comedy-hero, he fancied himself ('before I became accustomed to Corsican hospitality') in a tavern, and demanded so many dishes at table that 'Signora Tomasi looked in my face and smiled, saying with much calm-ness and good-nature, "Una cosa dopo un altre, Signor."—One thing after another, Sir.' A Goldoni scene, equally, perhaps.

His next halt up-country was a monastery at Canari, evoking a truly surprising remark, considering the kind of public his book was written for:

The religious who devoutly endeavour to 'walk with God' are often treated with raillery, by those whom pleasure or business prevents from thinking of future and more exalted objects. A little experience of the serenity and peace of mind to be found in convents, would be of use to temper the fire of men of the world.

Serenity and peace of mind are of course far from being the primal objects of the monastic life; yet one may well imagine the reception of this apologia by Wilkes and his cronies in due course; the pleasing jests, the brilliant epigrams, the cascades of laughter, the toasts to Friar Jacobus Boswell and his shaveling mates.

Thence, by way of Patrimonio, Oletta, and Morato, through 'wild mountainous rock country' to Corte, the capital, headquarters of Paoli and his Supreme Council, where Boswell presented his letter, in Paoli's absence, to a Signor Boccociampe, and retired to lodge at the Franciscan priory nearby. He liked the Franciscans, and they him. He sat in choir with the friars and admired the 'propriety' of the daily Office and the beauty of the tabernacle on the high altar, carved in wood by one of the brethren. 'I received many civilities at Corte.' He met, and admired, some of the Supreme Council. His hosts showed him the University, the Capuchin priory, and the Castle, with three condemned murderers lying in its prison, with whom he conversed; and then, having exhausted the sights of Corte, he resolved to approach Paoli at Sollacarò, over the mountains. For this purpose he needed a passport, and he reports a 'beautiful, simple incident' during his visit to the Great Chancellor for this purpose:

The Chancellor desired a little boy, who was playing in the room by us, to run to his mother, and bring the Great Seal of the kingdom. I thought myself sitting in the house of a Cincinnatus.

The Rousseau touch, perhaps? Boswell had already jested politely at dinner at the Barbaggi house at Morato ('No less than twelve well-drest dishes, served on Dresden china, with a dessert, different sorts of wine, and a liqueur, all the produce of Corsica') on the surprising Spartanism of Corsican life. On the way to Sollacarò he was to experience the real thing, lunching off chestnuts knocked from the trees when his guides felt like eating, lying with them over a crystal brook to wash down the Arcadian meal. 'It was just being, for a little while, one of the *prisca gens mortalium,* the primitive race of men.' One can see him glancing in the direction of the wild Philosopher at Motiers with a superior smirk. Rousseau might go lyrical over the Noble Savage; he, Boswell, was actually living with him.

At Bastelica a large company of the inhabitants attended Boswell to the monastery where he lodged. In 'an unusual flow of spirits' he harangued these frank and easy people in his best

Italian on the bravery with which they had purchased liberty, and gave them some useful hints on cultivating their island and engaging in commerce. At Ornano, his next stop, he came across 'a pretty droll society of monks', one of whom laughingly quoted a bishop's remark on the Reformation: *Angli olim angeli nunc diaboli*—'The English, formerly angels, now devils.' And Boswell says in his friendly way, 'I looked upon this as an honest effusion of spiritual zeal. The fathers took good care of me in temporals.'

On sighting Sollacarò his nerve gave way, for once, and he had some fears as to his reception. Taken into Paoli's presence in a black suit of ceremony, he found the General dressed in green and gold, having discarded the rustic Corsican costume since the arrival of the French in order 'to make the government appear in a more respectable light.' Paoli's greeting was polite, but reserved. He read Rousseau's letter and raked the strange visitor, who might easily have been a Genoese assassin, with a keen and penetrating eye. Having made up his mind about him after a brief exchange of talk, he dropped his reserve and became friendly and eloquent. He had, it seems, invited the author of the *Contrat Social* to Corsica to assist in drawing up a new legal code, but nothing came of it. The Philosopher, had Paoli known, was actually intriguing for the surrender of Corsica to France.

Presently they dined, plainly but substantially. By the time coffee was served all Boswell's timidity had worn off. The General handed him over, during his stay, to the care of the Abbé Rostini, who had lived in France. Boswell was excited and happy.

Particular marks of attention were shewn me as a subject of Great Britain, the report of which went over to Italy, and confirmed the conjectures that I was really an envoy. In the morning I had my chocolate served up on a silver salver adorned with the arms of Corsica. I dined and supped constantly with the General, I was visited by all the nobility, and whenever I chose to make a little tour, I was attended by a party of guards. I begged of the General not to treat me with so much ceremony; but he insisted on it.

That polite little half-assumption of Boswell's diplomatic status was evidently not discouraged by Paoli, with French and Geno-

ese spies in mind. We find Boswell before long taking his daily
ride on the General's own horse, caparisoned in crimson velvet
and gold lace, with an escort of guards. He is enjoying life
tremendously, without black moods. Moreover, it is one of the
only two periods of his existence unsullied by any ignoble incident whatsoever. And his host likes him more and more.

> Paoli became more affable with me. I forgot the great distance
> between us, and had every day some hours of private conversation
> with him.

Naturally the General does not escape scot-free. In the course
of long, intimate talks on the future of Corsica, on Greek and
British history, on glory and goodness, on the King of Prussia,
on Pennsylvania, on marriage, on the Corsican temperament, on
arts and sciences, on political philosophy, and many other
matters, he is called on, like Johnson, to examine and prescribe
for Boswell's mental state, his depressed speculations, and his
exhausted and recurring distaste—he was now 25—for existence.
Paoli's reply to morbid self-pity is characteristic.

> All this (said Paoli) is melancholy. I have also studied metaphysicks.
> I know the arguments for fate and free-will, for the materiality and
> immateriality of the soul, and even the subtile arguments for and
> against the existence of matter. Ma lasciamo queste dispute ai oziosi—
> but let us leave these disputes to the idle. Io tengo sempre fermo un
> gran pensiero—I hold always firm one great object. I never feel a
> moment of despondency.

He did not labour the point, and passed on to recommend
Livy and Plutarch. Boswell knew well enough what Paoli's *gran
pensiero* was, though courtesy forbade Paoli's dilating on it. He
had already illuminated Boswell's mind at the dinner-table by
stating 'with graceful energy' the principal arguments for the
Being and attributes of God. Paoli with his perfect manners
could have turned Boswell into a decent member of society with
far more ease than Johnson. It was not to be Boswell's fortune
to experience Paoli's influence continuously enough.

Meanwhile the guest of Free Corsica continued to gyrate and
to charm. He mixed freely with peasants and soldiers, did all he
could to 'make them fond of the British', answered all their

questions, jested with them, played them Scottish airs with vary-
ing success on the German flute (*Gilderoy, Corn Riggs are
Bonny, The Lass o' Patie's Mill*), and once, in response to popular
demand for an English song, delighted his audience with
Garrick's 'Hearts of Oak', which he afterwards translated for
them into Italian. '"*Cuore di quercia*", cried they, "*bravo,
Inglese!*" It was quite a joyous riot. I fancied myself to be a
recruiting sea officer. I fancied all my chorus of Corsicans aboard
the British Fleet.' The General was not present on this occasion.
Though he smiled readily, he did not (like most really great men,
comments Boswell accurately) often laugh. He could hardly have
helped laughing at and perhaps applauding this variety performance, which shows Boswell in his most attractive light as a
good fellow receiving and radiating harmless pleasure.

So, sped by Paoli's good wishes and the obliging kindness of
his secretary, Father Guelfucci of the Servite Order, a man of
'talents and virtues, united with a singular decency and sweetness
of manners', Boswell at length began the return journey, meeting
some of his former monastic hosts again with reciprocated
pleasure ('I was not in the least looked upon as a heretick')
and meeting new ones, and finally reaching Bastia, where he
called on the French Commander-in-Chief, the Comte de
Marboeuf, with a letter from Paoli. He found Marboeuf, an
elegant Breton, 'openhearted' and charming, and his officers as
friendly and polite as himself. The French were preparing the
way to the purchase of Corsica by making themselves popular;
Marboeuf, for example, had a gentleman's agreement with Paoli
over the apprehension of criminals in each other's territory.
Boswell was memorably entertained at Bastia and cured of a
tertian ague by the French garrison doctor, who refused to
accept a fee.

At the end of November he left for Genoa and thence, without
pausing, by way of Marseilles and Lyons, direct for Paris. The
three weeks he spent there sufficed to erase with ease from that
waxy mind the recent impress of Paoli, as will appear almost
immediately.

Meanwhile we may finish with the Corsican episode. In the
*Life* Boswell tells how his loud enthusiasm for Paoli and liberty

irritated Johnson, who was distinctly churlish and provincial over it, and perhaps a little jealous of the accompanying publicity. This did not quell Boswell, who continued to think and talk and write Corsica, who called on the astonished Pitt for propaganda purposes in the costume of a Corsican chief on February 21, 1766, who raised a £700 subscription in Scotland to supply the Corsicans with artillery from the Carron foundries—almost an incredible feat, as more than one English commentator has remarked—and whose *British Essays in Favour of the Brave Corsicans* (1768) came out a few months before the Genoese sold Corsica to France, when Paoli's last gallant hopeless stand for independence was nearly over.

'Foolish as we are', said Lord Holland, raising his eyebrows, 'we cannot be so foolish as to go to war because Mr. Boswell has been in Corsica.' One more gift to those who accuse the foreign policy of Britain, champion of liberty and small nations, of cynical opportunism and humbug; this time wrongly, for Corsica was no Poland. Paoli escaped to London in 1769 and became a social lion and an honoured member of Johnson's circle. In the years to come Boswell will see a fair amount of this great and noble man; but not enough.

Boswell arrived in Paris on Sunday, January 12, 1766, and put up in the Rue Pierre-Sarrazin, near St. Germain-des-Prés, moving soon to the sign of the Dauphin in the Rue Taranne, close by. One of his first inquiries was a discreet one. They directed him to 'Madame Heket's.'

5

Paris in that damp and foggy January of 1766 which made Horace Walpole so querulous had a deal of novel amusement to offer Mr. Wilkes's young friend, with or without Mr. Wilkes's expert guidance.

It was a noisier, more vivid, smellier, more 'Gothick' metropolis than London, though vast planning-schemes were in progress under Gabriel and Bouchardon. While the Cité was still the old Paris of decorative, elaborate signs overhanging dark, narrow, twisting, deafening cobbled streets, courts, and alleys, the Paris

Villon knew, the developing quarters of the Madeleine and the
École Militaire, for example, displayed wide, airy vistas lined
with tall, gracious new buildings. But even in the older quarters,
and especially in the Marais, you came suddenly on quiet
gardens, conventual or patrician, full of birdsong and lilac. At
least half a dozen parks, like the charmingly-named Jardin de
l'Infante, the Tuileries, and the Luxembourg, were open to the
public, and all round Paris were wide leafy promenades. As in
London, no pavements existed as yet, except on the bridges.
From the Faubourg-St. Honoré a broad walk amid Le Nôtre's
plantations crossed the plain of the Champs-Elysées, dusty in
summer and muddy in winter, to the Butte de l'Etoile, standing
some sixteen feet higher than the present site of the Arc de
Triomphe.

The racket of Louis XV's Paris exceeded that of London; its
tempo was quicker, its pitch more shrill, its citizens more restless,
more cynical, more insatiable for novelty and amusement, with
some thirty-five newspapers, daily and weekly, to feed this
passion,[1] and the cafés and their politicians and chess players
increasing in number and noise as France staggered into bankruptcy. Theatres, art-exhibitions, concerts, executions, masked
balls, and breakings on the wheel in the Place de Grève were
among the more seemly pleasures of the town. Boswell's visit
coincided with one of those periodical outbreaks of anglomania
which introduced horse-racing on the Newmarket plan to the
Plaine des Sablons, on the St. Germain road, in February of
this year.

How many of these diversions engaged Boswell's attention
during these three weeks we do not know. The Parisian entries
in his journal are brief, scrappy, and for the most part, decorous.
His earliest call of ceremony was at the Scots College, that
ancient foundation of David, Bishop of Moray, moved in the
seventeenth century from the neighbourhood of the Sorbonne
to the Rue du Cardinal Lemoine. The College had nearly thirty
years' existence still before it as a seminary for priests on the
Scottish Mission; in its chapel was the tomb of James II. During
his stay Boswell frequently enjoyed the hospitality of the Rector,
Father Alexander Gordon, attended Mass more than once in

[1] London at this time had about twenty, morning, evening, and weekly.

the chapel, and met Lord Alford and several other fellow-Scots at the Rector's table.

It is curious he notes none of the entertainments of Paris, barring Madame Heket's and a certain 'Montigni's' ('sad work'), and does not once mention the theatre, of which he was so fond. Perhaps the Parisian stage disappointed him. To any London playgoer it would seem, indeed, the thinnest of bread-and-butter. Although London taste had improved and Garrick had put the cruder bawdy out of fashion,[1] the Londoner in Paris would still miss the jolly drunken scenes, the scenes of attempted seduction or rape, the coarse backchat, the gibes at filial duty and the marriage-tie and family life and the clergy to which he was accustomed, for the French Censorship insisted on a tiresome standard of decency. A pleasing illustration of the gulf between the Paris and London theatres is quoted by Professor F. C. Green.[2] In Destouches' comedy *L'Amour Usé*, adapted for the Haymarket as *The Contract* in the 1750's by the Rev. Thomas Francklin, one of the many eighteenth-century divines whose simple duties enabled them to dabble in playwriting, there is a love-scene as follows:

*Isabelle:* Est-ce bien lui? Ne m'a-t-on pas flattée? Non, c'est une vérité. Vérité charmante! Je vous revois donc, mon cher, mon bien aimé Lisidor!
*Lisidor:* Ma belle, mon aimable, ma charmante Isabelle!
*Isabelle:* Je suis dans une folie—
*Lisidor:* Et moi, dans un transport—
*Isabelle:* Qui me bouleverse le sens.
*Lisidor:* Qui me fait extravaguer.
*Isabelle:* Je n'en puis plus!
*Lisidor:* Je me meurs!

Spicier fare, what the hack Conway called 'the Cayenne Humour', was required for the London palate, and Mr. Francklin duly supplied it.

[1] Through all his life one of Garrick's favourite parts was that of Sir John Brute in a slightly modified version of Vanbrugh's *Provok'd Wife*, the comedy which partly evoked Jeremy Collier's historic onslaught on the profane and shameless London stage.
[2] *Minuet:* a Critical Survey of French and English Literary Ideas in the Eighteenth Century. London, 1935.

*olonel:* She comes, she comes, the charmer of my heart! O Eleanora!
(*They embrace.*)

*eanora:* My dearest Colonel, is it then given me once more to
behold—(*aside*) He's a horrid creature!

*olonel:* After so many years of tedious absence, again to look on
those dear eyes, to taste those balmy lips! (*embrace again.*) She
stinks like a pole-cat! (*aside.*)

The exquisitely pure and subtle filigree of Marivaux would
em tame enough after this. Whether any of his comedies were
ing performed in January 1766 I cannot discover. Beau-
archais, of course, was not yet on the horizon. Boswell would
ve just missed seeing the greatest actress in France, Mlle.
airon, who had resigned from the Comédie-Française a little
me before, following the famous strike and uproar which de-
ghted the town and landed her, with Le Kain, 'the French
arrick', and three other actors for a week in the prison of
e For-l'Evêque, where *le Tout-Paris* rallied to La Clairon's
pper-parties and the streets leading to the prison were blocked
ith ducal coaches.[1] Chastened by this object-lesson, Mlle.
umesnil and the comedian Préville and Bellecourt and the
maining members of the company would be walking through
piece by Legrand or La Chaussée with less than their normal
nchalance, one imagines. —

At the Opéra some imperious Davilliers or Dangeville would
e singing in Gluck's *Orfeo,* or Rameau's *Indes Galantes,* or
ousseau's *Devin du Village.* At the Opéra-Comique, which
ad recently absorbed the Italian Comedy, Carlino Bertinazzi
as playing Arlequin to the Inamorata of Mme. Favart. The only
ther public theatrical performances, as in London, were at the
irs, especially the great Fair of St. Germain, where ropedancers,
arionettes, quacks, mountebanks, *parades,* and knockabout
rce derived from the Commedia dell' Arte diverted the masses;
ut this fair did not open till February, and the others much later.

[1] Funck-Brentano, *La Bastille des Comédiens* (*Le Prison du For-
Evêque*); Paris, 1920. The squabble leading to this incident is too involved
be dealt with here. French stage-players at this period were servants
the Crown, and disciplined accordingly. Garrick, who was in Paris in
765, offered his brother-star refuge from the Lieutenant of Police, but
e Kain could hardly miss a public performance of this magnitude, and
racefully gave himself up.

In any case the entertainment Boswell was chiefly interested i
would take him, with or without Wilkes, more often to th
Tuileries Gardens and the new Boulevards, from the Temple t
the Porte St. Martin. Along this fashionable promenade th
cafés, side-shows, and gay ladies were plentiful; the Palais-Roy:
was not yet the centre of Parisian raffishness. Not that Boswe
need depend on any roving encounters, much as he esteeme
adventure of the kind. Wilkes, apart from having been a pe
like Rousseau and Hume, of the fickle great ladies who, i
Horace Walpole's charming phrase, 'violated all the duties
life and gave very pretty suppers', had plenty of acquaintanc
in *le monde où l'on s'amuse*. That anecdote Boswell tells in th
*Life* of Wilkes's supping with a young peer and his Opera gi
on the eve of parting belongs to this period, and doubtle:
Wilkes could command the key of more than one nobleman
*folie* in the leafy Parisian suburbs as often as he felt incline
He did not take Boswell into any of the smart philosophic:
drawing-rooms, where his own popularity had waned a trifle b
now; but he was undoubtedly a mine of information on the town
more accessible amusements, if not a valued guide.

Boswell had resumed contact with Wilkes soon after his arriva
His classical friend was now living with a Mlle. Chassagne in th
Rue des Saints-Pères, off the Quai Malaquais; desperately sho:
of money, more heavily in debt than ever, and dependent entirel
on subsidies from Lord Temple and the Whigs, with an occa
sional mysterious *douceur* from the French Government, fc
what services nobody seems to know.[1] Boswell found him mood
and depressed, but his 'perpetual gayety' soon reasserted itsel
Before long Wilkes was ridiculing the Incarnation, and at th
top of his form. One diary entry a few days later is typic:
Boswell. Calling on Wilkes on January 27 and picking up
belated copy of *The St. James's Chronicle*, he was stunned t
read a brief notice of his mother's death. Still stunned, he dine
with the Dutch Ambassador, and at six o'clock rushed (his ow:
word) away in a fever to Madame Heket's, where the charm
of a certain Constance allayed his grief.

That same week Boswell called on Horace Walpole—'in spit

[1] Horace Walpole and others accused him years later of being a Frenc
agent, which he vigorously denied.

of my teeth and my doors', as Walpole complained to Gray—in his *hôtel garni* in the Rue du Colombier, now the Rue Jacob, to extract some information concerning the misfortunes of ex-King Theodore of Corsica. But the frigid Walpole, 'either from pride or stupidity', deigned to say very little. Mr. Hume had recently left the Embassy to accompany Rousseau to England, and so escaped. Not so Lady Berkeley, Lord Alford, and a few other English and Scots notables.

On January 31 Boswell left for England, escorting Rousseau's mistress, Thérèse Levasseur, whom he had met again in Paris. During the journey they misbehaved themselves quite ignobly, as appeared from a long passage in the journal which Colonel Isham managed to peruse before it was destroyed by another hand. As every admirer of Rousseau is aware, Mlle. Levasseur, Rousseau's prop and stay, cook-housekeeper, nurse, and guardian for over thirty years (a difficult feat), was a coarse, plain-featured, illiterate harridan, now aged about forty, whose one virtue is supposed to have been fidelity to '*mon Mari*'. Wilkes must have laughed consumedly on receiving Boswell's account of this adventure, applauding his young friend's return to common sense after all that hymn-singing and mixing with monks and priests in Corsica and being 'elevated' by the devout Paoli.

I pause to reflect how difficult it is, as one surveys the relations between Wilkes and Boswell, not to fall into romanticism and to descry the tempting parallel of Mephistopheles and Faust. Some of the polite raillery Goethe puts into the tempter's mouth throughout his play are essential Wilkesery. 'I am the Spirit that Denies—and rightly, since everything that exists is fit only to be destroyed . . . However bad the company thou art in, thou shalt feel thyself a man among men . . . My friend, the time has come to indulge ourselves in a little discreet debauchery . . . Civilisation, which polishes the whole world, has extended even to the Devil . . . One dare hardly name to chaste ears what chaste hearts can never tire of . . . I wish thee much pleasure in lying to thyself from time to time . . . I can think of nothing more ridiculous than a devil who despairs . . . *O sancta simplicitas!*' An urbane and perfect Mephistopheles, Mr. Wilkes, shrugging and grinning and undermining.

It is easy to understand why Boswell was permanently

fascinated by Wilkes. What Wilkes saw in Boswell to warrant a lifelong friendship is not less easy to discover, I think. He found in him endless amusement. The agreeable scatterbrain, the gay drinking-companion,the quaint Scots chatterbox, the admirable and untiring listener had absurd recurrent urgings towards Christianity and a better life, and Wilkes must have derived kindly pleasure from rallying these intempestive and reactionary impulses. Boswell's addiction to a monster of probity and credulity like Johnson, we may be sure, inspired frequent and amusing Wilkesian epigrams, at which Boswell would roar as heartily as any others of the retinue. A weathercock, a whirligig; and the same unseen spirit-chorus which mourned for Faust may have hovered over him often as he laughed with Wilkes at the supper-table, the romantic might imagine with a sigh.

> Weh! Weh!
> Du hast sie zerstört
> Die schöne Welt
> Mit mächtiger Faust
> Sie stürzt, sie zerfällt!
> Ein Halbgott hat sie zerschlagen!
> Wir tragen
> Die Trümmern ins Nichts hinüber
> Und klagen
> Uber die verlorne Schöne! . . .[1]

Unfortunately reality, as so often, spoils the symphony. This Faust will never turn on the mocker in fury and loathing, crying 'Thou thing of filth and fire, dog, execrable monster!' They remain close friends till Boswell-Faust quits this life, and two years later Mephistopheles-Wilkes himself attains Christian burial after a last ribald jest or two. The memorial-tablet in Grosvenor Chapel, South Audley Street, may, I believe, be viewed today.

So Boswell returned to England with the unattractive Levasseur, dumped her forthwith at Chiswick, where Rousseau was

---

[1] 'Alas, alas! Thou hast destroyed it, the happy world! Thou hast shattered it with mighty force, it lies in ruins! A half-god has tumbled it down! We bear away the fragments into Nothingness, weeping over lost beauty!' (*Faust*, Pt. I, Sc. IV.)

staying, hastened to call on Johnson in Johnson's Court, Fleet
Street, and was kindly received. Johnson had written to him in
Paris urging him to end his rambling and return home for the
sake of his father, who was ill. They supped at the Mitre again,
and again a few nights later, when Temple was present. Here
Boswell thoughtlessly put his foot in it.

I having mentioned that I had passed some time with Rousseau in
his wild retreat, and having quoted some remarks made by Mr.
Wilkes, with whom I had spent many pleasant hours in Italy, Johnson
said (sarcastically), 'It seems, Sir, you have kept very good company
abroad, Rousseau and Wilkes!' Thinking it enough to defend one at a
time, I said nothing as to my gay friend, but answered with a smile,
'My dear Sir, you don't call Rousseau bad company. Do you really
think him a *bad* man?'

Johnson did think so, describing the Philosopher vigorously as
a rascal who ought to be hunted out of society, a man as bad as
Voltaire. One may imagine Boswell pulling himself up on the
edge of the abyss. Another incautious word or two and he would
be babbling of things which would have crisped Johnson's wig
with anger and disgust, and possibly ended their acquaintance
that night. Psychiatrists say the temptation to rush into this
kind of peril is almost overwhelming to a type like Boswell. No
doubt he wiped a little sweat off his forehead more than once
during this Mitre supper, and blamed the fire. Nobody reading
the *Life* would gather that the Doctor knew nothing whatsoever
of his disciple's private life. Boswell was nearly betrayed to
Johnson a little later, as we shall see, by the playful Wilkes,
whose geniality was not, as I have already noted, without a
touch of sadism. To see the wretched Boswell writhing like a
butterfly on a pin and imploring him to be discreet and merciful
was doubtless an exquisite joke. However, Mephisto tired of the
sport and let him off.

The Corsican fever held Boswell now firmly in its grip, despite
the Doctor's testiness. Puffing himself in paragraphs to the
*London Chronicle,* surrounding himself with romantic mystery,
calling on Pitt in masquerade, boasting of his friendship with
Paoli, and all the rest of it made him a public figure at last. Mr.
Corsica Boswell. The Eighteenth Century quaintly bestowed

titles on the eminent, taken homerically from their feats and works: Athenian Stuart, Shakespeare Steevens, Leonidas Glover, Dog Jennings (the dilettante who bought the antique Greek marble alleged to represent Alcibiades' dog), Palmyra Dawkins, Hermes Harris, Dictionary Johnson. Mr. Corsica Boswell had arrived. Unfortunately a return to Scotland was imperative. His mother was dead, his father was ill, and his bond required him to seek admission forthwith to the Society of Advocates. He left for home accordingly in April, got through the double viva-voce, paternal and legal, without trouble, was admitted an advocate on July 29, and almost immediately plunged into a passionate intrigue, about which he keeps Temple fully posted. She is a Mrs. Dodds, a woman with three children, deserted by her husband (which makes it all right, as Boswell points out light-heartedly to his clerical friend). His preoccupation with the 'dear Infidel', the 'sweet little mistress', very nearly gives him that light push over the mental borderline which so often threatened him, for the adored one, though handsome, very lively, and 'admirably formed for amorous dalliance', is a bouncing virago with a certain reputation. Rumours concerning her come to Boswell's ears in February 1767, after he has taken a house for her and the family, designing, he tells Temple, to be 'safe and happy, and in no danger either of the perils of Venus or of desperate matrimony'.

Incoherent, jerky letters pour from him before long. Philosophy, he says, 'teacheth us to be moderate, to be patient, to expect a gradual progress of refinement and felicity, and in that hope I look up to the Lord of the Universe, with a grateful remembrance of the grand and mysterious propitiation which Christianity hath announnced'; but meanwhile the sweet little mistress is driving him crazy with jealousy. He is half inclined to say 'Damn her, lewd Minx.' He is tormented and disgusted. He hates her lack of refinement. 'She is ill-bred, quite a rompish girl. She debases my dignity.' On the other hand how can he do better than 'keep a dear Infidel for my hours of Paphian bliss'? Yet since the last draught of Paphian bliss he has cooled off, he says. 'This is a curious epistle to a clergyman!' It certainly is, and one may imagine Temple settling his bands now and again with a dazed expression as his confidant rambles on. Shall

Boswell tell the charmer he is himself an inconstant being? Shall
he let his love gradually decay? 'Had she never loved before,
I would have lost every drop of blood rather than give her up.
There's madness! There's delicacy!'

He assures Temple that he is equally pursuing the law.

It must be confessed that our Court of Session is not so favourable
to eloquence as the English courts; yet the Outer House here is a
school where a man may train himself to pretty good purpose. . . .
I already speak with much ease and boldness, and have already the
language of the Bar much at command. I have now cleared eighty
guineas. My clerk comes to me every morning at six, and I have
dictated to him forty folio pages in one day.

Incidentally he fears that furnishing a house for the 'sweet little
mistress' will cost a great deal and is 'too much like marriage',
though he has taken the house and cannot draw back. Skipping
a parenthesis or two touching on Robertson's *Charles the Fifth*,
Rousseau's quarrel with Hume, the amiable Dr. Gregory of the
Department of Medicine, and Hume's praise of the Corsican
book, we come to this:

Temple, will you allow me to marry a good Scots lass? Ha! Ha! Ha!
What shall I tell you? Zelide has been in London this winter. I never
hear from her—she is a strange creature.

One more parenthesis concerning 'brother Davy', a prodigious
fine fellow, home from Spain for Christmas, and he returns to
Mrs. Dodds. They have quarreled. He told her how unhappy he
was. Her eyes were full of passion. He took her in his arms and
embraced her with transport. The same evening he gave a
supper-party to some friends to settle an old wager that he would
be free from venereal disease for three years, got roaring drunk,
spent the night with a drab ('Bless me, what a risque!') and
next day breathed the whole story into his charmer's ear in an
orgy of Rousseauesque emotion and was forgiven.

I confess Boswell is becoming tiresome. In his next letter he
is going to marry one of two ladies—either his Yorkshire relative,
Miss Boswell, or charming Miss Catherine Blair of Adamtown,
near Auchinleck. I do not propose to follow all his babblings to
Temple on this theme. His 'late Circe' is with child ('What a

fellow am I!') and he provides for it and ends the affair. Miss
Blair and her mother have visited Auchinleck's 'romantick
groves', and he has drunk the fair one's health so vigorously that
he finishes the night in a brothel. He orders Temple to visit
Adamtown and praise him effusively, at the same time em-
phasising his butterfly nature. ('Ask gravely, "Pray don't you
imagine there is something of madness in that family?"') The
pursuit of Miss Blair, 'my Princess', complicated to some extent
by the recent appearance of the late-adored Zelide in England
and a letter from the Siena angel, is now a major issue. He has a
formidable rival, a rich East Indian Nabob named Fullerton.
Presently Boswell is calling on Miss Blair in a green-and-gold
suit, attended by a servant in claret-coloured livery and gold-
laced hat. But Miss Blair is elusive and difficult.

An ensuing letter (December 24, 1767) contains a sentimental
dialogue between Boswell and his Princess which, whether he
touched it up or not, is so surprisingly free from the ritual 'La,
Sir!' and 'Madam, I protest!' of the eighteenth-century theatrical
love-scene as to be worth setting down in part, I think. Perhaps
this is how eighteenth-century lovers actually talked to each
other. The dialogue begins with the Princess's coy remark 'No,
I really have no particular liking for you; I like many people as
well as you.'

*Boswell:* Do you indeed? Well, I cannot help it; I am obliged to you
    for telling me so in time. I am sorry for it.
*Princess:* I like Jeany Maxwell [Duchess of Gordon] better than you.
*Boswell:* Very well; but do you like no man better than me?
*Princess:* No.
*Boswell:* Is it possible that you may like me better than other men?
*Princess:* I don't know what is possible.
    (By this time I had risen and placed myself by her, and was in
    real agitation.)
*Boswell:* I'll tell you what, my dear Miss Blair, I love you so much
    that I am very unhappy if you cannot love me. I must, if possible,
    endeavour to forget you. What would you have me do?
*Princess:* I really don't know what you should do.
*Boswell:* It is certainly possible that you may love me; and if you shall
    ever do so, I shall be the happiest man in the world. Will you make
    a fair bargain with me? If you should happen to love me, will you
    own it?

*Princess:* Yes.

*Boswell:* And if you should happen to love another, will you tell me immediately, and help me to make myself easy?

*Princess:* Yes, I will.

*Boswell:* Well, you are very good (often squeezing and kissing her fine hand, while she looked at me with those beautiful black eyes).

*Princess:* I may tell you, as a cousin, what I would not tell to another man.

*Boswell:* You may indeed. You are very fond of Auchinleck, and that is one good circumstance.

*Princess:* I confess I am. I wish I liked you as well as I do Auchinleck.

No doubt the essential technique of the fan was in operation all this while, and the fine black eyes flashed and languished and rolled, were averted or hidden, according to the rubrics. The scene ends with Boswell saying that he is in earnest and that whatever happens, they must never quarrel again.

*Princess:* Never.

*Boswell:* And may I come and see you as much as I please?

*Princess:* Yes.

And the dissatisfied lover sums up to Temple:

My worthy friend, what sort of a scene was this? . . . She said that to see one loving her would go far to make her love that person; but she would not talk anyhow positively, for she had never felt the uneasy anxiety of love. We were an hour and a half together, and she seemed pleased all the time . . . I admire her more than ever . . .

His Princess, though she does not talk at all like a leading lady of Sheridan's or Goldsmith's, is obviously a girl of sense. 'How long must I suffer?' he cries to Temple. 'Kate has not fire enough; she does not know the value of her lover!' One sees the bewildered clergyman rolling a bemused eye round his study. Not that his advice mattered one way or the other. Two months later Miss Blair definitely discards Boswell for her Nabob, and Zelide, the 'charming Dutchwoman' of Utrecht, steps into first place again.

6

One would think Boswell's clerk, Mr. Lawrie, had little to do at this time but twiddle his thumbs and yawn through the dusty office-window at the bustling street-life of Edinburgh. Not so. A *cause célèbre* was engaging the Scottish legal and social world, and the busybody Boswell, simultaneously engaged on his *Account of Corsica,* a less attractive work than the *Journal,* must needs plunge into the thick of it, dictating and publishing a pamphlet, *The Essence of the Douglas Cause,* dashing off a fictional version of it called *Dorando,* and showering paragraphs on the Edinburgh newspapers. He was not professionally engaged, but he attended all the hearings and displayed himself sufficiently in the limelight to earn, later on, a freezing cut from the Duchess of Argyle [1] at the Duke's own table. The *Essence* is said by lawyers to present the case quite competently.

The Douglas Cause, involving the heirship of Mr. Archibald Douglas to the family estates as against the Duke of Hamilton, excited Edinburgh so much that it soon became a party-question and the Hamilton apartments at Holyrood were sacked by the mob and the judges' windows—including Lord Auchinleck's—smashed. The case had a scabrous side. The Hamiltons had to prove Archibald Douglas illegitimate, and Horace Walpole remarks of the subsequent appeal to the Lords that Lord Sandwich, who had studied the 'midwifery' of the business, scandalised the Bishops excessively. The Hamiltons' case was that Archibald Douglas and his twin-brother, who died young, were the offspring of a glass-manufacturer and a French rope-dancer, and had been purchased from them by the Douglases. The House of Lords at length reversed the Court of Session's verdict (by the President's casting-vote), the Douglases triumphed, and Edinburgh was illuminated. The case, including bribery by both sides on a lavish scale, cost £500,000 at least in modern money and fills eighteen thick volumes of law-print. The unreliable Ramsay of Ochtertyre, whose whimsies we have noted before, tells a story about Boswell's heading the mob which broke his father's windows after the verdict of the Court of Session and Auchinleck's tearful pleading with President Dundas to commit James to the Tolbooth. As father and son were equally pro-Douglas this seems obvious nonsense.

[1] Formerly Duchess of Hamilton. One of 'the beautiful Gunnings', she was married to the impatient Hamilton at midnight with a curtain-ring on the operative finger. On Hamilton's death she married Argyle.

In February 1768 the Foulis brothers of Glasgow printed and the Dillys in London published the *Journal of a Tour to Corsica,* and Boswell's literary reputation, after years of tedious scribbling, was made at last. Before October the slim book was in its third edition, as it deserved. Johnson esteemed it highly, like Bonaparte after him. The finical Gray confessed to Horace Walpole that it 'pleased and moved me strangely', adding spitefully that any fool may write a most valuable book by chance', and that the conversations with Paoli were exchanges between 'a Green Goose and a Hero'. But as old Auchinleck growled, Jamie had ta'en a toot on a new horn', and a highly successful one.

Boswell hastened to London to enjoy his triumph, heralding his arrival on March 23 by paragraphs in the daily papers. James Boswell, Esq., is expected in Town.' (*London Chronicle.*) Yesterday James Boswell, Esq., arrived from Scotland at his lodgings in Half Moon Street, Piccadilly.' (*Public Advertizer.*) This journalistic side-industry we have not noted before, and need not mention again. It is a constant. He was always an indefatigable publicity-agent for James Boswell. He found Johnson was in Oxford and followed him there, after a few days' relaxation. The Doctor was a little cool. Boswell had annoyed him by printing one of his letters in the *Journal* without permission. He obtained forgiveness forthwith, also Johnson's sanction for the publication of all his letters, after death, in a projected biographical work Boswell mentions vaguely for the first time: the *Life,* already taking shape, dimly, as a 'future'.

Happy and intoxicated with fame and Johnson's returning kindness, Boswell writes to Temple:

My book has amazing celebrity. Lord Lyttelton, Mr. Walpole, Mrs. Macaulay, and Mr. Garrick have all written me noble letters about it. There are two Dutch translations going forward, and Zelide translates it into French.

At last he could mingle with the rest of Johnson's literary intimates as an equal. Moreover he was being taken up. Old General Oglethorpe, founder of Georgia, Pope's friend, called and solicited his acquaintance, among others.

I am really the great man now. I have David Hume in the forenoon, Mr. Johnson in the afternoon of the same day. I give admirable dinners

and good claret, and the moment I go abroad again, which will be
in a day or two, I set up my chariot. This is enjoying the fruit of my
labours, and appearing like the friend of Paoli.

His guests at this time include Johnson, Hume, Oglethorpe,
Benjamin Franklin, Garrick, Bennett Langton, Sir John Pringle,
Dr. Percy and Dr. Douglas, two bishops-elect, Dr. Hugh Blair,
and Thomas Davies; for though Boswell tends to patronise the
actor-bookseller to whom he owes so much, he does not drop him.
At one of these dinners Johnson is in magnificent form, tossing
and goring everybody. And Boswell's other existence, the secret
one, the racketty one, goes on simultaneously. 'To confess to
you at once, Temple', he writes on April 16, 1768, 'I have, since
my last coming to town, been as wild as ever.' Ten days later:
'Your moral lecture came to me yesterday in very good time,
while I lay suffering severely for immorality.' He is not meeting
the adored Zelide, but they correspond. He blames her levity,
she retorts acidly. Postscript to the April 16 letter:

I knew you are determined to have me married. What would you
think of the fine, healthy, young, amiable Miss Dick, with whom you
dined so agreeably? . . . She wants only a good fortune.

*Miss Dick?*
He returned to Auchinleck a week or two later, having made
a solemn vow in St. Paul's Cathedral to refrain from 'licentious
connections' of any kind for six months, and plunged forthwith
into the legal business of the Summer Session, gambling, and a
fresh infatuation. 'The finest creature that ever was formed, *la
Belle Irlandaise* . . . formed like a Grecian nymph', Mary Anne
by name, surname unrecorded, is the visiting daughter of a
Dublin barrister, and, writes this hare-brained Macheath to
Temple, 'here every flower is united.' He carves her name on a
tree and cuts off a shining lock of her hair against her will, like
Pope's Baron. 'I have given up my criminal intercourse with
Mrs. ——; in short, Maria has me without any rival.' The shadowy
Miss Dick is out of circulation already, if she was ever in it, and
Zelide quits the stage for ever. A letter to Temple four months
later announces that Miss Blair is again princess of Boswell's
heart and that he is in debt, due to play, and in low spirits, due

to drinking, 'a habit which still prevails in Scotland'. But 'from henceforth I shall be a perfect man; at least, I hope so.' He adds suddenly: 'Am I right to insist that my dear little woman shall stay?' And who should the dear little woman be but Mrs. Dodds, the Paphian, whom he still feverishly loves but admits to be 'unworthy of Paoli's friend'? Poor Temple.

Into this confused whirl of law-business, gambling, drinking, Corsican business—including the raising of that £700 subscription which brought the hard-pressed Paoli welcome ordnance—and women business, comes a decision at last. In April 1769, having taken a trip to Dublin to visit *la Belle Irlandaise,* during which Lords Leinster and Charlemont and other notables praise and entertain the author of the Corsican Journal very gratifyingly, Boswell makes up his mind to marry, finally and irrevocably. His choice, if the reader is not too dizzy by now to catch up with Lothario, is obvious. It is his cousin, Margaret Montgomerie.

Miss Montgomerie of Lainshaw, a relation of the Eglintouns, was gentle, kindly, patient, sensible, and rigid. She needed all these qualities in the years to come. No flaming beauty, she possessed all those Scottish virtues which inspire admiration and fear in subject races. The engagement was accepted by both families. The cousinship of the parties does not seem to have perturbed them. Lord Auchinleck perhaps was ready to risk anything to get the wild youth settled. So a marriage was arranged for November, and Boswell came to London in the early autumn of 1769 for Johnson's blessing and one last fling, to find Johnson away at Brighton with the Thrales. Looking round for more immediate entertainment, he noted that a Shakespeare Jubilee celebration was to take place at Stratford-upon-Avon in the first week of September, and was to include a masquerade. All the fashionable world (said the newspapers) would be there. So would he, with the costume he had brought from Corsica in his baggage; the striking costume which had already raised the eyebrows of Pitt and won derisive cheers from the loungers of Whitehall.

7

Amusing as are certain modern manifestations of what has unkindly been called the Shakespeare Racket at Stratford-upon-Avon, they miss by some octaves the high note of comedy which marked the Shakespeare Jubilee celebrations at that spurious shrine on September 6, 7, and 8, 1769, when aubades and serenades, public breakfasts and dinners, fireworks, bells and cannon, oratorio and odes and oratory, a Grand Masquerade and a grand horse-race celebrated Shakespeare's immortal glory, amid torrential rain, with hardly a word of Shakespeare's spoken from beginning to end.

By 1769 Stratford's main industry had already taken on that mildly diverting aspect now inseparable from it. The natives had not yet tapped the international market or entered the picture-postcard and brass toasting-fork period, but Shakespeare's famous mulberry-tree was yielding immense dividends in the shape of snuff-boxes, walking-sticks, and other curios. It had been hewn down in 1756 by Dr. Johnson's fellow-countryman, the Rev. Francis Gastrell, who then occupied New Place, in a spasm of hate. Three years later the bitter clergyman pulled down New Place itself and left Stratford 'as the villain in melodrama should leave the stage, amid a storm of hisses.' [1] The Jubilee of 1769, so called because it happened five years after the bicentenary of Shakespeare's death, was Garrick's inspiration, and indeed Garrick's show throughout. Aptly did Gray call it Vanity Fair, and truly symbolic of Garrick's lifelong attitude to Shakespeare is the Gainsborough portrait now in Stratford Town Hall, showing Garrick leaning elegantly crosslegged against a sylvan pedestal crowned by the Swan of Avon's bust, the right arm, hat in hand, thrown round it in protective benignity; *ego et poeta meus*.

In September 1769 the great actor was enjoying one of his temporary retirements from the stage. His Stratford performance was partly the result of those often mysterious public recalls to which eminent actors must gracefully and instantly submit, and partly a return-courtesy to the municipality of Stratford, who had bestowed the borough's freedom on him in the previous year.

[1] *Amazing Monument,* by Ivor Brown and George Fearon. London, 1939.

Garrick certainly worked like a slave over the Shakespeare Jubilee, guaranteeing most of the expenses and losing a fair amount of money; for the weather, itself in Shakespearean and jubilee mood, put up a spirited and almost non-stop performance based on the opening scene of *The Tempest* and the storm-scene in *King Lear*. During three arduous days Garrick was Chief Steward, poet, orator, pageant-master, chorus-leader, Master of Ceremonies, and unwilling providence to his brother George, a confirmed sponger who 'touched' the Town Clerk—as he would say merrily nowadays—for a hundred pounds, which his famous brother was apparently expected to pay back.[1]

Foote, who swore he was charged nine guineas for six hours' sleep by the racketeers of Stratford, duly waxed funny over the result of his rival's labours:

A Jubilee is a public Invitation, circulated and arranged by Puffing, to go posting without horses to an obscure borough without representatives, governed by a Mayor and Aldermen who are no Magistrates; to celebrate a Poet, whose Works have made him immortal, by an Ode without poetry, Musick without melody, Dinners without victuals, and Lodgings without beds; a Masquarade where half the people appear bare-faced, a Horse-Race up to the knees in water, and a gingerbread Amphitheatre which tumbled to pieces as soon as it was made.

That, of course, is 'pretty Fanny's way'; yet the sufferings of the Beau Monde for Shakespeare's sake, far exceeding those of Lord Lilac in the poem, deserved an ode to themselves, and would have drawn tears from any observer of sensibility had not the weeping skies half drowned the world already. The rains began on the second morning of the Jubilee, as coaches and chaises from London and the country were still pouring into Stratford, and hardly stopped until the last gilded wheel had been heaved out of the mud for the homeward journey. Some of the rich and great had to sleep in their coaches, for the town was packed by 'incredible multitudes', the happy natives were charging what they liked, and the noise and discomfort were considerable.

At 5 a.m. on Wednesday, September 6, a discharge of artillery

---

[1] With David, George Garrick had been one of the first three pupils at Samuel Johnson's 'academy' at Edial, near Lichfield, in 1736.

on the river-bank opened the Festival, and Mr. Garrick's Drury
Lane company, 'fantastically dressed', paraded the streets, singing:

> Let Beauty with the Sun arise,
> To SHAKSPEARE tribute pay,
> With heav'nly Smiles and speaking Eyes
> Give Lustre to the Day!
>
> Each Smile she gives protects his Name,
> What Face shall dare to frown?
> Not Envy's Self can blast the Fame,
> Which Beauty deigns to crown.

To this aubade succeeded a rollicking ditty of more obvious
Garrick vintage (he should have attended to Shropshire as well):

> Ye Warwickshire Lads and ye Lasses,
> See what at our Jubilee passes,
>    Come revel away, rejoice and be glad,
> For the Lad of all Lads was a Warwickshire Lad!
>    Warwickshire Lad!
>    All be glad!
> The Lad of all Lads was a Warwickshire Lad!

By this time the sun was well up. Children ran from house to
house distributing programmes, the band of the Warwickshire
Militia struck up with fife, brass, and drum, and all Stratford
began to deck itself with ribbons and favours and to prepare for
the Public Breakfast at nine; admission one shilling, provided a
guinea had already been subscribed to the Entertainment Fund
and another half-guinea to the Masquerade.

Shortly after eight Mr. Garrick arrived at the breakfast-rooms,
to be received by the Mayor and Corporation, to be invested
with his Steward's insignia, a gold-framed Shakespeare medallion
from the inexhaustible mulberry-tree and a wand of office, and
to make a suitable oration, amid more bell-ringing. The company,
including the Dukes of Dorset and Manchester, Lords Grosvenor,
Beauchamp, Spencer, Denbigh, Carlisle, and Pigot, Sir Watkin
Williams Wynn, Bart., the great Welsh Jacobite, and many more
notables, including James Boswell, Esq., of Auchinleck, then
sat down to eat and the band struck up gay airs. After breakfast

the company adjourned to the parish church to hear Dr. Arne's oratorio *Judith,* with the composer conducting. Mr. Boswell later expressed the view in *The London Magazine* that prayers would more fitly have opened the Jubilee, followed by a short sermon. The nobility and gentry doubtless thought Garrick's plan better value, seeing that the entire Drury Lane orchestra was performing with full choruses and leading singers, including the celebrated Mrs. Baddeley.

The oratorio over, there was a procession, headed by Garrick and his wand, to the new Rotunda on the Bankcroft, designed for the occasion in wood and named 'Shakespeare's Hall': an impressive and decorative, if gimcrack edifice, with a chandelier of eight hundred lights and a painted ceiling and cornices, planned to hold a thousand people. During the procession there was another Garrick chorus:

> This is a Day, a Holiday,
> Drive Spleen and Rancour far away ...

Outside the alleged birthplace of the presumed author of *Hamlet* the procession halted and appropriate lines were chanted:

> Here Nature nurs'd her darling Boy,
> From whom all Care and Sorrow fly,
> Whose Harp the Muses strung! ...

In the Rotunda the tables were spread for the 'grand Public Ordinary' at three o'clock, with turtle-soup and Madeira; but it seems that the main repast, supplied by the landlord of the White Lion at 18s. 6d. a head, was a disappointment, consisting notably of poor beef and worse port. By six o'clock the company were leaving to dress for the Assembly, and the eminent pyrotechnician Signor Domenico Angelo, who had brought down from London two waggon-loads of fireworks, was looking to his rockets and squibs. They went off with a great bang at 10 p.m., when the Assembly opened and the minuets began, to be followed at midnight by country-dances, as at Bath and Tunbridge Wells, till three in the morning.

So far, so good. But soon after dawn on the Thursday the rain began. Before noon, an after-breakfast Procession of Shakes-

peare's Characters having been called off, it was drumming
fiercely on the wooden roof of the Rotunda as Garrick, wand
in hand, standing gracefully on the platform beneath a Shakespeare statue, began his Jubilee Ode. He wore an elegant gold-
laced suit of brown and a modish periwig. On either side of him
was the chorus, with the orchestra, under Dr. Arne, in front, for
the Ode was partly choral. Arne's baton rose. Orchestra and
chorus crashed into the prelude.

> To what blest Genius of the Isle
> Shall Gratitude her Tribute pay,
> Decree the festive Day,
> Erect the Statue, and devote the Pile? ...

The music ceased and the noble voice began declaiming. Outside the packed Rotunda the rain redoubled its fury. Inside
there was swaying and heaving; part of a wall collapsed and
some benches gave way. But amid a rapt hush the magic periods
continued, like the voice of a demi-god in ecstasy (Boswell):

> Now swell at once the choral Song,
> Roll the full Tide of Harmony along;
> Let Rapture sweep the trembling Strings,
> And Fame, expanding all her Wings,
> With all her Trumpet-Tongues proclaim
> The lov'd, rever'd, immortal Name:
> SHAKSPEARE! SHAKSPEARE! SHAKSPEARE!
> Let th' inchanting Sound
> From Avon's Shores rebound ...

Avon's shores were at that precise moment being turned into a
swamp by the rapidly rising river. The rain fell ever more
heavily. Dr. Arne and his troops successfully fought it in a
tempest of melody.

> Wild, frantick with Pleasure,
> They trip it in Measure
> To bring him their Treasure,
> The Treasure of Joy!
>
> How gay is the Measure,
> How sweet is the Pleasure,
> How great is the Treasure,
> The Treasure of Joy!

And so the Ode rose to a triumphant harmonious finale and
ceased, amid thunders of applause. It was followed immediately
by a panegyric of Shakespeare, delivered by Garrick in rhythmic
near-Johnsonian prose, combining classical polish with fire and
ending with a ringing challenge to any who dare dispute the
Swan of Avon's fame. Upon which, by a curious piece of stage-
management, the Drury Lane comedian, Mr. King, attired in
blue-and-silver, rose up immediately and began a mock-serious
denunciation of the Bard, amid indignant hoots and catcalls;
this item had evidently gone a little wrong, since many provin-
cials in the audience did not gather what the gentleman in blue
was driving at. However, Garrick soon rose again, and in a
mellifluous poetic Epilogue, addressed to the ladies, brought the
ceremony to a close. It had not lacked a few low-comedy mis-
haps. Another bench or two had given way. Some highly-born
posteriors met the floor. A rickety door fell on Lord Carlisle.
Outside the rain awaited patricians and commonalty alike in
sheets and torrents, but the spirit of the Island Race was un-
quenchable. By five o'clock, after another White Lion dinner,
the assembly was singing glees and catches under Garrick's
indefatigable direction:

> Untouched and sacred be thy Shrine,
> Avonian WILLY, Bard divine! . . .

Soon after six Signor Angelo touched off his fire-works again,
in a gallant attempt to carry out the programme, but the English
climate won. Fizzy smoke and smell and a few dispirited 'illuminated Transparencies' drew a meagre crowd. Most of the Beau
Monde had already returned to their lodgings to rest and dress
for the great event of the Jubilee, the Grand Masquerade at
eleven o'clock in the Rotunda. 'The river was now overflowing,
the meadows were a quagmire. The Rotunda had to be approached by duckboards. Carriages were bogged. It was all
most unfortunate. But primed with hot brandy and Shakespearean ardour, the nobility and gentry faced the midnight
music to the number of a thousand.' [1] Of these many wore no
disguise but mask and domino. Not so James Boswell, Esq., who
has been far too long in the background of this chapter. Describ-

[1] *Op. cit.*

ing the Jubilee in a seven-column letter to *The London Magazine* for October, Mr. Boswell spreads himself especially on the Masquerade, to illustrate which he supplied a choice engraving of himself in costume:

One of the most remarkable masks upon this occasion was James Boswell, Esq., in the dress of an armed Corsican Chief. He entered the Amphitheatre about twelve o'clock. He wore a short dark-coloured coat of coarse cloth, scarlet waistcoat and breeches, and black spatter-dashes; his cap or bonnet was of black cloth; on the front of it was embroidered in gold letters *Viva la Libertà,* and on one side of it was a handsome blue feather and cockade, so that it had an elegant as well as a warlike appearance. On the breast of his coat was sewed a Moor's head, the crest of Corsica, surrounded with branches of laurel. He had also a cartridge-pouch, into which was stuck a stiletto, and on his left side a pistol was hung upon the belt of his cartridge-pouch. He had a fusee slung across his shoulder, wore no powder in his hair, but had it plaited at full length with a knot of blue ribbons at the end of it. He had, by way of a staff, a very curious vine all of one piece, emblematical of the sweet Bard of Avon. He wore no mask, saying it was not proper for a gallant Corsican.

So soon as he came into the room he drew universal attention . . . He was first accosted by Mrs. Garrick, with whom he had a great deal of conversation. There was an admirable dialogue between Lord Grosvenor, in the character of a Turk, and the Corsican, on the different constitution of the countries so opposite to each other— Despotism and Liberty . . .

A lot more of it, and then the Boswell Note:

Mr. Boswell danced both a minuet and a country dance with a very pretty lady, Mrs. Sheldon, wife to Captain Sheldon, of the 38th Regiment of Foot, who was dressed in a genteel domino, and before she danced threw off her mask.

There is one interesting incident at the Masquerade which Boswell does not clear up. He had in his pocket a copy of an original forty-six-line poetic appeal for Corsica, beginning:

> From the rude banks of Golo's rapid Flood,
> Alas! too deeply ting'd with patriot Blood,
> O'er which, dejected, injur'd Freedom bends,
> And sighs indignant o'er all Europe sends,
> Behold a *Corsican!* . . .

Did he intend to recite his verses to the gay and apparently indomitable Rotunda crowd? Did he intend to have copies printed for distribution? One account says he actually began to recite, but was shouted down, which is likely; the company had had quite enough poetry. He contents himself in *The London Magazine* by praising his verses as being 'well suited to the occasion' and preserving 'the true Corsican character'.

He left Stratford for London the day after this personal triumph, abandoning the rest of the limelight—programme including the crowning of Shakespeare's statue by Garrick, a horse-race in nearly a foot of water for the Jubilee Cup, and another dogged night of revelry in the Rotunda—to the Profession. He had more luck in getting away, apparently, than some of the Beau Monde, whose ornate coaches were stuck in the mud and the bog-holes for hours.

From the *Public Advertizer* of October 4 (contributed):

On Sunday last General Paoli, accompanied by James Boswell, Esq., took an airing in Hyde Park in his coach.

The last stand for Corsica was over. A French force of 20,000 under Count Vaux had occupied the island to seal its purchase by France in May 1768. Paoli, fighting to the last, had managed to make his way to Leghorn, and thence, saluted by British men-of-war, to take ship to London. On the night of September 10, 1769, Boswell introduced him to Johnson, who greatly admired the General's lofty port and easy elegance, with 'the brand of the soldier, *l'homme d'épée*'. Boswell's gratification was extreme. His better self was in command. He was the intimate and confidant of two of the noblest characters in Europe, brought together by his own exertions. The dissolvent grin of Wilkes must have seemed fainter and more faraway than that of the Cheshire Cat in her penultimate phase. But it would return.

8

It was in this same autumn of 1769 that another dramatic performance occurred which, although Boswell gives it scant attention in the *Life*, shocked the entire Johnsonian circle and the Doctor himself profoundly. Joseph Baretti, one of their number, the touchy, highly cultured, ferocious-tempered Italian lexicographer and man of letters, 'my Baretti', of whom Johnson was so strangely fond, was tried at Old Bailey for murder.

Boswell, to whom it would have given much pleasure to see Baretti hanged, and vice-versa (according to Mrs. Thrale) wastes little space on the affair. His cool lack of interest robs the *Life* of a fascinatingly Hogarthian page, swarming with the redoubtable fauna of the Haymarket and Leicester Square [1] district of the period. I cannot resist pausing a moment to contemplate this little drama. The Newgate Calendar supplies nearly all its salient features.

Baretti, in the Old Bailey dock, pleaded not guilty. His statement was that a little after 4 p.m. on Friday, October 8, having spent the day in literary work, chiefly on the second edition of his Italian-English dictionary, he strolled to the Royal Academy Club in Gerrard Street, Soho, and waited about half an hour for his friends, warming himself at the club-room fire. As nobody came, Baretti left for the Orange Coffee-House in the Haymarket, where his letters were directed at this time. As he was returning a little later up the Haymarket to Gerrard Street, some eight or ten yards from the corner of Panton Street a woman of the town accosted him, and getting no reply, assaulted him viciously. In his pain and fury Baretti struck her on the arm. She began instantly to yell and abuse him for a 'damn'd Frenchman and woman-hater'. A passer-by gave him a blow and another a shove, a hostile mob sprang up at once—this was in broad daylight, we may recollect, and in the heart of fashionable London—and the shortsighted Baretti was being dragged off the high pavement towards 'a great puddle' in the roadway to be ducked and trampled on when he got away, beaten and pursued by the mob, and dived into a shop in Oxenden Street round the corner, where in his confusion and terror he knifed one Evan Morgan, who died shortly after.

Having been rescued by a constable, Baretti, escorted by the mob, was taken to Bow Street, where Sir John Fielding, the novelist's half-brother, committed him forthwith to the Bridewell

[1] Leicester Fields was first called Leicester Square in the 1720's. Throughout the 18th century both names were used indifferently. It was a ground to be avoided after nightfall.

in Tothill Fields, after he had been allowed to send to Gerrard Street for Sir Joshua Reynolds and some other friends. From the Westminster prison he was taken to Newgate, and on October 20 he appeared at the Old Bailey. His friends rallied generously to him. Boswell may sum up:

Never did such a constellation of genius enlighten the aweful Sessions-House, emphatically called JUSTICE HALL: Mr. Burke, Mr. Garrick, Mr. Beauclerk, and Dr. Johnson; and undoubtedly their favourable testimony had due weight with the Court and Jury. Johnson gave his evidence [as to Baretti's character] in a slow, deliberate, and distinct manner, which was uncommonly impressive. It is well known that Mr. Baretti was acquitted.

What is not so well known is what actually happened in Oxenden Street. The incident of the knifing as reported in the Calendar is obscure. Whether the victim, Evan Morgan, was one of the mob of Baretti's pursuers, or a passer-by, or the shop-keeper, or a looker-on inside the shop is not clear. He owed his death, according to Baretti, to 'his own daring impetuosity', which may possibly identify Morgan—a Welshman, and there-fore a hornet irascible as Baretti himself—as the shopkeeper, stabbed presumably while rushing to throw the fugitive out. The stabbing was done with a pocket fruit-knife, in a moment, Baretti confessed, of complete demoralisation.

His escape from the steps and the string, as Moll Flanders would say, did not sweeten Baretti's temper noticeably. Having refused a £100-a-year academic post at Dublin he entered the Streatham Place household as tutor in Italian to the Thrale girls in 1773, accompanied the Thrales and Johnson to Paris in 1775, and towards the summer of 1776 turned 'very odd and cross' and was frequently rude to Mrs. Thrale, finally packing his 'cloke-bag' one morning in a violent rage and leaving the house. The quarrel, due, according to Baretti, to insufficient financial recog-nition,[1] was patched up some four years later, but not suffi-ciently to prevent Baretti from making a venomous attack in *The European Magazine* on Mrs. Thrale after her marriage to Piozzi in 1784, and sending his late friend and employer 'a

[1] As he reserved the right of coming and going as he pleased, he was paid no salary, but received periodical money presents.

letter full of the most flagrant and bitter insult'. His death in May
1789 moved Mrs. Piozzi only to charity.

Poor Baretti! I am sincerely sorry for him, and, as Zanga says, 'If
I lament thee, sure thy worth was great.' He was a manly character,
at worst, and died, as he lived, less like a Christian than a philosopher,
refusing all spiritual or corporeal assistance.[1]

Reynolds's portrait, painted for the gallery at Streatham Place
and showing Baretti scowling at a book held some two inches
before his nose, had moved Mrs. Thrale years before to excuse
his oddity in playful and nearly prophetic verse:

> Baretti hangs next; by his frowns you may know him,
> He has lately been reading some new-published poem;
> He finds the poor authour a blockhead, a beast,
> A fool without sentiment, judgment, or taste . . .
> Yet let us be candid, and where shall we find
> So active, so able, so ardent a mind?

From which it is clear that this difficult character was not
completely impossible. His atheism, which was of a peculiar
kind for a considerable man of letters—he did not know, apparently, the author of the *Pater Noster*—does not seem to have
irritated Johnson as Hume's and Foote's did. But Johnson's likes
and dislikes are often mysterious.

[1] In a less kindly tribute discovered among her private papers Mrs.
Thrale applies to Baretti Pope's lines on Menelaus in the *Iliad:*

> So burns the vengeful Hornet, soul all o'er . . .
> Untam'd, untir'd, he turns, attacks, and stings.

# Chapter Five

---

# LOTHARIO MARRIED

## 1

1770. THE RAKE BOSWELL IS MARRIED AND REFORMED AT LAST. FOR more than a year his copybook will be without a blot, his behaviour faultless, his settling down to 'a comfortable life as a married man, and a lawyer in practice at the Scotch Bar', all that could be wished. The quotation is from a letter to Johnson in 1772, the first for many months. Boswell's effort to live a decent family life and to build up his practice is tremendous, like his effort at Utrecht. Mrs. Boswell's steadying presence and his father's and Johnson's approval are behind him.

Unquestionably, apart from the matter of their cousinship, Miss Montgomerie was the best possible wife Boswell could have chosen; a quiet, shrewd, level-headed, unexciting partner, as we have already noted, and not incapable of heroism—did she not for his sake endure three years later the least endurable kind of guest a Scottish housewife could be faced with, in the person of the tumultuous and slovenly Doctor with his Choctaw habits? Only one recorded comment was wrung from Margaret Boswell, and it is eloquent. 'I have seen many a bear led by a man; I have never before seen a man led by a bear.'

Boswell loved and esteemed her unwaveringly, even when he began deceiving her in due course. His diaries and letters till her death in 1789 are full of tender references to her and her children, anxiety for her health—she became a tubercular invalid not long after marriage and never recovered—acknowledgments of the qualities of 'my valuable Wife', and gratitude for her help and forbearance. She had no easy life with James Boswell, apart from his drunken bouts, but her affection remained. 'My dearest Mr. Boswell', she writes to him a little before her death. 'My dearest Life', he replies, thanking her for her kind letters. The parallel with the Steele *ménage* will readily occur; yet Steele, whose life was raffish enough, has been awarded high marks for his attachment to his wife and children, whereas Boswell still awaits this recognition. Mrs. Boswell was, perhaps a trifle unpliable, sometimes a trifle grim; but her husband's feelings for her are almost uxorious, and his remorse at hurting her, as he frequently did, utterly sincere.

However, her trials are not yet, and there is nothing but humdrum marital felicity in the house at Chessel's Buildings in the Canongate. Boswell goes daily to his office, is immersed in his work, and drops writing even to Johnson for eighteen months; he is the complete eighteenth-century Scotch lawyer, like Rankeillour in *Kidnapped* and Stewart in *Catriona*, fond of a good plea, a well-drawn deed, his books, his bottle, a crack with other lawyer-bodies, and perhaps a round of golf on Saturday evenings, though I find no evidence that Boswell ever played this rancid game. He still takes pleasure in the society of Hume, who is now back in Edinburgh, but his old morbid introspections and nerve storms are gone. His father has recently married again—another cousin, elderly Miss Elizabeth Boswell of Balmuto—and Boswell behaves with careful diplomacy towards his bleak stepmother, observing with satisfaction to Temple that she shows no signs of multiplying. On September 1, 1771, he informs Temple that his first (legitimate) child is born and has lived only two hours, a matter of deep distress to him and his wife. In September Temple and his wife visit the Boswells and he enjoys 'hours of elegant friendship and classical sociality'. In August of the next year—a daughter, Veronica, has been born to Boswell meanwhile—Paoli comes to Scotland with the Polish Ambassador, is shown round by Boswell, and arrives at length at Auchinleck, 'to the joy of my worthy father and me at seeing the Corsican Hero in our romantick groves'. Old Auchinleck's joy may be doubted. He had dismissed Paoli some time ago as a 'landloupin' scoun'rel' as finally as he later dismissed Johnson as 'Ursa Major' and 'a dominie, man, an auld dominie—ane that keepit a schule an' ca'ed it an Academy!' Grim poker-faced

politeness to the popish landlouper was doubtless the best the
judge could muster. Paoli returned to Edinburgh, slept at the
Boswells' house, and left again for London, and Boswell duly
recorded the entire visit in *The Scots Magazine*. In March 1772
there was an appeal to the Lords from the Court of Session in
which Boswell was concerned, and on the 21st he was in Johnson's
study again at 7 Johnson's Court, Fleet Street, being warmly
greeted.

Their talk, about a thousand things, is in the *Life*. To attempt
to skim the cream of it, as I have said before, is not only difficult
but absurd. They went about together, they dined with Paoli
and Oglethorpe and a dozen other notables, they discussed
everything under the sun, and everywhere Boswell drew the
Doctor out unwearyingly. What matter if the question be foolish, so long as the great man rises to it? The comparison of the
showman putting the bear through his tricks is obvious enough,
and has been freely used. Once again I cannot follow the deduc-
tion that Boswell was exploiting the Doctor for his own glorifica-
tion, the more so as the Doctor so frequently made him look a
fool. Naturally Boswell's native egotism is involved, for, like
every other man, he was not all of a piece; but it is subordinate.
To dismiss a Bach recital by Casals as a piece of exhibitionism
would be an insult to an inspired instrument revealing and inter-
preting a master. The tendency to make Boswell merely an
exploiter derives, I think, from a puzzled feeling that such a
man should not be capable of exalted motives; which seems
poor enough psychology, since even the lowest types of God's
creation, a bawd or a financier or a journalist, may be capable
of nobility.

We must not forget what Boswell had to contend against. To
Wilkes, and in some degree to Hume and Dempster, Johnson
in his moral aspect was a figure of fun, a bigoted old fool, a
reactionary, a clerical, a *calotin*, what the intelligentsia today
would naturally label a fascist, since Johnson often went into a
church without the intention of burning it down; a type who
believed, talked, and practised the kind of obsolete nonsense no
man of intelligence who admitted Progress could possibly endure. Every time Boswell supped with Wilkes I do not doubt
that he had to put up with a stream of exquisite raillery on this

topic; yet he stuck to Johnson, and paraded his devotion to Johnson, and openly revered him, despite 'my classical friend'. Hume's attitude to Johnson was consistently illiberal, as Boswell puts it; he would hardly speak enthusiastically of a man who detested and challenged his most cherished sophistries. Dempster, early in the *Life*, is represented as admiring Johnson's conversation, at least by hearsay. He was a vaguer and less aggressive type than the other two, and found it easy to compromise, the more so as Johnson apparently did not object, after that first revulsion, to his company.

I ask to be excused again for believing that against three such antagonist forces only a noble and exalted motive could prevail, and that Carlyle is right. That streak of pure gold in this unfortunate fellow's composition is the secret of his attachment to Johnson. As for the *Life* and the immense labour which went to produce it, we may find an explanation presently.

One of the richest stretches of the *Life* embraces the years 1772-3. In 1772 the intimacy between Boswell and Johnson was at its height. The talk was varied and magnificent, like the company. On Good Friday, finding Johnson occupied with his folio Greek Testament, Boswell 'beheld him with reverential awe, and would not intrude upon his time'. A week or so later, having introduced 'some of the usual arguments for drinking', as he was fond of doing ever since the Sage had left off wine, he earned a smart rap over the knuckles. He presents Johnson's interlocutor simply as 'a gentleman', an incognito he occasionally assumes in such circumstances:

'You know, Sir, drinking drives away care, and makes us forget whatever is disagreeable. Would you not allow a man to drink for that reason?' JOHNSON. 'Yes, Sir, if he sat next *you*.'

Johnson's facial expression is not recorded. He may have said it with a smile. Many of the rebuffs Boswell received from him, which seem unkind in cold print, may actually have been no more brusque or harsh than the box on the ear a cat gives her favourite kitten, and I think a great many of Johnson's bullyings would sound quite differently had we been able to see his face. It is to be noted incidentally that of Boswell's two darling vices, he brings up drink for discussion frequently but lechery only once or twice, on one of which occasions he demurely agrees with Johnson that it produces nothing but misery. Had Johnson discovered anything of Boswell's other life there would have been far more than a passing rap to record.

However, at the moment Boswell was behaving himself quite well, and a rap from the Doctor, playful or not, need not perturb him unduly. On Monday, April 20, his diary records that he met Wilkes again—for the first time, apparently, since his Paris visit, and whether by accident is not clear—at the Lord Mayor's banquet, and sat next to him. Wilkes rallied him gaily on his new respectability. Boswell retorted equally gaily that he was now a Scotch married man, a Scotch lawyer, and a Scotch laird. They at once resumed their old cordiality, though they do not seem to have met again during this particular London visit of Boswell's; perhaps because Wilkes was now a very busy public man, perhaps because Boswell was really trying to reform.

Certainly his admiration for Wilkes had not lessened. His gay friend had become a more spectacular public figure than ever, with fanatical supporters all over the country and even abroad. Having returned from exile to be elected M.P. for Middlesex in March 1768, to the riotous joy of the mob, which forced half London to illuminate and had to be fired on by the troops, Wilkes elaborately surrendered himself to justice. His outlawry was reversed first of all by Chief Justice Lord Mansfield, influenced possibly by the Government's sweating anxiety to deprive Wilkes as far as possible of the halo of martyrdom, under a providential subtlety of British Law.[1] On the charges of seditious and criminal libel a bothered judge of the King's Bench was forced to commit Wilkes to a comfortable apartment in the King's Bench Prison for twenty-two months, enabling him to give rollicking supper-parties to his mistresses and his friends, who instantly paid the incidental £1,000 fine. Here, amid a constant stream of congratulations and hampers of luxuries and gifts of all sorts, the jovial Wilkes and his supporters planned further embarrassments for Court and Government. By 1772 he had been elected

[1] A flaw was discovered in the Sheriff's writ. Instead of reading 'at the County Court for the County of Middlesex' it should have read 'at the County Court *of Middlesex* for the County of Middlesex.' This blunder made the outlawry decree null and void.

for Middlesex three times more and been each time repudiated by the Commons, the last time permanently. He had won the powerful backing of Chatham and 'Junius', upset the Ministry, and been elected an Alderman of the City of London, whose enormously wealthy merchants were traditionally *frondeurs* and anti-Court.

For his services as Alderman of the Ward of Farringdon and Sheriff, Wilkes had since been presented with a silver cup worth £100 by the Common Council. His debts had been paid in full by his admirers, and his power over public opinion, as it is called, was such that Benjamin Franklin observed at this time that had Wilkes been a good man and the King a bad one, George III would have been off his throne. The over-ambitious young King himself recognised 'the Devil Wilkes' as a personal and redoubtable enemy. Wilkes parried the Royal hate with mocking aplomb and his *mots* flew round the town. 'Pray, Madam, do not ask me', he said to a lady of fashion who invited him to a card-party. 'I am too ignorant to distinguish between a king and a knave.' One can hear the stamping of the Royal foot from here.

Radicalism and republicanism, at any rate in theory, were Wilkes's 'platform' at this period, as we perceive; but his tongue was often in his cheek, and any earnest Left Winger of today would turn in fury from an enemy of tyranny whose comments on modern Left Wing totalitarianism would be interesting. Moreover Wilkes's politics were to change in due course. In the 1780's he veered to what was almost Tory Imperialism, and in the 1790's nobody denounced the 'bloody mobocracy' of the French Revolution more forcibly. But even in his demagogic period Wilkes never cherished the naive modern illusion that you usher in millennium by changing the Constitution.

So Wilkes in 1772 was courted and flattered more than ever. His picture hung in every printshop and every alehouse. Ladies of fashion carried his squinting image engraved or painted on watches and fans and brooches and patch-boxes, beaux tapped it on their snuff-boxes; it adorned jugs and mugs, teapots and punch-bowls, and was nobly apotheosised in Battersea enamel and Chelsea porcelain, with attendant Cupids. In France all the philosophers and smart ladies acclaimed him. In America chil-

dren were christened after him and his health was drunk
annually under the Liberty Tree at Boston, Mass. South Carolina
contributed £1,500 to pay off his debts, North Carolina named
a county after him. One might imagine this public idol had
not much time for people like Boswell now, but there is
abundant evidence that Wilkes in his short-lived glory never
dropped anyone who amused him as Boswell did. And Boswell's
company would be all the more diverting since Johnson's recent
gallop to the Government's aid with his anti-Wilkes broadside
*The False Alarm,* of which production Boswell remarks in the
*Life* that 'even his vast powers were inadequate to cope with
constitutional truth and reason, and his argument failed', despite
the 'extreme coarseness of contemptuous abuse' Johnson employed against Wilkes. To quote from such an attack in the
disciple's chuckling presence, with appropriate comment, would
be a pleasure few wits in such circumstances could deprive
themselves of.

However, Boswell seems to have kept away from him during
this visit, and we remind ourselves that he was queerly capable
of taking a definite line for a brief period, and sticking to it.

Before leaving London in August he renewed his attempt to
get Johnson to visit Scotland, a proposal which had been hanging
in the air recently. The Doctor wrote to him on August 31 re-
gretting that the 'state of my body' was not equal to his 'pleasing
expectations', but expressing hopes for the following year, 'for
I am very sincere in my design to pay the visit, and take the
ramble'. With this promise to brace him Boswell returned to his
legal work, to the study of Scottish feudalism, and to the composition of a pamphlet which I have not read, entitled *Reflections
on the Bankruptcies in Scotland.* In the February following we
find him at a masked ball in Edinburgh given by Sir Alexander
Macdonald of Sleat and attended by seventy 'Persons of Quality'.
The Macdonald was a connection of Boswell's, having married
his Yorkshire relative and one-time love, Miss Bosville; his
skinflint behaviour in Skye will in due course be the only blot
on a perfect experience.

April 2, 1773, found Boswell in London again. Late on the
night of April 3 he is drinking tea with blind old Mrs. Williams

in the house in Johnson's Court [1] and waiting for the Doctor to come home; the privilege he had formerly envied Goldsmith is now a commonplace. April 9 being Good Friday, he breakfasted with Johnson on milkless tea and cross-buns, attended Morning Service with him at St. Clement Danes, and, fasting, turned over Johnson's books on their return; the Established Church had not yet borrowed the Good Friday devotion of the Three Hours from the Jesuits. The 'tremulous earnestness' of Johnson's piety impressed him forcibly. In the evening they attended church again. Johnson's pew, numbered 18 in the north gallery, close to the pulpit, to suit his hearing, was blasted with its brass memorial-plate from the earth by German bombs in 1940.

That Easter Sunday a piquant new experience fell to Boswell. Johnson invited him home to dinner. 'I generally have a meat-pye on Sunday', the Doctor explained, 'It is baked at a publick oven, which is very properly allowed, because one man can attend it; and thus the advantage is obtained of not keeping servants from church to dress dinners.' Boswell's description of the Easter Sunday meal is well known.

I had gratified my curiosity much in dining with JEAN JACQUES ROUSSEAU, while he lived in the wilds of Neufchatel; I had as great a curiosity to dine with DR. SAMUEL JOHNSON, in the dusky recess of a court in Fleet-street. I supposed we should scarcely have knives and forks, and only some strange, uncouth, ill-drest dish: but I found everything in very good order . . . We had a very good soup, a boiled leg of lamb and spinach, a veal pye, and a rice pudding. [2]

No doubt the Doctor had been fully aware of this amused curiosity and had taken steps accordingly. A dull jape of Foote's connecting 'black broth' with Frank, the Doctor's Negro servant, had failed to materialise. Only Mrs. Williams and 'a young woman whom I did not know' dined with them. Of Johnson's other quarrelsome pensioners at this time Levitt, the silent, meritorious quack, lived in the garret, Mrs. Desmoulins had her own room. On the Tuesday following Johnson and Boswell dined with Goldsmith at General Oglethorpe's and afterwards drank tea with the ladies, and Goldsmith sang two songs from *She*

[1] This court, which was not named after Dr. Johnson, stands on the north side of Fleet Street, behind Anderton's Hotel.

[2] His diary adds: 'Pickled Walnuts and Onions—Porter and Port wine.'

*Stoops to Conquer;* after which Johnson accompanied Boswell to his lodgings in Piccadilly and stayed, drinking tea, till a late hour. They dined together subsequently at Paoli's, at Thrale's, and at Oglethorpe's again. And then arrived a memorable evening, Friday, April 30, when they dined at Beauclerk's house with Lord Charlemont, Reynolds, and some other members of the Literary Club; for on this evening Boswell was to be proposed for the Club, a very great honour indeed.

This exclusive gathering of notable men was now nine years old. Its foundation members, whose numbers were soon greatly extended, were Johnson, Reynolds, Burke, Nugent, Beauclerk, Langton, Goldsmith, Chamier, and Hawkins. They supped one evening a week, at this period, at the Turk's Head tavern in Gerrard Street, Soho, and continued their conversation till 'a pretty late hour'. Boswell's chances of getting into the Club (one black ball excluded, and Garrick nearly missed election owing to his arrogance) were by no means good on the face of it; but Johnson was determined that he should be elected, with Beauclerk's help, despite the amiable doubts of Burke and the less amiable jealousies of Goldsmith and Garrick. Later, in Scotland, Johnson revealed that the members were well aware that if they black-balled Boswell he would have taken care they never got another man in.

After dinner at Beauclerk's the members departed to take the ballot, leaving Boswell to be entertained by Lady Diana Beauclerk, whose beauty, brains, and charm could hardly still his tremors. At length, receiving the message so ardently desired, he took a coach forthwith to Gerrard Street, where Johnson, leaning over a chair, 'with humorous formality gave me a *charge,* pointing out the conduct expected from me as a good member of the Club'. It is not difficult to guess the trend of this semi-serious homily. The entire Club had probably besieged Johnson feverishly.

So Boswell was now a member of The Club, and had a right to be proud. The Club still exists, and is more socially exclusive today, perhaps, than its founders intended. Some years ago it found Gilbert Keith Chesterton's joyous pride in his middle-class origin too much for delicate stomachs, so the candidature of that great man, the best intellectual talker since Johnson, fell through.

On Tuesday, May 10, Boswell returned to Edinburgh, having filled many pages of his journal with rich Johnsoniana, having heard the Doctor slander the charming Lady Diana in a careless moment, and having witnessed that remarkable scene of Johnson's roaring bout of midnight laughter in Fleet Street which he records with such consummate skill. This time he went home in sprightly anticipation. One of the two happiest periods of his life was to follow.

2

It was an elate and exulting disciple who strutted arm-in-arm with Dr. Johnson up through the dusky effluvia of the High Street of Edinburgh on the night of Saturday, August 14, 1773, from Boyd's Inn, Canongate, to Boswell's new apartments in James's Court. The almost unimaginable had come to pass. The indolent Doctor who lay abed daily till noon, detested any form of physical exercise, and swore that no life existed outside London, had been induced to heave his huge torso into a succession of post-chaises as a prelude to an expedition among the savage aboriginals of wild and rocky wastes as remote from the ordinary Englishman's experience as Hy-Brasil or the Moon; for which purpose he had bought two pistols, with gunpowder and bullets.

The impact of the Doctor's apparition on Mrs. Boswell, waiting apprehensively at her tea-table, was tremendous and unpleasant. We know exactly what he looked like that night. Lord Auchinleck's 'Ursa Major' is an admirable footnote to his son's description:

He wore a full suit of plain brown clothes, with twisted-hair buttons of the same colour, a large bushy greyish wig, a plain shirt, black worsted stockings, and silver buckles. Upon this tour, when journeying, he wore boots, and a very wide brown cloth great-coat, with pockets which might almost have held the two volumes of his folio Dictionary; and he carried in his hand a large English oak stick.

A bear, Mrs. Boswell agreed; an enormous, peering, rumbling, grimacing, and not very cleanly bear, whose tumultuous courtesy to his hostess, in whom he at once recognised a gentlewoman, failed to offset the uncivilised habits he almost immediately revealed, such as demanding and swilling tea in enormous quantities day and night, gorging his food with distended veins, flicking lighted candles over the carpet to make them burn better, keeping the servants up, lecturing at all hours, and rolling and grunting in the best bed till the sun was high. Actually Mrs. Boswell had disliked the Doctor long before she met him for his strange influence over her husband, to whom he stood for the lure of London and periodical escapes from domesticity. Politeness Johnson certainly got from Margaret Boswell, but no more, and he always knew it. Her stiff Scots backbone was not a little to blame. Other women found him captivating. The Johnson whose playfulness so often delighted Fanny Burney and Mrs. Thrale, whose merriment entranced Hannah More, that unofficial maiden aunt of the Established Church, never appeared *chez* Boswell. I think Mrs. Boswell froze the Doctor at first glance with a cold Scots eye and he never recovered. The fault is as much hers as his, and I am not disposed to regard her quite as the martyr some authorities do. Mrs. Thrale, who endured Johnson infinitely more, did so gaily to the utmost limit of patience, and always recognised the greatness of her awkward guest.

Since one of the most delicious books of travel-entertainment ever written is at everybody's hand, I do not propose to sketch a précis of Boswell's *Journal of a Tour to the Hebrides,* which came out in 1785, the year after Johnson's death; for the Doctor had frowned on its publication during his lifetime, partly because of its personal nature, partly, as Boswell wrote to Temple, because 'between ourselves, he is not apt to encourage one to *share* reputation with himself', and considered his own *Journey to the Western Islands of Scotland* (1775) vastly more important. The difference between these two books is, I think, that one esteems Johnson's, but one loves Boswell's. The one is full of grave, sound observation and shrewd reasoning; the other vibrates with pleasure and life and colour and amusement, frank self-revelation and picaresque incident. The account of the wanderings and escape of Prince Charles Edward after Culloden alone is a little masterpiece, shot subtly through with that pain for a lost and noble dream which every decent Scotsman feels, but which few admit, yet never tinged with that tinsel romanticism with which the Whigs, inspired by their master the Devil, have so cleverly enveloped the Stuart Cause, as Mr. Compton Mackenzie has remarked, turning it into a fairytale for greensick girls. Despite Boswell's care to underline his allegiance to Hanover—as we shall see later, he approached George III himself on the delicate matter of naming 'The Wanderer'—we guess what higher and finer loyalties quicken his pulse as he contemplates the vision of the gracious, gallant youth who could have done so much for Scotland ('Oh, God! Poor Scotland!'), and for England, too. If Boswell's spirit ever revisits the Highlands, I think it must hover longest over the memorial chapel on the green slope above Loch Shiel, where the west door stands always open and a tablet on the wall invites all true hearts that pass by to say a prayer for the repose of the soul of Charles Edward Stuart.

Boswell started north with Johnson on Wednesday, August 18, after prevailing on the Doctor to leave his pistols behind (a pity there was no battle with the hairy brigands Johnson imagined in the high hills; Stevenson could probably not have bettered Boswell's account). They returned on Tuesday, November 9, to Edinburgh, where Johnson dawdled away a fortnight more before taking the coach for London. They had gone by way of St. Andrew's, Aberdeen, Inverness, and Fort Augustus to the Hebrides, visited Skye, Rasay, Col, Mull, Inchkenneth, Iona, and Icolmkill, and come thence through Argyleshire by Loch Lomond and Dumbarton to Glasgow, and so, by way of Auchinleck, back to Edinburgh. Johnson thus saw 'the four Universities of Scotland, its three principal cities, and as much of the Highland and insular life as was sufficient for his philosophical contemplation'.

To choose one's favourite passage from the *Journal* is not easy. What more agreeable than the night-piece of the Atlantic storm which caught their boat between Skye and Mull, with Boswell hanging on like grim death to a rope they had given him to haul on, to keep him quiet, though he well knew it was merely fastened to the mast? Or the relation of the great all-night drinking-bout and the wild Gaelic dances at Corrichatachin under the Red Hills? Or the dinner-scene at Inverary Castle where the Duchess of Argyle treats Boswell with such icy and ill-mannered hauteur? Or the glimpse of Dr. Johnson that night at Col when he 'strutted about the room with a broadsword and target, and made a formidable appearance', increased by the large blue Highland bonnet Boswell took the liberty of clapping on that redoubtable bushy grey wig? Or the gay hospitality, the songs and reels at the Macleods' in Rasay? Or that tremendous clash at Auchinleck of which Boswell says, 'I cannot be certain whether it was on this day, or a former, that Dr. Johnson and my father came into collision', and the tactful curtain he drops on all but one incident of that memorable row? Or the vivid full-length portrait, stroke by stroke, of a typical Highland gentleman, Macleod of Rasay?

He was now sixty-two years of age, hale, and well proportioned,—with a manly countenance, tanned by the weather, yet having a ruddiness in his cheeks, over which a great part of his rough beard extended. His eye was quick and lively, yet his look was not fierce, and he appeared at once firm and good-humoured. He wore a pair of brogues,—Tartan hose which came up only near to his knees, and left them bare,—a purple camblet kilt,—a black waistcoat,—a short green cloth coat bound with gold cord,—a yellowish bushy wig—a large blue bonnet with a gold thread button.

And what, among a score more notable passages, of the companion-portrait of Macdonald of Kingsburgh?

He had his Tartan plaid thrown about him, a large blue bonnet with a knot of black ribband like a cockade, a brown short coat of a kind of duffil, a Tartan waistcoast with gold buttons and gold button-holes, a bluish philabeg, and Tartan hose. He had jet-black hair tied behind, and was a large stately man, with a steady sensible countenance.

If a small disappointment may be admitted, one could wish it had been possible for Boswell to be more enchanted by Kingsburgh's wife, 'the celebrated Miss Flora Macdonald'. Perhaps, like most of us, he imagined in advance a comely, strapping, high-cheekboned, high-coloured creature, romantic even in middle age. The heroine of the '45 turned out to be merely 'a little woman, of a genteel appearance, and uncommonly mild and well-bred'.[1] Johnson, the Staffordshire Tory, a Jacobite's

[1] Mildness may have been accentuated by depression. The Macdonalds, in low water financially, were on the eve of emigrating to America.

son, half a Jacobite himself, paints a slightly warmer portrait. 'Flora Macdonald, a name that will be mentioned in history, and, if courage and fidelity be virtues, mentioned with honour. She is a woman of middle stature, soft features, gentle manners, and elegant presence.' Possibly they were both a trifle disillusioned.

I found it strangely impossible, while following the traces of Johnson and Boswell here and there in the Highlands a little time ago, to avoid seeing two other old friends, two half-glimpsed shades, hovering constantly in their background. How pleasant had it been possible for the Doctor to encounter Alan Breck Stewart and David Balfour lurking in the heather! But in terms of time alone this agreeable fantasy would be impracticable. In 1773 the Chevalier Stewart, if alive, would be an elderly, greying exile, his dangerous missions over for good, attending the aged Ardshiel at 'Melons in the Isle of France' and brooding on the latest news from Rome, where the beloved unhappy Prince, having recently married the hussy Louise of Stolberg, was finding intermittent consolation for disappointments, disillusions, and despairs in the brandy-bottle, surrounded by spies of the British Government. By 1773 Cluny's Cage on Ben Alder would be in ruins and overgrown, Cluny himself dead in France long since, and David Balfour and his Catriona playing, perhaps, with their first grandchild in the House of Shaws.

Johnson and Boswell actually touched the fringes of the Appin country once, during their visit to Mull. The murder of the Red Fox, Colin Roy Campbell of Glenure, was still a topic in the 1770's of all that countryside, and then, as today, no native would ever reveal the murderer's identity. Though Boswell makes no mention of the Appin murder and is suitably awed by the magnificence of the great Argyle, he twice reports a strong distaste for Campbells which infallibly recalls *Kidnapped.* M'Lean of Corneck buys the lease of a part of Col belonging to Argyle at 'a very advanced rate, rather than let the Campbells get a footing in the island'. Scolding a servant, Sir Allan M'Lean of Inchkenneth crushes him with: 'I believe you are a Campbell!' Could Alan Breck have wished for more?

The *Journal,* is, as I have said, a happy book. Apart from the

[TITLE PAGE TO THE THIRD EDITION]

# THE
# JOURNAL
## OF A TOUR TO THE
# *HEBRIDES,*
### WITH
# SAMUEL JOHNSON, LL.D.

## BY *JAMES BOSWELL,* ESQ.

CONTAINING

Some Poetical Pieces by Dr. JOHNSON, relative to the TOUR,
and never before publifhed;

A Series of his Converfation, Literary Anecdotes, and Opinions
of Men and Books:

WITH AN AUTHENTICK ACCOUNT OF

The Diftreffes and Efcape of the GRANDSON of KING
JAMES II. in the Year 1746.

*THE THIRD EDITION, REVISED AND CORRECTED.*

O! while along the ftream of time, thy name
Expanded flies, and gathers all its fame,
Say, fhall my little bark attendant fail,
Purfue the triumph and partake the gale? POPE.

*LONDON:*

PRINTED BY HENRY BALDWIN,
FOR CHARLES DILLY, IN THE POULTRY.
MDCCLXXXVI.

Corsican journal, it records the only continuous period in
Boswell's history when he was free alike from melancholia and
ignoble weaknesses, barring that carouse at Corrichatatchin for
which the Doctor ('You drunken dog!') so indulgently forgave
him. In Corsica he had been under the golden influence of
Paoli; in the Hebrides he had Johnson all to himself, the
Rambler in holiday mood, the honoured and courteous guest,
he smiling, shrewd, and sometimes blunt observer. They
quarrelled only once, and a brief and childish fit of petulance in
Johnson was solely to blame. They savoured alike the ducal
luxury of Inverary and the squalor of Highland inns like the
hovel at Glenelg. They dined or supped with peers, chieftains,
scholars, lawyers, clergymen, soldiers, and burgesses. Only once
did they encounter a scrubby host: Boswell's relation by
marriage, Sir Alexander Macdonald of Sleat. Only once were
they lacking in the duties of guests, when they made themselves
deliberately some hours late for dinner at Sir John Dalrymple's
of Cranston. Perhaps the jocularity Boswell reports between
them on this occasion is not the best of manners, nor his excuse,
that Dalrymple had sneered at Johnson, strong enough. But this
incident, like other indiscretions scattered through the *Journal*,
is merely the essential Boswell and does not spoil a masterpiece.
Such lapses helped to increase a growing reputation for fecklessness in Edinburgh legal and social circles, doubtless, but the
Scots newspapers and magazines did not rise against the *Journal*
in one compact mass of Knoxian wrath as they had done against
Johnson's *Journey*, though the wits derived a little mild fun from
the softening, for the second edition, of a too-candid account of
Sir Alexander Macdonald's meanness, which account itself
apparently replaced, while the first edition was actually being
printed off, a still more scathing passage hastily suppressed.
Eventually Boswell was forced to deny, in *The Gentleman's
Magazine*, that Sir Alexander had ordered him with threats to
make a correction.

What the cultivated public thought of the *Journal*, despite a
few snarls from the critics, is shown by the fact that in three
months it ran through two editions, and a third followed in
August 1786. In 1787 a German edition was almost equally

successful. It does not detract much from Boswell's achievement
to recognise the contribution to it made by Edmund Malone.
By calling on this quiet, amiable [1] Irish barrister, scholar, and
critic, a member of the Literary Club greatly esteemed by
Johnson, to read his manuscript (and later, that of the *Life*)
for the press, Boswell did a very wise thing, and his acknowledgment stands for ever in his prefaces. Malone's first-edition copy
of the *Journal*, now in the library of that eminent Johnsonian
Mr. R. B. Adam of Buffalo, shows to some extent, from Malone's
own marginal and other notes for the second edition, what his
contribution was. Boswell supplied the material, the writing,
the style, the genius; Malone removed a number of Scotticisms
and other inelegancies and suggested corrections, and, most
valuable of all, advised on the arrangement of the material; for
Boswell, as we know, was no great hand at system or order.
So it is chiefly to Malone that we owe the smooth continuity of
the *Journal* and the *Life* alike. From his 'revision', as Boswell
calls it, the author sometimes differed totally and went his own
way, not always wrongly. His printed tributes to Malone are
just and necessary, yet far from complete, for that modest man
who shrank from claiming any share in Boswell's triumph
worked with Boswell daily over a long period.

A triumph the *Journal* undoubtedly is. Some connoisseurs rank
it higher as a work of art than the *Life*, even. From its pages
one perceives Boswell to be already a master. As a picture of
vanished Highlands (but even then emigration to America and
Canada was draining and destroying them) the *Journal* is a
valuable document, apart from its discreet decorations of history
and archaeology. As a living, breathing picture of Johnson in
all his moods it is almost perfect; as a picture of Boswell himself
at his best and happiest ('There is no house', wrote Johnson to
Mrs. Thrale, 'where he is not received with kindness and respect.
He has better faculties than I had imagined: more justness of
discernment, and more fecundity of images.') it has a certain
pathos. Facing his last page is a promise to the public of an
even greater treat to come.

---

[1] 'Too soft in his manners,' the connoisseur Boswell once remarked to
Farington, R.A., to be 'a favourite of the Ladies.' A Miss Bover refused
Malone's hand in 1795.

*Preparing for the Press, in one Volume Quarto,*
THE LIFE OF SAMUEL JOHNSON, LL.D.,
by JAMES BOSWELL, ESQ.,

r. Boswell has been collecting materials for this work for more than
venty years, during which he was honoured with the intimate friend-
ip of Dr. Johnson . . .

The great work, which will occupy his sober hours for the
ext six years, will contain the 'most authentick accounts' obtain-
le, from those who knew the Doctor best, together with 'many
etches of his conversation on a multiplicity of subjects' and a
reat number of letters. The advertisement ends, with prophetic
:curacy: 'He is confident that the publication of the whole of
r. Johnson's epistolary correspondence will do him the highest
onour.'

Well for him if he could have stayed on those sunlit, bracing
plands of moral and physical health and happiness he attained
uring the Hebrides tour. But almost before the rumble of
ohnson's coach-wheels on the road to London was out of
earing Boswell returned to his wallow, and the shadows re-
iveloped him.

### 3

It was sixteen months before he got to London again. Edin-
urgh's dullness and the daily legal grind brought on melan-
holy, which drove him to the bottle which increased it. All
irough 1774—the year his daughter, Euphemia, was born—
is private papers record frequent drinking-bouts, with a
equent sequel on the streets. Mrs. Boswell had to nurse
im each time back to sobriety, to listen to his groans and im-
lorations, and, once, to dodge a candlestick he threw at her.
[is remorse after each occasion was tearful and eloquent, his
ebauches were soon renewed, and his business began at length
) suffer. Some idea of the kind of lawyer he was becoming is
emonstrated by his conduct of the case of a sheepstealer named
)hn Reid, found guilty and sentenced to death. Reid became
loswell's *idée fixe*. When his hard work for a reprieve failed,
e visited his client in prison daily, drank whisky with him,
volved a wonderful plan for cutting him down alive and getting

doctors to restore him, attended him at length to the gallow (for which ceremony the condemned man wore shroud an nightcap, as the ghastly custom often was), got him a last gla: of wine to drink the company's health, saw him swing off an hang three-quarters of an hour, and finally just escaped a du with the son of the Lord Justice-Clerk by writing a foolis paragraph in the newspapers on the case; fortunately for Boswel a written apology settled it. There was humanity and kindne mixed in this behaviour. There was also, plainly, a kind of craz obsession.

In March 1775 he was in London again, seeing Johnson an another old friend. Let us return for a moment to the Island Mull on the morning of Thursday, October 21, 1773, and liste to the booming voice of Johnson, who is discussing City affair a trifle prematurely.

It is wonderful to think that all the force of government was re quired to prevent Wilkes from being chosen the chief magistrate London, though the liverymen knew he would rob their shops,- knew he would debauch their daughters.

Twelve years later, publishing the *Journal,* Boswell is apologi ing to his gay friend for this remark.

I think it incumbent on me to make some observation on this stron satirical rally on my classical companion, Mr. Wilkes. Reporting lately from memory, in his presence, I expressed it thus:—'They kne' he would rob their shops, *if he durst*; they knew he would debauc their daughters, *if he could*'; which, according to the French phras may be said to *renchérir* on Dr. Johnson; but on looking into m Journal, I found it as above, and would by no means make any add tion. Mr. Wilkes received both readings with a good humour that cannot enough admire. Indeed, both he and I . . . are too fond of *bon mot* not to relish it, though we should be ourselves the object of i Let me add, in justice to the gentleman here mentioned, that at subsequent period he *was* elected chief magistrate of London, an discharged the duties of that high office with great honour to himsel and advantage to the City.

Which will remind us that since we last saw Wilkes he ha made more conquests, and that Boswell's admiration for hi is still as keen.

In 1775 Mr. Alderman Wilkes was in his second year as Lord Mayor of London, after outwitting the Court party among the Aldermen in three desperate attempts to over-ride a majority-poll. The feat must have diverted him not a little. Though Ravenscroft's bawdy Restoration comedy *The London Cuckolds* was no longer ritually performed at Drury Lane on the evening of every Lord Mayor's Day—Garrick had abolished it some years before in favour of Lillo's moral melodrama of a City apprentice, *George Barnwell*—the new Chief Magistrate of London, survey-ing the fur-trimmed purple pomp of the conscript Fathers, could hardly help equipping more than one portentous, disapproving, bob-wigged head in fancy with the traditional set of antlers. Mr. Wilkes, Head Cit. Mr. Wilkes, Master-Cuckold. A wit of less breeding would have laughed till the Guildhall echoed, I think.

The Lord Mayor's procession of 1774 has been described, by those who love to coin a phrase, as a Roman triumph. It was a Thames spectacle, and both river-banks were packed with jubilant mobs, cheering their idol hoarse as the State barges passed from Queenhithe to Westminster and pelting the bourgeoisie with garbage with more than their traditional vim. At the ensuing Guildhall banquet there were many high empty places. A mysterious epidemic had swept the West End of town and their Royal Highnesses of Gloucester and Cumberland, together with the Lord Chancellor, the Chief Justices, the Arch-bishops and Bishops, the Secretaries of State, and most of the leading nobility had found themselves forced to decline my Lord Mayor Wilkes's invitation; at which my Lord Mayor grinned all the more pleasantly. He was soon to make his office a social as well as a political triumph. In the year following the Archbishop of Canterbury and five other bishops dined with him at the Mansion House and the pick of fashionable Society enjoyed his splendid entertainment at the Easter Ball. 'City hospitality' took on a new meaning, and Wilkes himself, till now thin as a shotten herring', was able to point merrily before long to 'a belly truly aldermanic.'

His beloved daughter Polly acted as his hostess. In the back-ground, for he was careful to keep them apart, was his latest mistress-in-chief, Marianne-Genevieve Charpillon, an ex-Parisian of Swiss extraction, long since settled in London, who has her

niche in the history of the higher prostitution. Not many
*horizontales* of the period could boast of having had Casanova
arrested for molestation.[1] As with the Corradini, Wilkes had to
keep Mlle. Charpillon's relatives as well during their four years'
liaison, for her mother, her grandmother, and herself—'three
generations of solid professional talent', as somebody remarked—
were inseparable.

A fortnight after taking office Lord Mayor Wilkes, having been
elected M.P. for Middlesex once again, entered Parliament in
triumph as the leader of a party of a dozen, the Wilkites, to
whom he always swore he did not belong. His record as Alderman and Sheriff had been good. He had really earned public
plaudits by checking profiteering on the corn-market, fighting
the widespread abuse of the press-gang system, and bettering,
to some extent, the condition of Old Bailey accused and other
prisoners. He carried the same energy into Parliament, where
he began at once to preach the cause of the American colonists,
then backed by the City, with such tireless vigour that he
became in due course a bore, and, as national sentiment changed
and the Court and the Jingoes prevailed, a back-number.

But in April 1775, when his second Guildhall banquet came
round, Wilkes was firmly in the saddle, and his invitations were
eagerly snapped up. Boswell was among his important guests,
and woke next day with a royal headache, for Wilkes had
patriotically banned French wines from the Guildhall table in
favour of port and sherry, both loaded, and heavy drinking was
the rule. Their friendship was proceeding comfortably, though
one would not suspect this from the *Life*, where over a space of
eight years (1770-1778) Wilkes is not mentioned at all. Boswell
was now taking to the bottle more vigorously, following an oath
of reformation made under 'a solemn yew-tree' in Temple
rectory garden at Mamhead, Devon, where he went down for
rest and fresh air after the Guildhall dinner, visiting Lord

[1] Casanova met Mlle. Charpillon in London in 1764, pursued her, gave
her presents, was held off, and finally, in a passion, threatened her with
his cane; for which she lodged a complaint at Bow Street and had him
arrested and cautioned by Sir John Fielding. In the memoirs of his old age
Casanova remembers this singular defeat with bitter resentment.

Pembroke at Wilton with Paoli on the way. A lapse during this short stay shocked even the shock-proof Temple. On his return to London in May Boswell appeared drunk one night at the Literary Club, whose minute-book still shows his almost illegible signature. 'I have had rather too much dissipation since I came last to town', he writes to Temple, ending with a typical Boswellism: 'I have only to tell you, as my divine, that I yesterday received the holy sacrament in St. Paul's Church, and was exalted in piety.' On May 17 he writes from the Thrales' at Streatham Place: 'I have been like a skiff in the sea, driven about by a multiplicity of waves . . . This morning Dr. Johnson and I return to London . . . I go with Mr. Beauclerk to see his elegant villa and library, worth £3,000, at Muswell Hill . . . I have a cause to come on in the House of Lords on Friday . . . on Saturday last I dined with John Wilkes and his daughter, and nobody else, at the Mansion House; it was a most pleasant scene . . . I had that day breakfasted with Dr. Johnson; I drank tea with Lord Bute's daughter-in-law, and I supped with Miss Boswell. What variety!'

Of Lord Bute's daughter-in-law, 'sweet, handsome, lively little Mrs. Stuart', who has now fascinated Mr. Boswell's goggling and tireless eye, he writes to Temple on May 22 from Grantham, on his way north:

I passed a delightful day yesterday. After breakfasting with Paoli and worshipping at St. Paul's, I dined *tête-à-tête* with my charming Mrs. Stuart, of whom you have read in my journal; she refused to be of a party at Richmond, that she and I might enjoy a farewell interview. We dined in all the elegance of two courses and a dessert, with dumb-waiters, except when the second course and the dessert were served. We talked with unreserved freedom, as we had nothing to fear; we were *philosophical*, upon honour,—not deep, but feeling; we were pious; we drank tea, and bid each other adieu as finely as romance paints.

Conscious (and compulsory) virtue swells in his bosom as he adds complacently:

She is my wife's dearest friend; so you see how beautiful our intimacy is.

He adds a charming postscript:

There is a Miss Silverton in the Fly with me, an amiable creature, who has been in France. I can unite little fondnesses with perfect conjugal love.

An illuminating phrase, and a sincere one.

Edinburgh depressed him on his return more than ever, and the frequent company of Hume and Lord Kames, and his work at the Bar of the General Assembly ('something low and coarse, but guineas must be had') were a relief. A coolness with his father was in progress. The old judge had turned unaccountably rude to Mrs. Boswell, whom he seemed to blame for his son's caprices. 'He harps on my going over Scotland with a Brute (think, how shockingly erroneous!) and wandering (or some such phrase) to London. In vain do I defend myself.' And he reminds Temple ruefully that Auchinleck holds the whip-hand. 'I always dread his making some bad settlement.' All this summer Boswell is the prey of moodiness and melancholy, mingled with vague longings, quickened by the talk of Hume and Kames, to be 'a man of consequence in the State.' Jealousy also contributes. His old college-friend, Henry Dundas, has just been elected King's Advocate. 'To be sure he has strong parts, but he is a coarse unlettered dog.' And he moans in his exile over 'the unpleasing tone, the rude familiarity, the barren conversation' around him, which only Hume's polished society can mitigate; reporting incidentally an interesting solution of Hume's for the American problem, expressed at Lord Kames's house:

He said it was all over in America; we *could* not subdue the colonists, and another gun should not be fired, were it not for decency's sake; he meant, in order to keep up an appearance of power . . . He said we may do very well without America, and he was for withdrawing our troops altogether and letting the Canadians fall upon our colonists. I do not think he makes our *right* to tax at all clear.

Both Hume and Kames, a rough-tongued old Whig, took that night to attacking Dr. Johnson, especially over 'absurdities' in his Dictionary, Hume expressing himself so insolently that Boswell was stung into quoting a recent reference of Temple's to 'the

Government's infidel pensioner, Hume'. For this was a different matter from Wilkes's raillery, and Boswell was a loyal soul.

The summer of 1775 is full of melancholia, as I have said, despite legal business which brings in £124 in two months. At a tavern-supper Boswell drinks too much hock and 'though I did not get drunk, I was intoxicated, and very ill next day'; a nice distinction for the Logic Schools. On Monday, August 14, he quotes to Temple a cheering letter from Wilkes, whom he had asked to authenticate a pedigree of the Boswell family for his brother David in Spain. Wilkes's reply shows what easy terms they were on.

The pedigree was authenticated with all due solemnity, and in a more beautiful manner than has been done before at the Lord Mayor's office, that the name of Boswell may be considered in as fair a light in Spain as it is in Scotland and England ... I expect in half an hour a score of worthy Liverymen, friends of Wilkes and Liberty, whom so liberal a Scot as you would rejoice to hear and make libations with.

To which Boswell adds a footnote: 'Mr. Boswell in a bumper—huzza! huzza! huzza!' but he is not in a very huzzaying mood. He is trying hard to get Lord Auchinleck to increase his £300-a-year allowance to £400 and to let him go to the English Bar; but the old judge, who at the moment is liable for a £1,000 debt incurred by his heir, has decided instead to lower his allowance to £200. 'I must not dispute with him, but he is really a strange man'. Apart from these daylight worries, Boswell is beginning to dislike going to bed.

I awake in the night, dreading annihilation, or being thrown into some horrible state of being.

Another gnawing preoccupation is the disposition of the Auchinleck estate, which his dissatisfied father (now 'visibly failing') is rather ominously considering. Amid his fears that Auchinleck may 'incommode and disgrace' him and impoverish his family by some strange settlement, Boswell, backed by Johnson's approval, stands doggedly for feudal principle and heirs male, and finally Auchinleck yields, with a grim precautionary clause in the deed against 'a weak, foolish, and extragavant person'; so all the strong beer Boswell has been drinking recently 'to dull my faculties' and appear politely good-humoured in the presence of his sour step-mother has not been thrown away. Meanwhile in October Margaret Boswell has given birth to a son, diplomatically christened Alexander, which improves her husband's relations with his father to some slight extent, though the judge still makes Boswell feel in his presence like '*a timid boy*, which is intolerable'. So the winter arrives and wanes, with the usual lapses and a curious new impulse of Rousseauism. He shows his wife a graceless entry in his journal, and although the operative words are more or less disguised in Greek characters, she guesses their import and is greatly hurt, and Boswell even more hurt at her being hurt. For he is sincerely fond of his wife, and his children, and his family hearth is never more sacred to him than when he is away from it, drunk, or quitting the arms of a drab. I think that when Mrs. Boswell got a letter from the innocent Johnson in May 1776 containing the words 'You will now have Mr. Boswell home; it is well that you have him; he has led a wild life . . . Pray take care of him and tame him; the only thing in which I have the honour to agree with you is in loving him,' she may have given a dry laugh.

4

The next landmark in Boswell's life is the death of his father in 1782 and his accession to the lairdship of Auchinleck. It is unnecessary to follow his gambols up to that time in detail; the chronicle is becoming monotonous. What he was like every time he saw Johnson is to be viewed in the *Life*. Away from Johnson, and each time he returned home, he fell automatically into the old ways and continued to build up a three-bottle reputation notable even at the Scottish Bar. In any other age or country his advocate's business would have come to an end long since. Fortunately for him, his brother lawyers drank as valiantly as anybody, as Eldon's and other memoirs show.

As some sort of a safety-valve Boswell now decided to take the public more regularly into his confidence. He did so in a series of essays to *The London Magazine* which began in 1777 and lasted till 1783. In these essays, signing himself 'the Hypochondriack', he unbosoms himself of a variety of richly-muddled thinking on many topics obsessing him—love, property, marriage, morals, travel, politics, and so forth, and of course drinking. His apologia for the bottle (1780) contains at least one key-clause:

I do fairly acknowledge that I love drinking; that I have a con-stitutional inclination to indulge in fermented liquors, and that if it were not for the restraints of reason and religion, I am afraid that I should be as constant a votary of Bacchus as any man ...

His conclusion, so far as he can be said to conclude, seems to be that wine is the solace of old age. It is not so interesting as the question raised by that prattle about reason and religion. Like every 'intimate' essayist, Boswell is posing for his public. He may be less prudent than Lamb and the other boozy essayists, who keep their drunkenness out of print entirely, but like them he is striking an attitude for the benefit of his readers. Is he also deceiving himself? Does he really believe that reason and re-ligion restrain him from excess? I think not, for his letters to Temple, in which debauchery and aspirations mingle so smoothly, reveal no actual self-deception in this matter. He is naturally not consistent. On the death of his uncle, Dr. John Boswell, a member of the odd Glassite sect, he remarks quaintly to Temple that although Dr. Boswell was fond of fornication and 'had no conduct', he has undoubtedly attained Paradise. Dr. John Boswell is the strict religious sectary, 'very licentious in indulging himself with women' and justifying it from Scripture, of whom Johnson, that monument of Christian common-sense, observed sardonically that there is 'no trusting to that crazy piety'. A hundred mad Messiahs from John of Leyden down have behaved like Dr. Boswell, with perfect sincerity. It is a logical product of private judgment, on which the Reformation rests, that certain types should not merely wallow in vice, which can happen to anybody, but should be able to prove righteous superi-ority by selected texts from the Old Testament. But Boswell never fell into this mania, and it seems to me perfectly under-standable that one of his favourite books all through his life should be Dr. Ogden's *Sermons on Prayer*. For he differs greatly from his uncle, being regularly oppressed by remorse, penitence, self-disgust, and a bitter longing for a sane, unclouded life. He can deceive himself luxuriantly over many things—a fascinating example will occur in due course—but he never attempts seriously to justify his own offences against Christian morals. Could Luther say as much?

He returned to London in March 1776, to bask in 'the full glow' of Johnson's talk and to feel himself 'elevated as if brought into another state of being', as well he might. They travelled together to Oxford, Birmingham, Lichfield, and Ashbourne in Derbyshire. Later they met again at Bath, with the Thrales. Back in London, Boswell added to his collection of notabilities a cynosure of the town, the celebrated and attractive Mrs. Rudd, heroine of a famous Old Bailey case, mixed up with the brothers Perreau, who were hanged, in a large-scale bond-forgery. His first visits to her ended in a perfect orgy of kissing; their desultory subsequent liaison lasted, with long intervals, till about 1786. Just before returning to Scotland again in April he brought about that feat of which Burke justly said that there was nothing to equal it in the whole history of the Corps Diplomatique. With infinitely delicate manœuvring Boswell managed to bring Wilkes and Johnson together at the Dillys' dinner-table in the Poultry.

The whole episode is brilliantly recounted in the *Life*. The scene at the beginning of dinner where Wilkes helps Johnson to veal is pure Molière. The gradual thawing, in the sunshine of Wilkes's famous charm—he played up to Boswell magnificently—of the surly, perturbed, and hostile Doctor is conveyed with great skill, and the finale, with a radiant Doctor thanking Boswell for a delightful experience, perfect. Wilkes, a finished actor, had given a performance Garrick might have envied. His deference to Johnson, his gaiety and his beautiful manners undoubtedly astonished and dazzled the old man. This was not the blasphemous foul-tongued ruffian Johnson had heard so much of; this was a gentleman and a scholar. We may well imagine the impresario Boswell's flush of triumph, for just before dinner the Doctor had looked ominous, and there might very well have been a terrific explosion. One would give something to have heard him discussing the evening over supper with Wilkes in due course.

The meeting with Johnson did not lead to any friendship with

Wilkes, for they were poles apart; but ever afterwards Johnson spoke amiably of him. Five years later they dined together again at the Dillys', again with reciprocal pleasure, and Wilkes called later on Johnson, received a gift set of his *Lives of the Poets*, and enjoyed a long literary talk. These were their only meetings, and it may be that the precarious truce between them would not have borne any more. They had found a few topics to agree upon, but inevitably sooner or later harmony would have gone up abruptly in smoke and flame, in angry bellowings from Johnson and a corrosive epigram from Wilkes.

After a period at home of the usual kind (but this time he excelled himself by appearing tipsy at a funeral) Boswell came in September 1777 to Ashbourne in Derbyshire to stay for ten days with Johnson at the house of Johnson's old clerical friend, Dr. John Taylor of the rich benefice and the plump horses and the stately purple-clad major-domo. His next visit to London was in March 1778; the year, as Mr. Vulliamy says, of the Great Dialogues, as every Johnsonian knows, the year of magnificent dinner-party and other conversations, and of Johnson's chance meeting with Mr. Oliver Edwards, the dull little lawyer whose name is surrounded with an imperishable halo for one single chance remark.

You are a philosopher, Dr. Johnson. I have tried too in my time to be a philosopher; but, I don't know how, cheerfulness was always breaking in.

During this visit Boswell was staying with Paoli in South Audley Street and 'entertained in elegant hospitality, and with all the ease and comfort of a home.' Even so his extra-mural amusements are reputed to have pained his kind host, whose intermittent influence undoubtedly saved Boswell many a fall, to the extent of making Paoli unwell, though his affection remained unchanged. The wayward guest returned to Scotland on May 19, being entertained on the way by the Chancellor of Lincoln Cathedral with 'the most flattering attention', though a complete stranger with only his name as a passport. He certainly had a gift.

This autumn another son, James, was born to Boswell. On March 15, 1779, he was in London again till May, amassing

more Johnsonian honey, though 'unaccountably negligent'. There
is one episode during this visit which illustrates that recurrent
gift of self-hypnosis in some matters very clearly, I think. He
put to Johnson a problem of conduct, explaining that when he
had objected to keeping company with a notorious infidel, 'a
celebrated friend of ours'—believed to be Burke—had remarked
that for ordinary men of the world this nicety would be excessive,
since 'it is not very consistent to shun an infidel today and get
drunk tomorrow'. Johnson dismissed this as sad reasoning.
'Because a man cannot be right in all things, is he to be right
in nothing?' asked the Doctor, raising his eyebrows. 'This doctrine would very soon bring a man to the gallows.'

Boswell moralises on this judgment very Boswellianly:

After all, however, it is a difficult question, how far sincere
Christians should associate with the avowed enemies of religion; for
in the first place, almost every man's mind may be more or less
'corrupted by evil communications'; secondly, the world may very
naturally suppose that they are not really in earnest in religion, who
can easily bear its opponents; and thirdly, if the profane find themselves quite well received by the pious, one of the checks upon an
open declaration of their infidelity, and one of the probable chances
of obliging them seriously to reflect, which their being shunned would
do, is removed.

Perhaps that complacent 'almost' supplies a key? Perhaps the
intimate of Wilkes and Hume considered himself immune from
corruption and a match for any infidel? One feels a phrase
analysing the Boswell Mind after the Proustian method might
profitably occupy our next few pages. Though Boswell is certainly no native of what François Mauriac has called the empty,
godless Proustian world ( *ce creux, ce vide* ), I fancy the method
which so slowly and inexorably dissected the dæmonic whimsies
of a Charlus and followed the determined flight from reality of
a Swann might at least lay bare in their order all the workings
of this brain, complex as a Prince Rupert clock. But this is a task
for one more patient than I.

A streak of military red enlivened Boswell's drab routine this
year, 1779. Colonel James Stuart, who was on a recruiting tour,
brought him down to London, via Leeds, and they left London

together a fortnight later for Chester, Stuart's regimental depot, where Boswell, as the guest of the officers' mess, of the Bishop, and of a prebendary with a 'very pleasing' niece, derived enormous pleasure from these contacts, visited and charmed the old ladies of Lichfield and others of Johnson's friends, and returned to Scotland at length 'quite enchanted'. From Carlisle he wrote to Johnson saying he had recently received the Sacrament in Carlisle Cathedral, and found it 'divinely cheering' to think there was a cathedral so near to Auchinleck; to which the Doctor, ever alert to handcuff fantasy, replied amiably, 'How near is the Cathedral to Auchinleck? . . . It is, I suppose, at least an hundred and fifty miles off. However, if you are pleased, it is so far well.'

In 1780 Boswell stayed at home and thereby missed the Gordon Riots, the roar of flame from 'mass-houses', mansions, and gaols, the bestial mob-orgies, the released criminals, the wreckings and lootings, the panic of London, and the admirable last-moment handling of the situation by his classical friend, who had been appointed City Chamberlain the year before, after four defeats. While the authorities sat supine and even complaisant—why should they worry over the harrying of Papists?—Wilkes took the matter into his own hands, commandeered troops, saved the Bank of England, which was important, and quelled the riots without mercy, jailing many of his own supporters, some of whom were hanged, and thereby hastening the end of his popularity with the proletariat. The Scottish lunatic who organised the terror and was duly acquitted in the King's Bench was a few years later convicted of libel and discovered at length hiding in Birmingham, bearded, circumcised, and a professed orthodox Jew. That Lord George Gordon died at length in Newgate seems only right and proper.

Chronic melancholia seized him again towards the end of the year, owing partly, perhaps, to a steady falling-off of his legal practice, and he diagnosed his case very fully for his *London Magazine* public. In March 1781 he was in London again, this time for nearly three months. During this period occurred his famous performance, drunk and slightly obstreperous, at the house of Miss Monckton, afterwards Countess of Cork, after dining with the Duke of Montrose. He relates the incident in the *Life* with a candour which has greatly annoyed the severe. A more discreditable incident, as some aver, was to mark this visit. In April, Henry Thrale, the wealthy Southwark brewer, who had been so warmly kind to Johnson for so long, and who incidentally was the only man in England able to quell the Doctor with a look, died of over-eating. The blow to Johnson was considerable. Apart from the loss of a dear friend it meant, as he well knew, the end of those halcyon days at Streatham Place. To Boswell, whose dislike of Mrs. Thrale was amply returned, it occurred a little later to compose for private amusement an *Ode by Dr. Johnson to Mrs. Thrale, upon their Supposed Approaching Nuptials,* parodying the Doctor's fondness for sonorous Latinate words. Having kept this production by him for seven years, Boswell published it anonymously in 1788, and later printed the opening stanza in the *Life,* also anonymously.

> Cervisial doctor's viduate dame,
> Opin'st thou this gigantick frame,
>   Procumbing at thy shrine,
> Shall, catenated by thy charms,
> A captive in thy ambient arms,
>   Perennially be thine?

Is Macaulay's shout that the fellow Boswell was utterly without shame or delicacy justified for once? Treacherous malice? Boozy mental decay?

While it is difficult to excuse Boswell completely, one feels there are one or two things Rhadamanthus in his anger may have overlooked. On the evidence of a playful threat by Wilkes in 1781 to show the poem to Johnson, and of a letter written by Boswell to Wilkes in 1783 containing an allusion to the *Ode,* it seems that Wilkes possibly had some active part in it. The poem itself bears out this theory. As a composition it ranks far above the feeble doggerel to which Boswell was normally addicted. If mildly ribald it is amusing, and not without literary skill; Calverley and W. S. Gilbert have written far worse. That Wilkes inspired and even collaborated in it seems to me more than likely. As to the more serious charge of hoarding this piece and hurling it like a bomb at Mrs. Thrale after her remarriage seven years later one must agree that if Boswell did so, he deserves to be soundly scolded, however Mrs. Thrale-Piozzi's sneers at him in print deserved it. To Wilkes it would seem an excellent jape, I think, like his threat to show the poem to Johnson. Boswell's diary simply records on May 9, 1788: 'Determined to publish Johnson's supposed Nuptial Ode.' How do we know that Wilkes, finding it one day on Boswell's table—no literary man can bear to throw away a good thing—did not insist on its publication, or even himself send it to the printer? Who could resist Jack Wilkes?

5

The death of Lord Auchinleck on August 30, 1782, evoked no hypocritical excess of grief from his heir, to whom Johnson remarked with sober realism, 'Your father's death had every circumstance that could enable you to bear it.' And, in fact, though Auchinleck had endured James's antics with surprising patience over some thirty years, his stiffnecked, tyrannous old age exhibited few lovable qualities. Boswell had almost tearfully deplored many times to Temple and to Johnson his utter inability to live on friendly or even easy terms with his father, whose disappointment in him was not hidden. Now a long ordeal was over, and Boswell could demonstrate the powers and duties of a Scottish laird.

The surprising thing is that he did so with remarkable efficiency, from the very beginning. The moody, drifting, bibulous figure over whose future Edinburgh legal circles shrugged and grunted turned overnight into an alert man of business and a liberal-minded and sympathetic landlord. Boswell had some time before regaled his *London Magazine* public with his ideas on landed proprietorship, which were strictly feudal; but a generous nature mitigated baronial principles, and his papers reveal him as almost the perfect squire. His poorer tenants soon had reason to bless him. Their problems and difficulties are his immediate preoccupation. He knows them and inquires after them, when absent, by name, like a Highland chief, and his agent is instructed to help, to be easy with arrears, and to distribute money and oatmeal and other gifts as directed. To Johnson

Boswell mentions one of these benefactions, the removal of a lonely old man from a remote cottage to a comfortable billet among friendly neighbours; one good deed out of many. At the same time the new Laird is firm with tenants who are trying to dodge their liabilities or to exploit him. One or two of these are to be prosecuted or removed forthwith. Nothing could be more businesslike than his procedure here, just as nothing could be more admirable than his anxiety and practical care for the needy and unfortunate on his estates.

Thus did responsibility, the feudal instinct, a kind heart, and family pride combine to produce a surprise very disconcerting to Boswell's intimates. It is not, I hope, cynical to surmise in addition that as a lifelong actor with an appreciative audience he admired himself extremely in his new patriarchal role. The Highland chieftains were shorn long since of their old powers of life and death and jurisdiction, yet even a Lowland laird's position was still sufficiently invested with authority to be agreeable. At the same time it naturally brought Boswell fresh worries. Lord Auchinleck had left the estate unencumbered, and the rent-roll was worth £1,500 or £1,600 a year, gross. This was enough for a man with a family who was prepared to live on his land, but certainly not enough for a man whose only dream was to escape to London at regular intervals, and a man moreover carrying a fair burden of debt, some of it due to his own generosity. Johnson's advice to him, as might be expected, was to stay at home and be prudent—'your estate and the Courts will find you full employment'. His brother David, 'honest David', the merchant from Spain, urged the same, Mrs. Boswell likewise. Mrs. Boswell, though herself far from well, was prepared, even, to endure another visit from the Doctor if it would keep her husband at home, and wrote to Johnson herself. The Doctor, now in his seventy-fourth year and his illnesses steadily increasing, replied to his enemy with pathetic gratitude.

Dear Lady,—I have not often received so much pleasure as from your invitation to Auchinleck ... If my health were fully recovered, I would suffer no little heat or cold, nor a wet or a rough road to keep me from you. I am, indeed, not without hope of seeing Auchinleck again; but to make it a pleasant place I must see its lady well, and brisk, and airy. For my sake, therefore, among many greater reasons, take care, dear Madam, of your health . . . Be very careful to keep your mind quiet; and do not think it too much to give an account of your recovery to, Madam, yours, &c.

After seven months of daily riding round his estate, instructing his agent, poring over accounts, ordering the welfare of his retainers, and looking after his trees and his 'coal work', a small surface outcrop, the new Laird considered he had earned a holiday. Thursday, March 20, 1783, found him accordingly in London again, calling next morning at Mrs. Thrale's house in Argyll Street. He found Johnson in his own room, looking pale and very ill. As ever, the sight of Boswell cheered and stimulated him, and he began at once to discourse on the agreeable life of a country gentleman; perhaps a trifle pointedly, for when Boswell countered with 'Yet, Sir, we see great proprietors of land who prefer living in London,' the Doctor was forced to concede that intellectual advantages might outweigh the others, and changed the subject.

Johnson's illness during this visit of Boswell's made him very fretful, and the conversations in the *Life* accordingly suffer, though there is one remark of the Sage's which might suitably be inscribed in gold over the principal entrance to the new House of Commons: 'It is wonderful, Sir, with how little real superiority of mind men can make an eminent figure in public life.' At this time—Boswell was once again a guest of Paoli's—occurred that amusing incident of the letter for Mauritius Lowe I have quoted in an early page. On Good Friday, April 18, Johnson and Boswell fasted and went to church together, and afterwards sat on the stone seats by Johnson's garden-door and discoursed placidly of a score of things, with the Doctor in the best of form. It was clear nevertheless that the old man's asthma and dropsy were increasing. On the evening of Easter Sunday, when Boswell dined with him quietly, he 'talked little, grew drowsy soon after dinner, and retired, upon which I went away.' He had recovered to some extent a week later, when Boswell next saw him, and was able to talk much as usual. The records of this visit in the *Life* are intermittently scrappy, disjointed and undated. Designing to repeat a famous experiment, to cheer the Doctor, and to gratify himself again with the triumph of his own audacity, Boswell tried to arrange one more meeting between Johnson and Wilkes, who at once suggested a dinner-party at his house in Prince's Court, overlooking St. James's Park. But Johnson had engagements on the dates Wilkes proposed, and Wilkes himself was ill towards the end of May, when Boswell had to return to Scotland.

A month later a severe stroke of palsy visited Johnson, depriving him of speech. He recovered, and on July 3 wrote to Boswell: 'Your anxiety about my health is very friendly, and very agreeable with your general kindness. I have, indeed, had a very frightful blow... I can now speak, but the nerves are weak, and I cannot continue discourse long... The physicians consider me as cured.' 'And such', says Boswell, 'was the general vigour of his constitution that in July he was able to visit Langton at Rochester.' Nor had Johnson given up hopes yet of accepting Mrs. Boswell's invitation. Answering a sudden burst of affectionate regard from Boswell a little before his return north, Johnson assured him that he would like nothing better in distress than to live in a cottage in the park at Auchinleck, toddle about, live mostly on milk, and be taken care of by Mrs. Boswell. 'She and I are good friends now, are we not?' added the Doctor cheerfully. No reply is recorded.

Amid his sincere anxiety over Johnson's condition Boswell, back in Scotland, started and began eagerly to pursue a fresh hare. On May 15 he had said suddenly to Johnson: 'I wish much to be in Parliament, Sir.' The Doctor was not enthusiastic.

'Why, Sir, unless you come resolved to support any administration, you would be the worse for being in Parliament, because you would be obliged to live more expensively.'

'Perhaps, Sir, I should be the less happy for being in Parliament. I never would sell my vote, and I should be vexed if things went wrong.'

'That's cant, Sir. It would not vex you any more in the House, than in the gallery; publick affairs vex no man.'

Boswell persisted that the turbulence of the reign, and the absurd recent vote of the House of Commons that 'the influence of the Crown has increased, is increasing, and ought to be diminished', had vexed him, though to be sure he neither ate, drank, nor slept less. The celebrated Johnsonian exordium beginning 'My dear friend, first clear your *mind* of cant', followed this. However, Boswell was determined to vex himself and to make a figure in politics. Fox's newly-introduced India Bill, which Wilkes was vehemently attacking in the House, gave him an opportunity. The Bill, of which the main provision was the handing over of the government of India to irremovable Commissioners appointed for four years, seemed to Wilkes to violate the charter of the East India Company and to bring the work of Governor-General Warren Hastings, as yet unimpeached, to naught. Boswell, taking a more Tory line, delivered himself of a *Letter to the People of Scotland on the Present State of the Nation* which in places is a typical piece of Boswellian bravura, with a concluding sentence of some pomp.

Holding an estate transmitted to me through my ancestors by charters from a series of Kings, the importance of a Charter and the prerogative of a King impress my mind with seriousness and with duty.

Amusing; though not, I think, so half-witted as it has appeared to some. Dundas, for example, quoted it later in the House and styled it excellent. The Laird, apart from expressing himself as a Laird of Auchinleck with right principles should, has his eye on the main chance, no more and no less than any other candidate for public life. The *Letter* is designed to catch important eyes in Whitehall and, with luck, a blue and rolling and popping Hanoverian eye in St. James's, and is meant to provoke such comment as 'Egad, this fellow should be useful to us, Dundas?' and 'Find out about this Mr. Boswell. He is the type of man We need.' A copy went forthwith to Johnson, who, though too desperately ill to look at political pamphlets when he received it, read it a fortnight later and approved.

Your paper contains very considerable knowledge of history and of the Constitution, very properly produced and applied. It will certainly raise your character, though perhaps it may not make you a Minister of State.

A copy went also to the younger Pitt, who had just become Prime Minister, and produced a polite acknowledgement.

I am extremely obliged to you . . . and have observed with great pleasure the zealous and able support given to the cause of the Publick in the work you were so good as to transmit to me.

Politicians' oil, no doubt; yet one hardly feels that a modern critic dismissing the *Letter* as 'another ominous proof of mental incoherence' is entirely justified. Was Johnson a fool? Or Dundas?

From the replies of Pitt and Johnson Boswell derived a thrill of happiness and hope. A new career seemed suddenly to be opening before him, and a brilliant one. His struggle with the Law, with a practice dwindling a little more every time he saw Mr. Lawrie, his clerk, need not necessarily fill the rest of his days. The grey perspective was brightening. He had evidently impressed Pitt. His old college-mate Dundas had taken note also. Then of course there was Burke . . .

Meanwhile there was the urgency of Johnson's latest letter, begging him to approach some of the leading Scots physicians for an opinion on his case. Boswell applied at once to Sir Alexander Dick and to Drs. Gillespie, Cullen, Hope, and Munro, lights of the Edinburgh School of Medicine, who all replied with opinions, prescriptions, and compliments to the venerable and illustrious patient. This duty off his mind, Boswell despatched a packet of medicines and turned avidly to the new game. A loyal address to the King composed by him for the patriots of Ayrshire was carried, to his gratification, by a large majority. This address Boswell decided to present to George III in person. Unfortunately Parliament had dissolved by the time he had got as far as York, and he scurried back to Ayrshire, having, as he wrote to Johnson from York on March 28, 'some intention of being a candidate to represent the county in Parliament'. This produced a characteristic letter from the Doctor, despite his condition. After thanking Boswell for his kindly solicitude about his health:

You are entering upon a transaction which requires much prudence. You must endeavour to oppose without exasperating; to practise temporary hostility, without producing enemies for life . . . One thing I must enjoin you, which is seldom observed in the conduct of elections;—I must entreat you to be scrupulous in the use of strong liquors. One night's drunkenness may defeat the labours of forty days well employed. Be firm, but not clamorous; be active, but not malicious; and you may form such an interest, as may not only exalt yourself, but dignify your family.

To Langton the Doctor wrote a week later, rather dubiously.

The man so busy about addresses is neither more nor less than our own Boswell, who had come as far as York towards London but turned back on the dissolution, and is said now to stand for some place. Whether to wish him success, his best friends hesitate.

As it turned out, Boswell's friends had no need to worry, as yet. The electors of Ayshire again chose their former representative, Colonel Montgomerie. Boswell's address to them, though suitably deferent, had harped somewhat on his family and his ambition, and had perhaps struck the wrong note. He came to London again early in May and found Johnson slightly better, but feeling lonely and cheerless and begining to dread the approach of death. To many this dread has seemed morbid, superstitious, and unworthy of a rational man, a prevailing modern impression being that the Four Last Things are the invention of unscrupulous medieval priests. But as a devout unquiet Christian Johnson was well aware of what faced him. It was not death in itself he dreaded, but the ensuing judgment. 'The better a man is', he argued, 'the more afraid he is of death, having a clearer view of Infinite Purity.' Some of his friends, like Dr. Adams of Pembroke, gave him what comfort and encouragement they could; nobody seems to have reminded him from the lives of the saints of the joy with which so many servants of God in every age welcome their summons from this world. Within the limits of their own narrowed conception of Christianity Johnson's friends did their best, but no one who loves the Doctor can help deploring the meagreness of the assurances they gave him. A Challoner by his bedside could have saved this *anima naturaliter catholica* many a bout of misery. His death, one is glad to think, was calm and happy.

However, apprehension was by no means Johnson's prevailing mood at this time. On May 15 Boswell found him in fine spirits at the Essex Head club, having dined the previous evening with Mrs. Garrick, the learned Mrs. Carter, Hannah More, and Fanny Burney, and enjoyed himself tremendously. He enjoyed himself

likewise during a stay at Oxford early in June, at the house of
Dr. Adams, his old tutor, now Master of his old college, who
welcomed him and Boswell with the warmest hospitality. Twice
during a sunny fortnight Johnson lapsed for a brief while into
his dark mood and displayed 'gloomy agitation', impelling
Boswell to remark, not for the first time, that his temperament
was naturally inclined to melancholy. He soon recovered, talked
delightfully, and before long was rapping Boswell's knuckles
for a gush of Rousseauism in the old familiar way.

'One set of savages is like another', proclaimed the Doctor,
apropos a newly-published work on the South Seas.

'I do not think the people of Otaheite can be reckoned
savages,' said Boswell.

'Don't cant in defence of savages.'

'They have the art of navigation.'

'A dog or a cat can swim.'

'They carve very ingeniously,' said Boswell.

'A cat can scratch, and a child with a nail can scratch.'

This was the old Johnson, the traditional Johnson, the Johnson
of whom Chesterton remarked, with a characteristic flash of
paradoxical perspicuity, that he was not a dictator but a demo-
crat, since he never feared to descend from his conversational
throne and fight as an equal. At the same time the Doctor's habit
of firing one final deafening broadside, right or wrong, and
declaring the battle over must have been excessively trying to
those of his opponents who had better arguments. But it is for
these things that we love him, after all.

They returned to London from Oxford on June 20, and met
three evenings later for dinner at the Literary Club, Johnson's
last appearance there. A day or so later he expressed a sick man's
longing, not for the first time, to winter in Italy. Boswell suppressed a chuckle. He had already taken the initiative. After
consulting Reynolds on the best way to bring it about without
offending Johnson's prickly pride, he had written to Lord Chancellor Thurlow asking if it were possible to apply to the King
to increase Johnson's pension of £300 a year sufficiently to allow
of his spending the coming winter in Italy with Sastres, his
humble Italian friend, thereby prolonging a valuable life. Lord
Thurlow replied on June 28 that he would certainly 'adopt and

press' the suggestion as far as he was able. Next day, having consulted Reynolds again, Boswell broke the agreeable news to Johnson and read him Thurlow's letter. The scene ends in a moving fashion.

He listened with much attention; then warmly said 'This is taking prodigious pains about a man.' 'O, Sir (said I, with most sincere affection) your friends would do every thing for you.' He paused, grew more and more agitated, till tears started into his eyes, and he exclaimed with fervent emotion, 'GOD bless you all.' I was so affected that I also shed tears. After a short silence, he renewed and extended his grateful benediction. 'GOD bless you all, for JESUS CHRIST's sake.' We both remained for some time unable to speak. He rose suddenly and quitted the room, quite melted in tenderness. He staid but a short time, till he had recovered his firmness; soon after he returned I left him.

And this is the Boswell whom some have exhibited as an exploiter; the Boswell whose reverence and affection for the Doctor, if (they say) it ever existed, had long since waned. Dining with Boswell at Reynolds's the following evening, Johnson glowingly discussed the Italian journey, the kind hearts of Boswell and his host delighting in the old man's loving gratitude. Early in July Johnson left London for a change of air at Taylor's at Ashbourne. Then came a sad disappointment. The Royal ear had not been gained. Thurlow, by way of mitigating the blow, suggested to Reynolds that if Johnson cared to mortgage his pension he might draw on him, Thurlow, for five or six hundred pounds at once. Johnson acknowledged and declined this offer in a letter of the noblest dignity.

Your Lordship was first solicited without my knowledge; but, when I was told that you were pleased to honour me with your patronage, I did not expect to hear of a refusal; yet, as I have had no long time to brood hope, and have not rioted in imaginary opulence, this cold reception has been scarce a disappointment; and, from your Lordship's kindness, I have received a benefit, which only men like you are able to bestow. I shall now live *mihi carior,* with a higher opinion of my own merit.

He declined Lord Thurlow's kindness because he was now feeling much better, and because to accept now would be to advance 'a false claim'. Pride alone dictated this attitude, for his asthma and dropsy were only temporarily alleviated. A lesser man might well have gone to Italy on such terms without hurting his conscience, and perhaps taken Boswell as well.

But Johnson and Boswell had already parted for the last time on earth. In a passage of the *Life* like the tolling of a distant bell Boswell records that after dining with Reynolds on Wednesday, June 30,

I accompanied him in Sir Joshua Reynolds's coach, to the entry of Boltcourt. He asked me whether I would not go with him to his house; I declined it, from an apprehension that my spirits would sink. We bade adieu to each other affectionately in the carriage. When he had got down upon the foot-pavement he called out, 'Fare you well'; and without looking back, sprung away with a kind of pathetic briskness, if I may use that expression, which seemed to indicate a struggle to conceal uneasiness, and impressed me with a foreboding of our long, long separation.

Nevermore. Six months later the Doctor was dead.

## Chapter Six

# DECLINE AND RISE

## 1

To admit that Boswell's 'Life of Johnson', so packed with riches, lacks its natural and artistic conclusion is grievous but inevitable. The work has no climax. The disciple was not at the master's death-bed. It is as if Plato's Phædo, answering the opening question, 'Were you present in person, Phædo, by Socrates' side the day he drank the poison in prison?' had been forced to answer 'Not so, Echecrates, I was unfortunately away in Boeotia at the time; but I have notes of the occasion from Cebes and Simmias, who were there.' Without doubt Boswell's absence in Scotland robs the *Life* of what should have been its great final scene. Why was he not at Bolt Court on the night of December 12-13, 1784, with old Mrs. Williams and the Negro Frank?

We know that on returning home on July 1, Boswell was the prey of forebodings and apprehensions concerning Johnson as well as his own future. He unburdened himself to Johnson to some extent almost immediately and received a gently chiding reply.

Write to me often, and write like a man. I consider your fidelity and tenderness as a great part of the comforts which are yet left me, and sincerely wish we could be nearer to each other . . . My dear friend, life is very short and very uncertain; let us spend it as well as we can.

Gamely struggling against the diseases which were over-whelming him, Johnson was spending his last summer and autumn in dogged visits to Oxford, to Lichfield, to Birmingham,

177

and to Taylor at Ashbourne. Returning to London towards the
end of November, he took to his bed within a few days and did
not leave it again. It was therefore not until early December that
Boswell need begin, if informed, to be seriously alarmed for him.
He had been desperately anxious for some time to cut his losses
at the Scottish Bar and try his luck at the English, and had
prevailed on Johnson this summer, after much argument, to
sanction the move to London in writing.

The condition [wrote the Doctor] on which you have my consent
to settle in London is, that your expence never exceeds your annual
income . . . The loss of your Scottish business, which is all that you
can lose, is not to be reckoned as any equivalent to the hopes and
possibilities that open here upon you. If you succeed, the question of
prudence is at an end.

So any impression that Boswell was wrapped up in self-pity,
self-indulgence, and a selfish neglect four hundred miles away
is inaccurate. On the contrary, he was expecting to regain contact
with London and Johnson as soon as he could wind up his affairs
at Edinburgh. Apart from which he says in the *Life*, 'I was
unfortunately so indisposed during a considerable part of the
year, that it was not, or at least I thought it was not, in my
power to write to my illustrious friend as formerly, or without
expressing such complaints as offended him.' In other words,
Boswell was heavily anxious and depressed, drinking rather
heavily to overcome it, and afraid to keep bewailing his misery
to his friend.

On November 5 Johnson wrote to him from Lichfield, in
affectionate reproach, his last letter.

My legs are extremely weak, and my breath very short, and the
water is now encreasing upon me. In this uncomfortable state your
letters used to relieve; what is the reason I have them no longer?
Are you sick, or are you sullen? . . . I am sometimes afraid that your
omission to write has some real cause, and shall be glad to know
you are not sick, and that nothing ill has befallen dear Mrs. Boswell,
or any of your family.

Bestirring himself at length in some remorse, Boswell wrote
back 'two as kind letters as I could'. By the time the second one
arrived Johnson was too ill to read. 'But I had the consolation

of being informed that he spoke of me on his death-bed with affection, and I look forward with humble hope of renewing our friendship in a better world.'

Strangely stoic, it sounds; but these words were written seven years after Johnson's death, 'strengthened in faith and joyful in hope', and Boswell's grief at the time, as we shall see directly, was unmistakable. To Dr. Percy he wrote in March 1785 that the light of his life had gone out, that he did not expect to recover from his loss, and that his great consolation was that he had already collected so assiduously such a store of Johnson's wit and wisdom. This has been interpreted in some quarters as if he were thinking only of the rewards he hoped to derive from the Doctor's remains.

Could he, if he had tried, have been present during Johnson's last hours? From Hawkins we gather that it was not until December 8 that Johnson knew he was dying, and made a new (and unsatisfactory) will. He certainly had a premonition on the 5th, when he received Communion in his bedroom with Langton, Hawkins, and a number of other intimates; but two days later he was scolding Dr. Brocklesby heartily for not operating for sarcocele and declaring 'I want length of life, and you fear giving me pain, which I care not for!' Had Boswell time? Like the post, the fastest journey between Edinburgh and London took three days. It was impossible therefore for Boswell to receive warning of the end in time to be in Bolt Court on the 12th, even if anybody had thought of warning him; which nobody did.

I make no apology for going into these questions of time and space in Boswell's behalf. They are not the only answer to suggestions of selfish forgetfulness. The news of Johnson's death was a severe shock, as we see from Boswell's diary under Friday, December 17, when the evening post brought him a long letter from Dr. Brocklesby containing 'the dismal news of my great and good Friend.' The Boswells had guests that evening and it was too late to put them off. Boswell managed to get through supper without betraying his emotion, and did not mention the news, except, as the guests were leaving, to Sir William Forbes, privately. 'My feelings were just one large expanse of Stupor. I knew that I should afterwards have sorer sensations.'

Johnson's funeral took place in Westminister Abbey three days later. Even by taking an expensive express postchaise early on the 18th, Boswell could not have got to London in time for this, and it seems clear moreover that his presence was not desired to any extent by pompous, managing Sir John Hawkins, the attorney-executor who took control of the funeral arrangements, and whom we shall meet again. By choice or necessity Johnson's other two executors, Sir Joshua Reynolds and Sir William Scott, apparently left everything to Hawkins. He took immediate steps to hamper Boswell, a coming rival, by securing all Johnson's existing private papers.

On December 28 Boswell read through Johnson's will, printed in a London newspaper, being still stupored and unable to realise his bereavement. A little hurt at not finding his name among the legatees, he reflected that others of Johnson's dearest intimates were left out as well, and that Johnson had during his lifetime given him more valuable tokens of regard than he had given other friends. And he took to his prayers.

A letter reached him from Charles Dilly, the London publisher, a day after Dr. Brocklesby's, demanding a 400-page octavo volume containing Johnson's choicest conversational feats, to be ready for the press by February; from which we perceive that the eighteenth-century book trade had little to learn from modern business-method. Boswell refused to be rushed. The work on Johnson he intended to publish, he reminded Dilly, required deliberation. Meanwhile his Hebrides journal, freed for publication by Johnson's death, was nearly ready as it stood for Malone's critical eye. As he turned to give his manuscript one more review his eye was caught by something which caused political ambition suddenly to wake and crow again. A Bill had just been introduced into the House of Commons to reduce the number of judges in the Scottish Court of Session from fifteen to ten, with corresponding increases in salary. Here was an opportunity for Lord Auchinleck's heir to show his grasp of affairs and to bring his name again before the curiously apathetic authorities.

In May 1785, accordingly, a half-crown pamphlet entitled, like its predecessor, *A Letter to the People of Scotland*, informed the public at large that Mr. Boswell of Auchinleck was in the

arena to fight 'this pernicious innovation' and infringement of the
Articles of the Union. But whereas his *Letter* of 1784 on the
India Bill was not devoid of learning and good sense, as we
have perceived, the *Letter* of 1785 is a truly rococo production;
breathless, fantastic, hysterical, sprouting italics and capital
letters and marks of exclamation and indignation in every other
paragraph. It appeals frenziedly 'in the name of GOD and THE
KING' to Pitt and Fox to put a stop to 'this conspiracy', which
may blow up their administration. It attacks Dundas, most
unwisely, and lavishes flattery and entreaties on Lowther, Lord
Lonsdale, Dictator of the North, who is implored to come forth
in his might and succour the nation in its need. It assures the
public of strong support against the Bill from 'my old classical
friend Mr. Wilkes, with whom I pray you to excuse my keeping
company, he is so pleasant', from the eminent Mr. Burke, Lord
Rector of the University of Glasgow, from 'my amiable and
honourable friend Dempster, that *rara avis* of the Scottish breed',
and from 'that brave Irishman, Captain Macbride, the cousin
of my wife'; which may have embarrassed that honest naval
officer not a little if he ever read it in the seclusion of his cabin.
It records a flattering unintentional compliment once paid the
author by 'my friend Lord Mountstuart', and mentions, in connection with Lord Eglintoun, that Mr. Boswell has 'the honour
and happiness to be married to his lordship's relation, a true
Montgomerie, whom I esteem, whom I love, after fifteen years,
as on the day when she gave me her hand'. It mentions the
author's hopes as a Parliamentary candidate for Ayrshire, goes
into the Boswell pedigree from Flodden down, and dwells on
Mr. Boswell's honesty and broadmindedness, as one ready 'to
discuss topicks with mitred St. Asaph and others; to drink, to
laugh, to converse with Quakers, Republicans, Jews and
Moravians'. It proclaims the said Mr. Boswell a Tory but no
slave or time-server, adjures his friends and countrymen—'in the
words of my departed Goldsmith, who gave me many noble
truths, and gave me a jewel of the finest water, the acquaintance
of SIR JOSHUA REYNOLDS'—to fly from petty tyrants to the Throne,
and winds up fortissimo with an impressive quotation from 'one
of the finest passages in John Hume's noble and elegant tragedy
of *Douglas*.'

Altogether the kind of haywire exhibition, to use the admirable American epithet, which would mildly interest a psychopath, and it serves to remind us, if we have forgotten it, that Boswell was undoubtedly, if intermittently, a trifle cracked. A 'follow-up' manifesto to the *Edinburgh Advertizer* ('My Friends and Countrymen, be not afraid! I am *upon the spot*. I am *upon the watch* . . . Collect your minds. Be calm; but be firm!!!') increases that impression. Whether, as I have seen it affirmed, this witch-dance automatically deprived Boswell for ever of all hope of legal or other preferment in Scotland and England alike I take leave to doubt. That is a modern view. The Eighteenth Century was more indulgent to eccentricity and racket than we, and more judges and public men than one came from the ranks of

> The hairum-scairum, ram-stam boys,
> The rattlin squad.

The effect of the *Letter* on Lord Chancellor Thurlow, whose own eccentricity took the form of imposing his illegitimate family on society whenever possible, may have been pure growling amusement ('Damn his blood!'). Certainly Thurlow never assisted Boswell to any legal advancement, though he once complimented him on a speech in an appeal-case. But this negligence was due to a rather crusty prejudice in favour of lawyers who know something of the law.

The *Letter* undoubtedly served a political purpose, notwithstanding the jeers and laughter it evoked from some of the wits. It caught the arrogant eye of Lord Lonsdale, that dark potentate, who was not accustomed to praise, and considerably affected Boswell's immediate future thereby, as will shortly appear. It reminded George III of Boswell's existence as well. On May 20 he attended a levee and was noticed by the King, who talked to him for some minutes, kindly and quite intelligently, about his literary plans. On returning to his lodgings Boswell thought deeply, and eventually wrote the King a respectful letter, containing a request. At the next levee, on June 15, he was questioned by His Majesty, at first a little sharply, then, as Boswell made himself clear, with 'the benignant smile of a Correggio angel', says the enraptured fellow. He had ventured to ask the King's views on a highly delicate personal matter, namely the manner in which he, Boswell, should refer to Prince Charles Edward Stuart in his forthcoming *Journal of a Tour to the Hebrides.*

George III displays himself in this little scene, as recounted in the Isham Papers, not unattractively. Having received without flinching the news that his loyal and respectful liege, Mr. James Boswell of Auchinleck, was cousin in the seventh degree to Prince Charles Edward, a delicate way of reminding His Majesty that he himself, *Georg. Rex III, Dei Gra. Britt. Omn.,* etc., etc., was Mr. Boswell's eighth cousin by the same token,[1] the King expressed no rancour or contempt for the *de jure* claimant to the British throne, so recently in arms against his house and so nearly successful, and indulged in no pomposity. When Boswell suggested referring in his book to 'Prince Charles', his Majesty seemed to knit his brows slightly. Then 'the Grandson of King James II', perhaps? Yes. Yes. That would do. The King approved that. He chatted a little longer with Boswell and observed finally, before turning away, 'I do not think it is a matter of consequence to my family how they [the existing Stuarts] are called. I think there can be no question as to the right'; which is arguable, perhaps, but certainly not ill-bred. Dr. Johnson's praise for George III's manners was by no means hyperbole, it would seem, even taking into account King George's marked liking for Scotsmen, derived from his mother, Lord Bute's close friend. It may be noted incidentally, before passing on, that the Bill which inspired Boswell's fantasy—he also presented to the King at this time an address against the Bill from the Auchinleck tenantry—was ultimately defeated. Perhaps the *Letter* had helped to achieve something real after all?

Social engagements before returning to Scotland this autumn included, as usual, a dinner or two with Wilkes. Boswell was particularly struck with the elegance of Wilkes's new establishment at Kensington Gore, opposite Prince's Gate, where Amelia

[1] Their distant common ancestor was John, third Earl of Lennox, grandfather of Darnley. In the *Hebrides Journal* Boswell remarks in a prideful footnote that 'THE ONLY PERSON IN THE WORLD' entitled to be offended at his delicacy in naming the Prince approved of 'my tenderness for what even *has been* Blood-Royal.'

Arnold was installed as reigning sultana. Wilkes had met Mrs
Arnold in 1777, a little before the end of the Charpillon affair
She was a homely, submissive, and adoring type, and she had
no apparent objection to her lover's pursuing simultaneously any
other women who caught his eye, which doubtless explains her
long reign. The little house at Prince's Gate impressed Boswell
with its airy good taste, its choice prints and china, its many
windows, and its extraordinary profusion of mirrors; for Wilkes
loved light and brightness and was impervious to the shock
of his features.

He was looking, notes Boswell, very old, though only just
turned sixty; still vivacious and charming, still indefatigably
witty against the Christian religion. Every day he walked from
Kensington Gore through Knightsbridge to the Guildhall and
back again in his City Chamberlain's uniform of scarlet, with
bag-wig, cocked hat, and glossy military boots. On the verge
of insolvency again, he was hospitable as ever, and it is no
surprise to find Boswell leaving Prince's Gate one August
evening this year very drunk, wandering among the Royal birthday crowd in Piccadilly and duly having his pockets picked.
One would like to know his complete reactions the morning
after an evening with Wilkes, the genial enemy not only of
Boswell's piety but of his King, whom Wilkes had attacked in
the House in 1777, during a debate on the Civil List, with more
audacity than usual. 'The Crown has made a purchase of this
House with the money of the people!' Wilkes had cried to an
embarrassed Commons, every man present knowing it to be
true. For five years also he had been thundering indefatigably
for peace with the American Colonies and the recognition of
their full rights. 'Force avails nothing! . . . Every friend of the
Constitution sees in the support of the American cause a vindica-
tion of the rights of Englishmen! . . . They [the Americans]
avoid us, as a tyrannical, unprincipled, rapacious, and ruined
nation! Their only fear is that the luxury and profligacy of this
country should gain their people!' Guffaws round the House at
such eloquence from such a champion of virtue were even more
excusable on another occasion, when Mr. Wilkes fervently
quoted Holy Writ in a speech in favour of relieving teachers
of the Dissenting sects from subscription to the Thirty-nine

Articles. His rhetoric—'pert but feeble', says Macaulay in his essay on Chatham—was curiously unconvincing, and by 1780, having been returned once more for Middlesex, Wilkes was a silent and isolated figure in the House, admitting himself a spent volcano. The Whigs, whom he had served so well, could give him no Government post, for George III was implacable. They could have found him some other snug place, but they did not.[1] He shrugged Whig ingratitude off as he shrugged off most things, with a cheerful grin. 'Wilkes and Liberty!' piped an old woman after him one morning as he walked through the City to his Guildhall office. 'Quiet, you old fool!' he growled amiably. 'That's all over long ago!' His popularity with the masses was extinct, but a little clique of faithful admirers remained; among them was Frederick, Prince of Wales, who hated his father far more than Wilkes did. The Americans also never ceased to admire him, as well they might, and he could have crossed the Atlantic and become Washington's successor, belike, but for his un-American morals.

Having attended one more levee in September, at which he eagerly promised the King a copy of his *Journal of a Tour to the Hebrides* on the day of publication, Boswell spent Christmas at Auchinleck with his family. He returned to London in January to be called to the English Bar at the opening of Hilary Term, 1786, for the great plunge was now taken.

2

It was, fortunately for Boswell, a pure formality without examination. One sees him, for once well-washed and freshly shaven, sprucely correct in a new forensic wig and gown and snowy, well-starched bands, creaking up Inner Temple Hall in square-toed silver-buckled shoes with two fellow-candidates to be received and to take the necessary oaths denouncing the Holy See of Rome—now occupied, all unawares, by Pius VI,

[1] During his Parisian exile in 1765 the Rockingham Whigs offered him £1,000 a year while the Whig government remained in office. Wilkes refused, regarding this as a bribe to shut his mouth; then, three months later, accepted. This pension ceased in 1767.

the future prisoner of the French Republic—and abjuring the Blessed Sacrament. The call ceremony over, Boswell and his two learned brethren, one of whom was the Hon. Daines Barrington, White of Selborne's fellow-naturalist and a friend of Johnson, gave the usual dinner in the Hall to their friends. Among Boswell's guests were Reynolds, Wilkes, Malone, Dr. Brocklesby, Dilly, his publisher, and Baldwin, his printer. The great chandelier was lighted in their honour.

On March 1, being Ash Wednesday, Boswell knelt with the crowd at the altar-rails in the chapel of the Neapolitan Embassy to have the sign of the Cross traced in ashes on his forehead before Mass by 'a holy Priest's finger', he writes in his diary, with the solemn ancient words *Memento, homo, quia pulvis es, et in pulverem reverteris*. He was taking his new career very seriously; but having begun to attend the King's Bench daily, notebook in hand, he found exhilaration slowly waning and depression taking its place. He was beginning to realise clearly, for once, to what he had committed himself at the age of 46, with most of his contemporaries at the Bar years ahead of him. Never very well acquainted, as he admits to Temple, with the 'forms, quirks and quiddities' of Scots Law, he had now to master a sufficiency of the widely-different complications of the English *corpus*, and he was not, except in rare spurts, given to study or concentration.

It is true that Boswell had less to fear than a man in the same position today. The Bar was not yet a cut-throat competition, the Law's tempo was leisurely, and, as we observe from *Marriage à la Mode,* a fashionable Counsellor Silvertongue might occupy his mornings and evenings more agreeably than in the Courts. But Boswell had a vast deal of leeway to make up. Although the Chinese enigma of the Law was not still further complicated in the 1780's by the necessity, abolished a few years before, to plead in law-Latin, and although Blackstone's *Commentaries* had recently enabled the average student to make sense henceforth of at least part of a bewildering mass of mumbo-jumbo which recalls the Bridlegoose chapters in *Pantagruel,* the only way to learn one's way about the mazy procedure was, as Johnson had once warned Boswell, to haunt the Courts daily. 'You must be careful', the Doctor had said, 'to attend constantly at Westminster Hall; both to mind your business, as it is almost all learned there (for nobody reads now), and to show that you want business.'

Contemporary prints show the lawyers so engaged, pacing Westminster Hall, poring over the bookstalls which line it, and escorting fair clients and their lapdogs to and fro; at one end of the Hall sit the judges in elevated state, wearing cocked hats over their great full-bottomed wigs. The lawyers' elegant nonchalance, demonstrated especially in their gestures and the graceful disposal of their legs, may be to some extent artistic fancy; nevertheless I can well imagine the chilly, dank odour of Westminster Hall and the ease of its professional crowd intimidating a novice like Boswell as he contemplates the scene. He consulted Malone, himself a barrister, and Malone advised him strongly to go on circuit until he was better acquainted with English legal procedure. It is clearly due to Malone's advice that we find Boswell this very spring on the Northern Circuit, and the comic central figure of a celebrated anecdote.

The Northern Circuit at this period covered the counties of York, Lancashire, Durham, Northumberland, Cumberland, and Westmorland, and it is to the assizes at Lancaster this April that the story attaches. Like most legal stories, it borders on the dull. Its climax I am inclined, like Leslie Stephen, to regard with the liveliest suspicion.

The authority for the story is the famous judge Lord Eldon, formerly Mr. John Scott, who in his old age related to a Mr. Twiss, who wrote his memoirs, his reminiscences of a long and successful life at the Bar. In an early page Twiss records that during the Lancaster Assizes of 1786, as Scott and other jovial young members of his mess were on their way to supper, they found 'Jemmy Boswell' lying drunk on the pavement. Conspiring together over supper and raising a guinea and a half between them, they sent Boswell, with fees for himself and his clerk, a brief with instructions to move forthwith for a writ of *Quare adhaesit pavimento*, adding a few notes conveying that this required considerable learning. Having despatched his clerk to all the attorneys in Lancaster for books bearing on this matter, but in vain, Boswell did the best he could (the story proceeds) with the notes on his brief and duly moved for a writ of *Quare adhaesit* in full Court, to the astonishment of the Bench and the hilarity of the Bar, one of whom at length enlightened his Lordship, amid much laughter, echoed incidentally by the genial Thackeray, who swallows this story whole in *The Four Georges.*

One can believe the impossible, but not the improbable. I feel it utterly improbable that Boswell, whatever his follies when drunk, could be taken in when sober by such a Fourth Form jape; for though his Latin was never up to Honours standard he would certainly be at once capable of translating *Quare adhaesit pavimento,* even if no prosaic Lancaster attorney did so for his clerk's benefit, and perceiving its point. I do not doubt that the bright young sparks of Boswell's mess would seize any opportunity to make a butt of one who was their elder and superior in so many ways as a man of the world, a travelled man, an habitué of the best intellectual London society, a laird of ancient family, an intimate of Dr. Johnson, an acquaintance of Voltaire and Rousseau, a successful man of letters, and so forth, and I do not doubt that Boswell's sociable nature and fondness for the bottle gave them more chances than one. But I decline with oaths to believe that they could have led Boswell to make such a public exhibition of himself in his sober hours as Eldon's story asserts.

One turns for light to Boswell's Lancaster diary. There is an entry halfway down the page for Thursday, April 6:

Last night a feigned Brief had been left at my lodgings.

After that the page is blank, and the entries are not resumed for some little time. Unless pages are missing, this tantalising silence might certainly seem to indicate that something ignominious happened, more or less as Eldon describes. However, on looking at the entry for the previous night, April 5, when Boswell was supposed to be helplessly drunk, we find that having dined 'moderately' in mess he went afterwards to the Assembly Rooms, where he played whist and drank tea with the fashionables of Lancaster and was 'quite gay', and plainly sober. He may of course have got drunk after that, but as Eldon and his colleagues would have been at supper long before the Assembly ended, it seems unlikely that they could have found him on the pavement

on their way, as Eldon says; had they found him after supper
there might be something in it. I am apt to believe that at the
age of 73 Eldon's memory may have deceived him, and that a
Northern Circuit mess-legend of his youth may have assumed an
undue tinge of actuality in his aged mind.

In May Boswell returned to London to the King's Bench and
to those growing forebodings for the future which even a revival
of *The Beggar's Opera*, which he so constantly loved for its
containing 'so much of real London life, so much brilliant wit,
and such a variety of airs which, from early association of ideas,
engage, soothe, and enliven the mind', could not banish for
many hours. There is a poignant entry in his diary at the beginning of July, recording how he quitted the Courts at the end
of the day in blank, dazed misery and wandered about the City
half distracted, thinking of 'my dear wife and children', with
tears streaming down his face, and how he finally found himself
in the wilds of Aldgate, where he took a cheerless meal of tea
and dry buttered toast at a coffee-house and returned west to
grapple with his despair. Paoli, whose guest he was in Portman
Square, heard his groans with the usual sympathetic kindness,
and advised him with strong common sense. 'You are past the
age of ambition', said the General. 'You should determine to be
happy with your wife and children.' But next day or the day
after buoyancy returned, and cheered by 'an enchanting letter
from my wife', Boswell determined to stay in London. He at
once took a house in Great Queen Street, Lincoln's Inn Fields—
No. 56, demolished in 1915—and having written to his wife to
make preparations for coming south, moved into half-furnished,
rat-haunted apartments on a memorable week-end, July 9-11, and
began at last to tackle the *Life of Johnson* in desperate earnest,
living for three days on tea and toast.

His friends rallied round him with encouragement in this
mighty resolve. He dined frequently with Malone and Reynolds;
also with Wilkes in Kensington, where what one might almost
be excused for calling a choice repast, including turtle-soup,
venison, fruits, ices, champagne, and half a dozen other wines,
demonstrated that the best of everything was still good enough
for jovial Mr. Wilkes, as his many creditors agreed. This summer,

moreover, Boswell experienced an agreeable surprise. Lord Lonsdale had evidently been informed of the fanfare saluting him in the *Letter to the People of Scotland* of the previous year. His lordship's attention may also have been drawn to a discreet footnote in that recent literary success, the *Journal of a Tour to the Hebrides,* in which Mr. Boswell mentioned, apropos the ancient Lowther family, that 'a due mixture of severity and kindness, economy and munificence, characterises its present Representative'. Whatever Lonsdale's reason—curiosity most of all, belike, for in the world of hate in which he moved tributes of any sort were notably rare—he sent Boswell a note in July asking him to dinner; an invitation, or rather command, from which Boswell was forced by all the social conventions to excuse himself, since he and Lonsdale had never met. But his diary whoops and dances in boyish glee. 'The great Lowther has taken me up! I may be raised to eminence in the State!' The recurring mirage of political ambition, lately flickering rather dimly on his horizon, has suddenly flamed up, bright, hot, and near, and the indefatigable hunter of dreams springs up ardent as ever.

He needed a little stimulation to his self-esteem at the moment, perhaps. Despite the gratifying success of the Hebrides Journal, this year 1786 had dealt him a blow which hurt. In March was published *Anecdotes of the late Samuel Johnson,* by Mrs. Thrale, now Mrs. Piozzi, which contained at least one spiteful allusion to himself, amid a plethora of commas.

A trick, which I have seen played on common occasions, of sitting steadily down at the other end of the room, to write at the moment what should be said in company, either by Dr. Johnson or to him, I never practised myself, nor approved of in another. There is something so ill-bred, and so inclining to treachery in this conduct, that were it commonly adopted, all confidence would soon be exiled from society.

Almost equally catty was Mrs. Thrale's rendering of a conversation of July 1773 in which Johnson playfully discussed with her his future biographer. Mrs. Thrale's instant suggestion of Goldsmith the Doctor rejected on account of 'the dog's particular malice towards me, and general disregard for truth'. The unlikely Dr. Taylor of Ashbourne, the even more unlikely Dr. James (of

James's Fever Powder), and 'Jack Hawkesworth' were then vaguely canvassed, and the Doctor brushed the topic away with the pronouncement that either Mrs. Thrale should write his life, with Taylor's help, or that he would outlive them all and write it himself. The name of James Boswell is not mentioned by Mrs. Thrale at all. I do not doubt for a moment that it was suppressed deliberately, as a counterblast to Johnson's tacit approval of Boswell's biographical intentions, as displayed in the recently-published *Tour to the Hebrides*. Mrs. Thrale had strong feminine prejudices, and Boswell very nearly topped her black-list.

Apart from all else, Mrs. Thrale-Piozzi had so manipulated her presentation of the Doctor in general that Boswell confided to his diary, in a spasm of bitterness, that her picture of Johnson fawning on the Thrales and sacrificing his friends to the rich fleshpots of Streatham Place 'cooled my warmth of enthusiasm for my illustrious Friend'. But this mood was soon over. Mrs. Thrale's inaccuracies and bias were all too evident. Boswell promptly pointed out in *The Gazetteer* a few of 'the lively Lady's' mishandlings of fact, as he did later in the *Life*. Horace Walpole characteristically damned her book as a heap of rubbish, and the satiric Peter Pindar (Dr. Wolcot) proceeded to take both 'Bozzy' and 'Piozzi' to pieces in a long and ill-natured *Town Eclogue*, which first pillories the alleged rivals—

> At length rush'd forth two candidates for Fame,
> A Scotchman one, and one a London Dame,
> *That*, by th' emphatick Johnson christen'd *Bozzy*,
> *This*, by the Bishop's license, Dame *Piozzi*,
> Whose widow'd name, by topers lov'd, was *Thrale*,
> Bright in the annals of Election Ale . . .

—then makes them attack each other:

### Madam Piozzi

> Who told of Mistress Montague the lie—
> So palpable a falsehood? Bozzy—fie!

### Bozzy

> Who would have said a word about *Sam's* wig,
> Or told the story of the Peas and Pig?
> Who would have told the tale, so very flat,
> Of *Frank*, the Black, and *Hodge*, the mangy Cat?

MADAM PIOZZI

I'm sure you've mentioned many a pretty story
Not much redounding to the Doctor's glory;
Now for a *saint* upon us you would palm him,
First *murder* the poor man, and then *embalm* him!

And so forth, growing more and more shrill and personal, till
Mrs. Thrale gets the last word.

I suffer only—if I'm in the wrong,
So now, you prating Puppy, hold your tongue!

Homespun satire enough, and it did not prevent the *Anecdotes*
from capturing the town. The first edition sold out on the day
of publication, and George III himself had to go without a copy.
One can see Boswell gritting his teeth as he turns afresh to his
growing pile of manuscript, yet not too cast down. He had on
the stocks what he knew, in his calmer moments, to be a masterpiece which would dispose of Mrs. Thrale's chatter very easily.
Meanwhile here was Lowther, evidently interested. And had
not Burke said to him, Boswell, in 1781, 'We must do something
for you, for our own sakes'? Nothing had come of it so far. The
genial Burke had smiled and nodded and passed on, and, after
recommending Boswell to General Conway, let the matter fade
from his mind; but politicians were notoriously abstracted, and
could always be reminded. Then again there was Pitt, who had
been so kind over the *Letter* of 1784; and Dundas, who had
praised it, had said something in the same year about supporting
a candidature. Yes, the future was certainly brightening, despite
his failure so far at the English Bar. For Lonsdale, who had
launched the younger Pitt, wielded terrific power, and Lonsdale
had his eye on him.

He went up to Scotland in September to collect Mrs. Boswell
and the family. On Wednesday, September 20, the Boswells,
seven of them, left Auchinleck with Mrs. Bruce, the housekeeper,
in two postchaises, and, travelling by easy stages, arrived in
Great Queen Street five days later. And one afternoon towards
the end of November, as he was drinking tea with his friend
Charles Dilly in the Poultry, his man-servant arrived from
Great Queen Street with an urgent message. Lord Lonsdale was

desirous to get into touch with Mr. Boswell. Would Mr. Boswell please call at Grosvenor Square at his earliest convenience? O happy day! In a flutter of excitement Boswell hastened in a hackney-coach to Lonsdale's town house, to be received by Mr. Garforth, his agent, and to be invited to act as counsel at the Carlisle election, which Lonsdale was directing a week hence. Accepting eagerly, Boswell sped in high spirits to tell the news to Malone. The GREAT LOWTHER—his diary breaks into hurraying capitals—had taken him up at last.

There is no record of his performance during this election. He was quite capable of putting up a good one. His legal duties lasted a week, and he returned to London in a glow of content.

### 3

There is a quaint entry in Boswell's diary under the date Monday, April 23, 1787:

> 'Only water. Some *Life*.'

It indicates how steadfastly he was buckling down to the great work this spring, despite the new temptation to lose himself in political dreams. Naturally the water-diet is not a constant; but he is sticking more or less steadily to his writing, in his spare time from the Courts, with Malone at his elbow to assist and encourage him. Even in the Courts his luck is turning. On May 26 he got his first brief as junior in an action of trover, through a servant of Paoli's.[1] It is true that no fee was attached, and true also that because the attorney on his side forgot to warn him when the case was coming on in the King's Bench he was not there, greatly to the annoyance of his leader; but still, it was a beginning. Meanwhile he was making progress with the *Life*, and had so little time for correspondence that even Temple only got one letter this year, it would seem; a very short one, written in January, and chiefly interesting because having been in the Courts all morning, Boswell says, he is dining at Sir Joshua Reynolds's at four with the Poet Laureate. The Laureate in 1787 was the Rev. Dr. Thomas Warton, Johnson's friend, that stout

---

[1] *Trover*, n. (legal). Action to recover value of goods wrongfully taken or detained. (Fr. *trouver*, find.)—Oxford Dictionary.

little husky, redfaced, cheerful don of Trinity (Oxon.) who loved beer, tobacco, tavern-suppers, and 'the Gothick', and whose *Pleasures of Melancholy* are well known to poetry-lovers; though I believe some modern connoisseurs prefer his Ode on the marriage of George III, with its graceful tribute to our most prolific sovereign:

> While chiefs, like GEORGE, approv'd in worth alone,
> Unlock'd chaste Beauty's adamantine zone . . .

If Boswell needed any literary spur this year the booksellers, or as we should say nowadays, the publishers of London supplied it, when *The Life of Samuel Johnson, LL.D.*, by Sir John Hawkins, Kt., came out and sold two editions with some success. Fifty members of the London book trade had jointly jumped the claim of Boswell and Dilly and commissioned Hawkins to write a 'definitive' or 'official' biography of the Doctor, after approaching Dr. Percy and Sir William Scott in vain. A jolt for Boswell, undoubtedly, though he was expecting something of the sort. Hawkins, a foundation-member of the Literary Club and, as we have noted, one of Johnson's executors, with immediate access to those of his private papers remaining from the Doctor's bonfires, was an obvious choice for Dilly's trade-rivals.

Reading Hawkins's book today, one perceives that Boswell had little to worry over. The most charitable adjective for Hawkins's *Life* is 'worthy'. The pompous, priggish lawyer-musician (his huge five-volume *History of the Science and Practice of Music* is, or was, a standard work) admired Johnson but lacked the 'Johnsonian æther', and did not know how to use his material. His *Life* is flat-footed, square-toed, jog-trot, and tangential, and as Boswell, whom he so heavily snubbed, takes leave to remark accurately in the introduction to his own *Life*, 'a very small part of it relates to the person who is the subject of the book'. A reasonable amount of irrelevancy in biography is no crime, as we discern from the work of the master himself. Hawkins's perpetual asides are mostly neither illuminating nor amusing. At rare intervals in his 600 pages he produces a good anecdote, or some drily-attractive phrase such as 'Cave had no great relish for mirth, but he could bear it', and 'How comes it else to pass that no sooner is a playhouse opened than it becomes surrounded by a halo of brothels?' I would give him decent credit also for a remark on Johnson's 'unmanly relish' for tea. But for the most part he is a plodder and a pedant.

Nevertheless Hawkins's *Life of Johnson* cannot be dismissed entirely. If he reveals little of the essential Johnson, he gives us two scenes, one festive, one macabre, which are not too far from the Boswell mark: the account of the decorous all-night orgy at the Devil Tavern in 1750 in honour of Mrs. Charlotte Lenox, when Johnson's face at 5 a.m. shone with 'meridian splendour', and that grim final glimpse of the old dying man snatching lancet and scissors and stabbing at his dropsical legs under the bedclothes, to relieve his tortured breathing. Hawkins is right, moreover, in his criticism of the Doctor's dilatoriness over his will and that 'ill-directed benevolence' which resulted in spoiling a thankless and selfish Negro with a bequest of little short of £1,500 and stinting one or two needy relatives of their due.

On the subject of Frank Barber, Johnson's Negro servant, Hawkins, who disliked him intensely, incidentally raises a question countless Johnsonians have asked themselves. What were the precise duties of this Jamaican, whom Johnson had acquired from Dr. Bathurst, whose father had brought him to England? Butler? Footman? Valet? Handyman? Hawkins gives it up.

Diogenes himself never wanted a servant less than he [Johnson] seemed to do; the great bushy wig, which throughout his life he affected to wear, by that closeness of texture which it had contracted and been suffered to retain, was ever nearly as impenetrable by a comb as a quickset hedge; and little of the dust that had once settled on his outer garments was ever known to have been disturbed by the brush. In short, his garb and the whole of his external appearance was, not to say negligent, but slovenly, and even squalid; to all which, and the necessary consequences of it, he appeared as insensible as if he had been nurtured at the Cape of Good Hope.

Once and once only in Boswell's *Life* do we catch a glimpse of Johnson's Negro engaged in any kind of domestic service, apart from opening the door. It is on the great day of the Wilkes dinner, when Johnson, belatedly about to dress, roars 'Frank, a clean shirt!' Barber was therefore a kind of valet-parlourman, it would seem. Boswell's uniformly suave politeness in print towards 'Mr. Frank Barber' may seem a little strange, but there is perhaps a good reason why Boswell criticises neither the Negro nor Johnson's double spoiling of him—in life, by spending nearly £300 in an attempt to have him taught Greek and Latin,[1] and in death, by pampering him in his will. The reason, I think, might be detected in the fact that it was necessary to obtain Mr. Frank Barber's permission to borrow some of Johnson's papers from Sir John Hawkins. Mr. Barber was to be *ménagé*.

One can forgive Hawkins more readily for going off at a tangent to discuss Frank Barber than some of his other expeditions. But one is bound to agree that his full-length sketch of Lord Chesterfield, something of a cad, is admirable, and his account of the poet Dyer's blossoming 'with sober and temperate deliberation' from nonconformity into the gay life, exactly like one or two Yellow Book figures of the 1890's, has undoubtedly, as Henry James said of the fashionable actress, a certain cadaverous charm. What is difficult to forgive in Hawkins is his making no attempt to display the Doctor's personality, apart from harping overmuch on his hypochondria, still less to reproduce that splendid vigorous talk which Boswell does so brilliantly. As for his one and only reference (in the account of the Hebrides journey) to 'Mr. Boswell, a native of Scotland', that was soon to be avenged, for who reads Hawkins now?

The rival biographers knew each other slightly at this time and did not much care for each other. Hawkins's book stirred Boswell's indignation at its 'dark uncharitable cast'. Stung in addition by the deliberate slight on himself, he called on Hawkins to protest.

'Surely, surely, Mr. *James* Boswell?'

Hawkins's saturnine features relaxed a trifle.

'I know what you mean, Mr. Boswell; you would have had me say that Johnson undertook this tour with *The* Boswell?'

A palpable hit, to which no reply is recorded.[2]

---

[1] For which extravagance, Hawkins says, blind old Mrs. Williams often bullied the Doctor when complaining of Barber's misdeeds. 'This is your scholar!—your philosopher!—upon whom you have spent so many hundred pounds!' The Negro himself seems to have accepted all Johnson's kindness as his due.

[2] Anecdote by Miss Hawkins, the climax unconfirmed by Boswell's diary. The slight still rankled in 1789, when Boswell complained to Temple of

4

In August this year Boswell took his wife and twelve-year-old Sandie up to Auchinleck for a change of air, returning to London with them in September. In November he asked the omnipotent Dundas to dinner with Reynolds, Langton, Malone, and Sir John Dick, and Dundas came, and was 'frank and good-humoured'; well aware, it seems, of the question in his host's eye, and breezily determined to ignore it. It may have been due in some degree to undercurrents at this dinner that Boswell, restless and deeming the time ripe for some kind of self-assertion somewhere, boldly applied to 'the great Lowther' on December 1 for the vacant Recordership of Carlisle. Making a considerable favour of it (Lord Darlington was one of a crowd of applicants, he assured Boswell), Lonsdale gave it him a month later. A pleasant omen indeed, and unexpected. Had Boswell any idea of the nature of the man into whose hands he was delivering himself?

Georgian velvet, bag-wig, sword, blue riband, and star fail somehow to express the essential ego of Sir James Lowther, Bt., created first Earl of Lonsdale in 1784. His proper costume, one feels, is the stiff cloth-of-gold dalmatic of Basil II, *Bulgaroktonos,* the Bulgar-Slayer of Byzantium, or the silk robes and turban of Sulieman the Magnificent, or the bejewelled caftan and red morocco kneeboots of Ivan the Terrible; for even in appearance Lonsdale was a perfect Oriental despot born out of his true sphere. To that 'swarthy, Turk-like stateliness' of Boswell's first impression he added qualities which Smollett's friend, Dr. Alexander Carlyle of Inveresk, summed up in a well-known comminatory phrase: 'More detested than any man alive as a shameless political sharper, a domestic Bashaw, and an intolerable tyrant over his tenants.'

Political sharpers were not rare in the England of the Magnates, where out of 513 members of Parliament in a given

---

Hawkins's malevolence. '*Observe how he talks of me as quite unknown.*' Nevertheless we find Hawkins at two 'little parties for cards and music' given by the Boswell girls in 1791, and Boswell and he continued to meet at intervals, not unamicably.

year 307 owed their seats to patrons; [1] where seats were bought and sold for cash like hats, or peerages under a modern Liberal Government; where the Treasury itself was in the market, and Prime Minister Lord North, needing three Cornish seats in the general election of 1774, had to pay Lord Falmouth 7,500 guineas for them; where Old Sarum was not a proverb, and the political patron was a recognised caste. Domestic bashaws were likewise not unknown, nor tyrants over their tenantry. But no potentate in Georgian England coming under any of these three heads seems to have cracked the whip with the insolence of Lonsdale. If this temperamental bully (or 'humourist', as Boswell calls him, in the quaint eighteenth-century argot) did not have offending serfs knouted or bowstrung when the spirit moved, he was restrained by nothing but the absurdities of British law, and his towns of Whitehaven and Penrith went in terror of him. At Cambridge he had belonged to 'The Bucks', a gang of gold-tufted Mohocks whose pleasures when in liquor were to break into shops, stand passing women on their heads, and run amuck generally, against a background of low-bowing donnish backs. Lonsdale carried the same zest into public life, enjoying the fear and hatred which surrounded him. In the north, where he exercised despotic rule and defied his creditors from Whitehaven Castle and Lowther, his writs took precedence of George III's. His wealth was considerable, his ferocity a byword, and his power aptly conveyed in four lines by Peter Pindar:

> . . . even by the elements confess'd
> Of mines and boroughs LONSDALE stands possess'd,
> And one sad servitude alike denotes
> The slave that labours and the slave that votes.

Politically he could defy competition anywhere north of York. Among a profusion of other jobberies he had nine Parliamentary boroughs in his pocket, the holders being known in the Commons as 'Lonsdale's Ninepins', and the younger Pitt, whom he launched on his career by putting him in for Appleby in 1781, naturally had lifelong obligations to him. Lonsdale in fact ex-

[1] Figures quoted by Grey and Mackintosh in the Reform Petition of 1793. Of these 307 nominees, some of whom had never seen a constituent, 157 belonged, like their seats, to 84 patrons.

ercised, to quote Lord Rosebery, 'a sway which we can now hardly measure or imagine. In 1782 he had offered to build and equip at his own expense a vessel of war with 70 guns.[1] Boswell and Wilberforce have borne almost trembling testimony to the splendour of his Court, tempered by extreme awe, and which northern politicians haunted like a northern St. James's.'[2] A British newspaper baron of the 1940's, controlling and dictating every day in the year the thoughts and passions and impulses of some two or three million of the compulsorily-educated halfbaked, could probably raise an eyebrow at Rosebery's concept of absolute power. Lonsdale's age at any rate admitted it, admired, and trembled. It was this tiger into whose jaws James Boswell was now inserting his thoughtless head.

He was not to fall foul of the dictator yet awhile, for Lonsdale was undoubtedly attracted and amused by this vivacious new plaything. The recordership of Carlisle meanwhile enabled Boswell to preen himself with great satisfaction. It gave him a recognised position in the Lonsdale entourage, and was plainly a stepping-stone. The duties of a recorder in England somewhat resemble those of a *corregidor* in seventeenth-century Spain, without the tall ebony cane, the plumage, and the horsemanship. He is the principal legal officer of his borough or city and the sole judge at the sessions he summons quarterly, also deciding appeals from the local justices. Today a recordership is a Crown appointment, and the holder, who must have had at least five years' experience at the Bar, is generally a 'silk'. In the 1780's there was less fuss, and at Carlisle, at least, the office was almost honorary, as I deduce from the salary of £20 a year attached to it. Boswell's receipts are not recorded in the Corporation archives. It would seem that his salary was paid by Lonsdale's household treasurer. Except for sessions and election duties he could continue to live in London.

Is it difficult to see James Boswell enveloped in the majesty of the Law, administering justice *solus* with gravity and decorum? In the absence of any evidence to the contrary in the

---

[1] Costing—hull, masts, and rigging alone—some £50,000.
[2] *Pitt,* 1891. I cannot find any 'almost trembling testimony' by Boswell to Lonsdale's Court, though he certainly viewed Lonsdale for some time as a portent.

Carlisle archives it would seem that he carried out his duties, during his brief term of office, with entire satisfaction; and why not? He was not unused to making decisions, and his light acquaintance with the law need not hamper him to any extent, since he had efficient prompters on the bench below. I can see him enjoying his new role mightily to begin with, the very pearl and phoenix of Recorders, starched and stately, following the evidence with pursed lips and sphinxlike immobility, delivering judgment in ripe forensic periods, tempering severity with that kindness of his, and, after the day's work, unbending with his peers over a bottle of claret in the judges' parlour with his usual vivacity.

The only trace preserved in his private papers of the manner in which he carried out his duties is the greater part of his address to the grand jury at the Michaelmas Sessions, 1789; a dignified allocution, congratulating the city of Carlisle on the fact that the grand jury had a blank calendar before it, congratulating the country on the 'excellent Government under which we live', indulging in a little politico-historical reminiscence, and reminding the grand jurymen that to fear God and honour the King is the duty of every trueborn Briton. It is an address showing Mr. Boswell once more to be a stout champion of law and order, throne and altar, and it can have done him no harm in exalted circles.

Domestic troubles meanwhile were increasing. London plainly did not suit Mrs. Boswell, who was now approaching the final stages of consumption, and her condition made her husband's work very difficult. In February 1788, asserting to Temple that 'I am absolutely certain my mode of biography is the most perfect than can be conceived, and will be more of a Life than any work that has ever yet appeared', Boswell adds:

I have been wretchedly dissipated, so that I have not written a line for a fortnight; but to-day I resume my pen, and shall labour vigorously. I am now in strong, steady spirits, which make me confident, instead of being in despondency. Oh, my friend, what can be the reason of such depression as we often suffer? I am very, very uneasy, on account of the state of my affairs. When you come we will consult.

With a postscript:

My wife is, I thank God, much better; but is it not cruel to keep her in this pernicious air, when she might be so much better at Auchinleck?

Margaret Boswell was indeed a very sick woman. Nearly eighty years were to pass before English physicians became aware of the properties of Davos-Platz and the other Swiss sanatoria, yet one would have thought any doctor would have ordered her long since out of the smoky and insalubrious precincts of what is now Great Queen Street, Kingsway. In Boswell's diary we hear her continual hollow cough, and see the pain and worry on her husband's face as he toils at his manuscript in the next room. Perhaps her doctor was not to blame entirely. The native stubbornness of Margaret Boswell and a determination to keep an eye on her volatile mate had more than a little to do with her staying in London, I think. Nor did she suffer his vagaries in silence. Ill as she was, she was able to give Mr. Boswell a tall dressing-down at the end of this February. Only the main heads of this curtain-lecture are set down in his diary, with rueful precision; it must have lasted some time, and is extremely thorough. It touches on Mr. Boswell's dissipated ways and recent shocking idleness, though the *Life* he is neglecting seems to be his chief financial asset; Mr. Boswell's friends, who are undoubtedly fewer (*sic*) than in the old days, for people always shun a man in difficulties; his lack of money and increasing debts; the increasing expense of his family; and the increasing folly—had Paoli seen her lately?—of trying to live a London life when your estate and duty lie in Scotland. To such a tirade from such a typical Scots mother and housewife, Boswell's reply, if any, is not recorded. He might have defended himself to some extent, perhaps, by admitting that what was chiefly driving him to the bottle nowadays was his gnawing anxiety and increasing dread on her account. Perhaps he said nothing. He may even have succeeded in making her laugh, which would be much better. They were very fond of each other.

On May 15 he took her back to Auchinleck with Euphemia and the infant Betsy, a recent addition to the family, and having stayed there till July, left to go on the Northern Circuit again;

a dreary but inevitable engagement which meant dropping the *Life* for some weeks.

His diary is not being kept day by day at this time but summarised briefly over a period. Otherwise we should have been afforded, no doubt, some interesting lights on the opening day of the Warren Hastings trial at Westminster Hall, February 13, and perhaps some corrective to Macaulay's rhetoric. Boswell managed to get into this tremendous theatrico-legal show, for which seats were selling at fifty guineas apiece, through the influence of his friend John Courtenay, M.P. for Tadworth, who took him into 'the Managers' Box'. His hasty diary-note makes no comment on the proceedings, and five days later, when he attended again, he mentions merely that Burke spoke astonishingly well. He was passionately on Hastings' side, and even when Courtenay later revealed to him something of conditions in British India, which shocked him considerably, he had no doubt that his idol could give good reasons for his conduct, including his acceptance of that £100,000 present from the Nabob of Oude. From this time dates a temporary coolness with Burke, Hastings' relentless prosecutor. The relations between Burke and Boswell as a whole we may examine later. Before passing on I cannot help quoting one of the great man's *mots*, uttered this year at a dinner at Malone's and preserved by Boswell, one feels, as a warning. Finding himself seated near a ham, Burke remarked jovially, apropos of nothing, 'I am Ham-Burke (Hamburg).'[1]

After Boswell's return from the Northern Circuit the rest of the year is chiefly notable for feverish application to the *Life*. He was also trying to find a better house to live and work in, having somehow overcome his wife's objections on the London question. In January 1789 he tells Temple he has at length succeeded.

It is incredible what difficulty I found, in several weeks' wandering, to find a house that would answer; at last I fixed on one at £50, in Queen Anne Street West, Cavendish Square, very small but neat. It however would not accommodate the whole of my family, even with tolerable conveniency, but would serve as a sort of camp-lodging

[1] 'No, Sir; I never heard Burke make a good joke in my life.'—Johnson to Boswell, *Journal of a Tour to the Hebrides*.

till better could be found. In winter, the upholsterers and brokers take numbers of houses and furnish them with old trash, and by letting them furnished get great profits.

Evidently the Londons of George III and George VI are not so totally dissimilar as we often think. Apart from finding a house at what would nowadays be about £250 a year, Boswell has to find himself chambers, and here one of his principal current worries comes again to the fore.

I am in a most *illegal* situation, and for appearance should have cheap chambers in the Temple, as to which I am still inquiring. But in truth I am sadly discouraged by having no practice, nor probable prospect of it.

He confesses to Temple that lack, already mentioned, of mastery of the 'quirks and quiddities' of the Law which often makes him afraid of exposing his ignorance; yet the delusion of Westminster Hall, of brilliant reputation and splendid fortune as a barrister, still weighs on my imagination. I must be seen in the Courts, and must hope for some happy openings in causes of importance.' So dreams and illusions rule him still. He goes on:

Could I be satisfied with being Baron of Auchinleck, with a good income for a gentleman in Scotland, I might, no doubt, be independent. But what can be done to deaden the ambition which has ever raged in my veins like a fever? In the country I should sink into wretched gloom, or at best into listless and sordid abstraction.

Which has moved a modern authority to remark that 'the mental health of this unfortunate man depended on a fiction that was hardly plausible'; though why the very normal and reasonable fear of degenerating into a turnip by being forced to live in a remote northern countryside, even on a sufficient income, should provoke such contemptuous pity I cannot conceive. Better-balanced men than Boswell have recoiled from such a prospect. For this cultivated and eager fellow, whose true spiritual home was London, relegation to the backwoods merely meant relapsing into the vegetable state and acute melancholia more speedily than most. Anyhow, he is determined to battle for better things. Lord Chancellor Thurlow, he tells Temple, has not yet come up to the scratch, but he will shortly try him again. Meanwhile he is very near the end of the rough draft—the work 'without nice correction'—of Johnson's *Life*, and has just completed the Introduction and Dedication to Sir Joshua Reynolds, a difficult task well done. When the rough draft is ready, he and Malone will begin preparing the first half for the press. And that political business is warming up as well. Boswell has been discreetly canvassing his chances during his late visit to Auchinleck, and sees a chance of slipping into a Parliamentary seat for Ayrshire if the rather involved manœuvres of the local Whig and Tory machines give him power to 'cast the balance', as they look like doing. Pitt, he complains, is neglectful, and Dundas a sad fellow; yet if all else fails there is still a nearer possibility. 'Should Lord Lonsdale give me a seat he would do well, but I have no claim upon him for it'. As a matter of fact three of Lonsdale's string of M.P.s, one of them Colonel Lowther, the great man's brother, had recently assured Boswell that a seat at the next election was almost certain. It may have been after supper. It may even have been a joke.

He can therefore afford to be a little scornful of Pitt. Does that reference to Pitt's neglect sound like typical Boswellian fanfaronnade? Apart from annoyance at Pitt's ignoring one or two polite hints at an interview, Boswell had some backing, apparently, for the belief that Pitt should already have done something for him. Fantastic as it sounds, he tells Temple that 'the excellent Langton' recently called it disgraceful and utter folly in Pitt not to reward and attach to his administration 'a man of my popular and pleasant talents, whose merits he has acknowledged in a letter under his own hand' (this was the formal acknowledgment of Boswell's India Bill pamphlet of 1784). Nobody has been able to explain this astonishing remark of Bennet Langton's. He was too grave, good, and sober a man to have been under the influence of drink when he uttered it, and he could hardly be accused of flightiness or a desire to jape; that one nocturnal frolic with Beauclerk and Johnson at Covent Garden many years ago seems to have been the one and only burst of frivolity of a lifetime. Either, then, Langton was being ironic, which is likewise utterly foreign to his character, or he meant it; and since he meant it, his view of Boswell must have been unique in London.

Here I pause to reflect sympathetically that there was one notable man at least whose high opinion of Boswell seems to have embraced his political genius at this period as well. The tribute occurs in a communication this year to Boswell's second cousin and agent, Bruce Campbell of Milrig, from none other than the admired poet, Mr. Robert Burns. The letter, ardent in its pride at 'the honor of drawing my first breath almost in the same parish with Mr. Boswell' and hinting at an introduction, encloses a set of verses by the poet, his junior by twenty years. They have to do with a political garden-party attended by the three Parliamentary 'propects' for Ayrshire the previous summer. Addicts of Burns's verse will recognise *The Fête-Champêtre* as one of his less breath-taking compositions. It helps to demonstrate nevertheless Boswell's prestige in his own countryside in this year 1788. Reviewing the candidates, the poet cries:

> Or will we send a man o' law?
> Or will we send a sojer?
> Or him wha led o'er Scotlan' a'
> The muckle Ursa Major?

Though Boswell, to whom Campbell of Milrig passed on the covering letter, endorsed it '*Mr. Robert Burns, the Poet, expressing very high sentiments of me*', and filed it away with his private papers, he did not return Burns's admiration and nowhere, so far as I can discover, mentions him or his works. Nor, apparently, did Ayrshire's two most eminent sons ever meet. This is not too difficult to comprehend from Boswell's standpoint. There was nothing the polite virtuoso and citizen of Europe detested and avoided more all his life than the raw home-bred product in any form. His letters and diaries record more than one expression of disgust after encountering some uncouth Sawney ('wull ye hae any jeel?') in London. If he ever read Burns's verse the native Doric gave him pain, I imagine. Yet the two might well have taken to each other. They had letters and intelligence and charm in common, they belonged to the same freemasons' club in Edinburgh, and they each had a notable fondness for women and the bottle. If it ever became known in Scotland that Burns admired Boswell so much, the fact might make an excuse for double bumpers henceforth at Burns Nicht gatherings, perhaps. I modestly place the suggestion before the great distilling combines.

5

To summon up a clear picture of James Boswell and his fortunes at the beginning of 1789 the balance-sheet method of Robinson Crusoe might be useful. His assets are the Auchinleck estate, the Great Work, now taking recognisable shape, and the growing, glowing possibility of a Parliamentary career. His debits are a very sick wife, whom he loves and esteems, a dreary daily grind at the Bar—the brief of 1787 has not repeated itself—the growing expense of his family, and a load of debts. For his two young sons, Alexander and James, are now in London to be educated, and their bills at the Soho Academy are already not negligible. A public school will very soon have to be chosen for them; Boswell has in mind Eton or Westminster. His eldest daughter Veronica, now sixteen, is also with him, superintending his household. On February 16 he tells Temple that he is hesitating about going on the Northern Circuit again. It will cost fifty pounds and he will have to endure four weeks of 'rough, unpleasant company'. It will also mean holding up the *Life* and leaving his family.

We know Boswell's feelings for his family; he was strongly attached to all of them. Were his children equally attached to him? There is not much evidence at the moment, apart from a dutiful letter or two. I conjecture they must have regarded him at this time with a teasing, tolerant affection at least. To the eighteenth-century child the spectacle of a male or even female parent the worse for liquor at intervals was normal enough, and however much Boswell drank and wallowed in depression he was a kind and indulgent and good-humoured father, and something more, as we shall perceive in due course. He mentions to Temple about this time, with a wry grimace, that Alexander (Sandie), his eldest, is becoming restive and opposing him, 'and no wonder'. It is the normal obstinacy of a growing boy of spirit towards a parent he may be fond of, but sees through. On the whole, I think, the Boswell children must have been fairly happy, despite their mother's illness and 'Papa's moods'. There is a glimpse in this February letter of the ever-kind Paoli, now in his 66th year, sending his coach for the family, with David Boswell, and entertaining them to dinner in Portman Square on the evening when London was illuminated for George III's recovery from his first illness. An agreeable dinner-party it must have been. One sees the flushed childish faces in the candlelight, the gleaming silver and glass, the dark, smiling, courteous, grizzled General toasting Miss Veronica at his right hand, the voluble Boswell at the other end of the table cracking simple jokes and laughing uproariously, the stolid David sipping his wine, the two small boys in their best velvet and ruffles kicking each other under the mahogany and eating enormously. Zoffany should have painted the scene.

*Tout passe.* On March 5 Boswell is writing to Temple in great distress. Margaret Boswell is worse, and he is making ready to set out for Auchinleck at once, if necessary. 'It vexes me to think I should appear neglectful of so valuable and affectionate a wife and mother, by being here; but God knows how sincerely and tenderly I regard her.' He blames himself for being so far away, but what else could he have done, with the *Life* to finish and the prospect of a capital prize out of 'the great wheel of the Metropolis' before long? And the old refrain appears again. 'I must acknowledge that owing to the melancholy which lurks about me, I am too dissipated and drink too much wine. These circumstances I must refrain, as well as I can.' He has already begged a trusted physician, Dr. Campbell, to call on his wife 'as if on a visit of compliment (for she will not have one to attend her, thinking it of no use)', and to send him a candid report. On March 31 he is in the depths of despair, for the doctor's report, just received, is alarming. His wife herself, though she writes 'My fever still continues, and I waste away daily,' begs him stoically not to leave London yet. But he can bear it no longer, and is to set out for Auchinleck 'the day after tomorrow', he tells Temple, taking Veronica with him. He has to be back in London on May 25 to appear as Recorder of Carlisle in a King's Bench case. He is racked with anxiety, and there are clouds newly rising over his political future as well.

As to myself, Dundas, though he *pledged himself* (as the modern phrase is) to assist me in advancing in promotion, and though he last year assured me, upon his honour, that my letter concerning the Scotch Judges [the *Letter* of 1785, in which, it will be remembered, Boswell had unwisely attacked Dundas] had made no difference; yet, except when I in a manner compelled him to dine with me last winter, has entirely avoided me, and I strongly suspect has given Pitt a prejudice against me.

The letter ends with a typical Boswell inconsequence.

Do you not think that the air of the west of England might do my wife good? But I fear she could not be persuaded to leave Auchinleck. How different are she and I! I was the *great man* (as we used to say) at the late Drawing-Room, in a suit of imperial blue lined with rose-coloured silk, and ornamented with rich gold-wrought buttons. What a motley scene is life!

So while Mrs. Boswell is dying in Scotland, Mr. Boswell is peacocking at Court in his finery? Is this as selfish as it seems? He was striving to climb, after all, for his family's sake as much as his own, and to be seen at Court was essential for one who still hoped to catch the eye of the Ministry. He could answer his conscience sufficiently, I think; though, as with Mr. Edwards the lawyer, cheerfulness must have kept breaking in, despite his worry, amid such a brilliant scene.

He duly set out for Auchinleck on April 2 with Veronica, and found his wife extremely ill, with no hopes of recovery; and black remorse devoured him. He writes to Temple from Lowther on May 22, in a passion of self-accusation after protesting his love and esteem for her.

I can justify my removing to the great sphere of England, upon a principle of laudable ambition; but the frequent scenes of what I must call dissolute conduct are inexcusable, and often and often, when she was very ill in London, I have been indulging in festivity with Sir Joshua Reynolds, Courtenay, Malone, etc., etc., etc., and have come home late and disturbed her repose. Nay, when I was last at Auchinleck, on purpose to soothe and console her, I repeatedly went from home; and both on those occasions, and when neighbours visited me, drank a great deal too much wine.

All this is confirmed in his diaries with groans. At least once his wife got up, ill as she was, to attend to him. The knowledge that she was doomed made nightly solitude in his dreary house unendurable. If his reaction cannot be excused, it may be understood to some extent, perhaps, by those who are themselves imperfect. Moreover Boswell is bound now to attend constantly on his exacting patron. His future depends on it, and his wife has herself elected to take second place to The Career, which is to be a glory to them all; this will be one more burden of remorse on Boswell's shoulders in due course. For the moment his personal shortcomings overwhelm him, and Temple might, and should, have been his confessor as he adds, beating his breast, that only last Saturday, calling on some political grandee in the neighbourhood of Auchinleck, he fell off his horse while riding home in the dark without a servant, and bruised his shoulder severely. Now he is waiting at Lowther till the Earl, with whom he is to travel to London for his King's Bench case, makes up his mind to start.

In his baggage is a congratulatory address to the Prince of Wales on assuming the Regency during George III's recent bout of insanity, composed on behalf of all his colleagues at Carlisle.

This will add something to my *conspicuousness*. Will that word do? As to Pitt, he is an insolent fellow, but so able, that on the whole I must support him . . . What a state is my present!—full of ambition and projects to attain wealth and eminence, yet embarrassed in my circumstances, and depressed with family distress, which at times makes everything in life seem indifferent. I often repeat Johnson's lines in his *Vanity of Human Wishes*:

> 'Shall helpless man, in ignorance sedate,
> Roll darkling down the torrent of his fate?'

And he returns to his gnawing anxiety:

How dismal, how affecting it is to me to see my cousin, my friend, my wife wasting away before my eyes! And the more distressing it is that she is as sensible as ever, so that we cannot see *why* this is. I entreat all the comfort you can give.

Mrs. Boswell died on June 4. On being warned that the end was near, Boswell with his two sons made an express postchaise journey from London, arriving at Auchinleck in 'sixty-four hours and a quarter', too late to see her alive. He pours out his grief to Temple on July 3. His absence from her was not inexcusable; she herself had pressed him to return to London with Lord Lonsdale; yet at the thought that he had not been with her at the end he wept and upbraided himself bitterly. Her death was peaceful. Even now he can hardly realise it.

To see my excellent wife and the mother of my children, that most sensible, lively woman, lying cold and pale and insensible, was very shocking to me. I could not help doubting it was a deception. I could hardly bring myself to agree that the body should be removed, for it was still a consolation to go and kneel by it, and talk to my dear, dear Peggie.

He adds, characteristically, that the funeral was remarkably well attended, with nineteen carriages following the hearse, and 'a large body of horsemen and the tenants of all my lands'; a remark which has uplifted a few cold eyebrows, as if Boswell's satisfaction at the honour paid his dead wife by the county were something ignoble.

He now has to think of the disposal of his family. His second daughter, Euphemia, he tells Temple, will stay in Edinburgh to finish her education. Veronica, the elder, wishes to be boarded with a lady in London. The youthful Betsy will go to a boarding school at Ayr for the time being; he would like to send her to a cheap French or Flemish convent school in a year or two, and finally to 'one of the great English boarding-schools'. Alexander is going to Eton this winter, James will remain at the Soho Academy. Boswell himself is thinking of going the Northern Circuit again, and he has to be on duty at Carlisle at Michaelmas. Amid a whirl of planning and indecision his 'great and patheticl deprivation' torments him more than ever.

He stayed on at Auchinleck some weeks after the funeral—having received a polite note of condolence from Lonsdale inviting him to report at Lowther at his own convenience—to take part in a Parliamentary election to replace Colonel Mont gomerie, retired. Dundas was 'insolently forcing' upon the county a candidate from outside, Sir Adam Fergusson, and Boswell and his two fellow-candidates determinedly but un successfully opposed him. His next immediate obligations were to report at Lowther and join the Northern Circuit at Carlisle. He accordingly set out towards mid-August for Lowther, where the first humiliation at the hands of Lonsdale, or his satellites, awaited him. Writing on August 23 from the Bishop of Carlisle's country house at Rose Hill, he tells Temple that being in great distress of mind and shrinking from 'the rough scene of the roaring, bantering society of lawyers', his first act on arrival was to consult Lonsdale about cutting the Circuit. Lonsdale not unsympathetically advised him to do so, and kept him a few days at Lowther, where there was an unusually large house-party. The Court included the customary buffoons, and it seems that Boswell was their mark. The letter goes on:

A strange accident happened: the house at Lowther was so crowded, that I and two other gentlemen were laid in one room. On Thursday morning my wig was missing; a strict search was made, all in vain. I was obliged to go all day in my nightcap, and absent myself from a party of ladies and gentlemen who went and dined with the Earl on the banks of the lake—a piece of amusement which I was glad to shun, as well as a dance which they had at night. But I was in a ludicrous situation. I suspected a wanton trick, which some people think witty; but I thought it very ill-timed to one in my situation. Next morning the Earl and a Colonel, who I thought might have concealed my wig, declared to me upon honour they did not know where it was; and the conjecture was that a clergyman who was in the room with me, and had packed up his portmanteau in a great hurry to set out in the morning early, might have put it up among his things. This is very improbable; but I could not long remain an object of laughter, so I went twenty-five miles to Carlisle on Friday, and luckily got a wig there fitted for me in a few hours.

This is the kind of simple jest popular among Surtees' fox-hunters, and Boswell doubtless was right in suspecting a play-boy. Eighteenth-century man, with his cropped or shaven head, was as unable to appear in society without his wig as without his breeches. Whether Lonsdale inspired or connived at the theft of Boswell's, it would strike his lordship as a jape of no more social importance than one played on a groom. So poor Boswell, skulking round in his nightcap, humiliated and miserable, was the jest of the entire Court.

However, he got away from Lowther, bought his new wig, and, as the guest of the Bishop of Carlisle, enjoyed a few days' peace.

But alas, my grief preys upon me night and day . . . Though I often and often dreaded this loss, I had no conception how distressing it would be. May God have mercy upon me! I am quite restless and feeble and desponding. I return to Lowther tomorrow for two days, to show that I am not at all in a pet, and then I am to return to Auchinleck for a little time.

He rambles on despondently. He longs to be laid by his wife; life seems unsupportable and he dreads, as well he might in 1789, that Eton may make his son extravagant and vicious. And for once he faces reality with a groan.

Every prospect that I turn my mind's eye upon is dreary. Why should I struggle? I certainly am constitutionally unfit for any employment. The law life in Scotland, amongst vulgar familiarity, would now quite destroy me; I am not able to acquire the law of England. To be in Parliament, unless as an independent Member, would gall my spirit; to live in the country would either harass me by forced exertions or sink me into a gloomy stupor. Let me not think at present, far less resolve. The *Life of Johnson* still keeps me up; I must bring that forth, and then I think I may bury myself in London, in total obscure indifference, and let the savings of my estate accumulate for my family.

And he sends up a desperate prayer for resignation to God's will, relapsing immediately then into fresh longings for his wife's presence.

She used on all occasions to be my comforter; she, methinks, could now suggest rational thoughts to me; but where is she? O, my Temple I am miserable.

Now more than ever, aching for his dead, he needed the invincible philosophy he nearly grasped in 1759; the universal religion which would have revealed to him the tremendous mystical meaning of the phrase 'the Communion of Saints' in the Creed he so often glibly repeated, with so many other practical benefits. He will continue to haunt the Embassy chapel of London frequently till his death, and it is clear that he always had some dim, vague, longing realisation of the majestic drama of the Mass and its significance; but he makes no further attempt to seize the privileges of the Faith he approached thirty years ago. No one can question the sincerity of his intermittent gropings; the pathos of his situation is that he so nearly found the answer.

He stayed another night at Lowther in the ensuing October, with his elder son Sandie, on the way to London and Eton, and found his missing wig. 'The way in which it was lost', he tells Temple grimly, 'will remain as secret as the author of *Junius*'; from which one may deduce that he knew Lonsdale's Mohocks had been toying with him.

On October 15 he took Sandie to Eton, having called on Dr. Jonathan Davies, the Headmaster, a few days before, and, a most agreeable surprise, found himself highly considered by the Fellows, with whom he dined and made a creditable figure. 'I certainly have the art', he remarks delightedly to Temple, 'of making the most of what I have. How should one who has had only a Scotch education be quite at home at Eton? *I had my classical quotations very ready.*'

Sandie's first impressions of his new school were not so pleasant, we shortly observe. Savagery was the keynote of the Public School system at this period, and long afterwards. Diet of the roughest, ritual floggings innumerable, and a recognised bullying-convention warranted to turn tender infants into half-witted trembling wrecks in one month helped to forge Britain's future proconsuls in a manner only comparable to that of a modern Prussian military academy. 'I have scarce observed a boy', said the great Chatham, 'who was not cowed for life at Eton.' Riots were frequent at all the great schools, and vice was, so to speak, not inconspicuous. The vociferous Dr. Davies has not attained the folk-tale celebrity of one of his immediate successors at Eton, Flogger Keate, he of the red face, the stentorian voice, the great cocked hat, and the fearsome brows; yet it may be noted that the terrible Keate was not unpopular. In the memoirs of that gallant Regency buck, Captain Gronow of the Guards, there is a jovial glimpse of Keate as the guest at dinner in Paris of a group of Old Etonians on Wellington's staff, whacking the bottle and crying '*Floreat Etona!*' with the best of them, and merrily swearing he had not flogged them half enough. So the System was evidently accepted by its survivors, and even a sensitive creature like Gray, brooding over the distant prospect of Eton's skyline, utters no word of past sufferings.

> Gay hope is theirs by fancy fed,
> Less pleasing when possest;
> The tear forgot as soon as shed,
> The sunshine of the breast;
> Theirs buxom health, of rosy hue,
> Wild wit, invention ever new,
> And lively cheer, of vigour born;
> The thoughtless day, the easy night,
> The spirits pure, the slumbers light,
> That fly th' approach of morn.

The dreamy, persecuted Shelley was to have equally kindly memories of Eton in after-years.[1] To another eminent Old Etonian, Henry Fielding, the Public Schools as a whole were nothing but the nursery of all evil and the source of all calamity, as we gather from *Joseph Andrews*, and Cowper's reminiscences of Westminster speak of vice, lying, and turbulence. Elderly gentlemen's recollections of the Old School are apt to be tinted either roseate or sable—compare, in a later period, Lord Salisbury's shudders over his Eton days of the 1840's and Kipling's lyrical view of Imperial Service College—and an eighteenth-century parent had very little choice.

With the new burden of Sandie's education, and Jamie's soon to follow, Boswell was becoming worried over money. Calculating to Temple he says: 'I must reckon my children at £100 a year each—£500; after which I reckon I cannot command more than £350.' Plainly the £100 for each child was to cover total annual expenses and not school-fees alone; otherwise Boswell would be spending in modern money about £100 a year more at least on Sandie's schooling than the £300 Eton costs today. One can understand his worrying, in any case. More than ever now he needed those elusive briefs.

[1] Chiefly, perhaps, as he told his old schoolfellow Captain Gronow at Genoa in 1822, of 'the excellent brown bread-and-butter we used to get at Spiers's', and the beautiful Martha, 'the Hebe of Spiers's . . . I loved her to distraction!'

Fortunately he was now forging steadily ahead with the great
ork, with Malone's daily assistance. 'Yesterday afternoon', he
lls Temple on October 14, 'Malone and I revised and made
:ady for the press thirty pages of Johnson's *Life*. He is much
leased with it; but I feel a sad indifference, and he says I
ive not the use of my faculties.' As he adds almost immediately
iat he has drunk far too much wine recently, this is not difficult
► explain. At the same time, we must remember, he was not
)aring himself. The advertisement to the First Edition of the
*ife* tells us something of his labours.

Were I to detail the number of books I have consulted, and the
iquiries which I have found it necessary to make by various channels,
should probably be thought ridiculously ostentatious. Let me only
)serve, as a specimen of my trouble, that I have sometimes been
)liged to run half over London, in order to fix a date correctly.

Running 'half over London' in the year 1789 was a more
:haustung process even than it is in the age of taxicabs, I
iagine. Traffic-regulations were non-existent, and the rate of
:ogress depended entirely on the skill, nerve, and violence of
ie's hackney-coachman. But as the Eighteenth Century did
)t suffer from modern neuroses it is likely that Boswell, sitting
ick while his coachman disentangled himself blasphemously
om a rival charging suddenly out of a side-street, would not go
iddenly into hysterics.[1]

There is a comic story in Fanny Burney's diary of Boswell on
ie war-path a little later, in the winter of 1790. He had been
)wn to Eton to see Sandie, and having business at Windsor on
s way back to town he bethought himself of Miss Burney, now
iduring her gilded servitude as maid of honour to Queen
harlotte. With her usual sub-acid tinkle when referring to Mr.
oswell, whom she never liked, Miss Burney relates how she
iddenly found him accosting her with a bow on her way to
. George's Chapel, and rattling away with hardly a pause.

I am happy to find you, Madam. I was told you were lost!—closed
the unscalable walls of a royal convent! But let me tell you, Madam,

[1] Though London hackney-coachmen often went mad, one of the Bedlam
►ctors told Fuseli, R.A., owing to the constant shaking affecting the pineal
and.

it won't do. You must come forth, Madam! You must abscond from
your princely monastery and come forth. You were not born to be
immured, like a tabby cat, in yon august cell! We want you for the
world! . . . My dear Madam, why do you stay?—it won't do, Madam!
You must resign!—we can put up with it no longer.

By degrees it emerges that the plump, breathless gentleman
with the 'serio-comic face' is in Windsor to get permission to
print Johnson's interview with George III in the Royal Library
in 1767. But Miss Burney herself is not going to escape.

Yes, Madam; you must give me some of your choice little notes of
the Doctor's; we have seen him long enough upon stilts; I want to
show him in a new light! Grave Sam, and great Sam, and solemn Sam
and learned Sam—all these he has appeared over and over. Now I
want to entwine a wreath of graces across his brow; I want to show
him as gay Sam, agreeable Sam, pleasant Sam! . . .

They walked together towards the Queen's Lodge, Boswell's
prattle never ceasing. At the gate he lugged out a bundle of new
proofs and proceeded to declaim choice extracts, with gesticula
tions and imitations—he was, like Garrick and that unnamed
lady of quality Johnson knew who afterwards went mad, an
excellent mimic—of Johnson's own manner. A small crowd
gathered to stare and giggle. Poor little Miss Burney was covered
with shame and confusion. Suddenly the face of her tyrant
Mrs. Schwellenberg, the old, stout, painted harridan who bullied
her Majesty's maids of honour like the Prussian sergeant-major
she may have been, loomed at an upper window, and glancing
round an instant later Miss Burney saw, to her terror, the King
and Queen and their attendants approaching from the Terrace
so Miss Burney fled forthwith. Next morning she perceived
Mr. Boswell in the distance, again on the watch for her, but
managed to evade him. Jane Austen might have invented the
Windsor comedy scene, one feels. Boswell is a perfect replica
in some aspects of Miss Bates in *Emma*. He failed to get much
out of Fanny Burney, who for all her delicate fluttering was no
fool, and was determined to keep her Johnsonian anecdotes for
publication herself.

One more instance of Boswell's nerve and determination at
this period is his descent in April 1788 on Horace Walpole in

Berkeley Square. Walpole, who had snubbed him in Paris twenty years before, did so again. 'Boswell, that quintessence of busybodies', wrote Walpole to Conway, 'called on me last week, and was let in when he should not have been. After tapping many topics, to which I made as dry answers as an unbribed oracle, he vented his errand; "*had I seen Dr. Johnson's Lives of the Poets?*"' Yes, Mr. Walpole had seen the work in question, and was icily furious at Johnson's criticisms of his great friend Gray, about whom Boswell wanted some information. Mr. Walpole, who had been recently looking at Johnson's *Prayers and Meditations*, discussed him a little with his visitor instead. He inclined to despise and pity the Doctor's spiritual anxieties, and thought no man should ever choose to review his own life. '*Genteel, fastidious, and priggish*', noted Boswell accurately in his diary that evening.[1] Like John Scott, Lord Eldon, who with shrinking legal delicacy declined to define taste at Boswell's request 'because I knew he would print it', Mr. Walpole did not talk for publication.

How many other rebuffs and insults, veiled or unveiled, Boswell endured in his quest one cannot tell. Many rich pages of the *Life*, if we did but know, were won at the cost of exhausting hard work and unflinching courage. In November 1789 he wails to Temple wearily: 'You cannot imagine what labour, what perplexity, what vexation I have endured in arranging a prodigious multiplicity of materials, in supplying omissions, in searching for papers buried in different masses, and all this besides the exertion of composing and polishing. Many a time have I thought of giving it up.'

Those who see him at this time as a muzzy and rapidly degenerating sot should read his letters again, perhaps.

He decided to relinquish his house in Queen Anne Street West at the end of 1789, his family being disposed of as we have seen, and to take good chambers in the Inner Temple, 'to have the appearance of a lawyer', he says bitterly. 'O Temple! Temple!

[1] Relating this interview to Miss Mary Berry in 1791, after politely damning the *Life of Johnson*, Walpole puts a more cutting edge on it. Boswell hummed and hawed, and then dropped, "I suppose you know Dr. Johnson does not admire Mr. Gray?" Putting as much contempt as I could into my look and tone, I said, "Dr. Johnson don't!—humph!"—and with that monosyllable ended our interview.'

is this realising any of the towering hopes which have so often been the subject of our conversations and letters?' Yet the mirage flickers on, and hope springs eternal in this artless breast. 'I live much with a great man, who *upon any day that his fancy shall be so inclined*, may obtain for me an office which would make me independent.' The italics are mine. Boswell already has a few illusions less about Lonsdale, evidently. His money worries are certainly no fewer, and moreover Sandie is hating Eton. 'You cannot imagine how miserable he has been; he wrote to me for some time as if from the galleys and intreated me to come to him. I did what was better; I sent his Uncle David, who was firm, and brought me back a good report that there was no reason to pity him.' From which we perceive that Sandie's father is no fool over his children. As for Jamie, the younger son, he wants to go to Eton, like his brother, but Boswell thinks not. Jamie is to go to Westminster, on the advice of Dr. Warren, who has three sons there.

To that, there is the objection of danger to his morals, which, however, is answered by the boys there not being worse than at other schools, and by the first people in the nation continuing to keep their sons there.

Cowper's reminiscences seem to confirm this slightly pessimistic view. Actually Westminster's atmosphere was a little more disciplined and dignified than that of any of its competitors, as befitted Westminster's claim to a more venerable history.[1] So to Westminster eleven-year-old Jamie ('an extraordinary boy... much of his father... quite my companion') will go in the coming year, and will be duly unhappy in his first term, and his

[1] Founded in 1339, 43 years before Winchester and 101 before Eton; but the Abbey monks had had a school since the 8th century. After the final expulsion of the monks Queen Elizabeth founded Westminster School afresh, in the original monastic buildings. The Benedictine line of Westminster has never been extinguished. The last survivor of the Abbey monks, Dom Siegebert Buckley, while in prison in 1607 admitted two priests, Sadler and Mayhew, to the Westminster *familia*, making them heirs to all spiritual rights and thus preserving the succession unbroken to the present day. The lineal descendant-house of Westminster Abbey is now Ampleforth Abbey, York, which has been granted arms by Heralds' College accordingly.

father's heart will be sore for him till he duly gets over it. Boswell himself had by now fallen violently in love with Eton, whose flattering attentions were renewed this winter, when he dined at the Headmaster's house with 'an excellent company' of ladies and gentlemen and greatly enjoyed himself.

Into the inner Boswellian circle this winter—a very social one, though no more so than any other—comes a new and genial figure, discerned at Boswell's dinner-table one evening with Malone, Reynolds, and Flood, the Irish politician. We hear a great deal henceforth of Governor Richard Penn of Pennsylvania, a grandson of the great William, 'a sensible and worthy fellow', an epicurean of jovial and elegant manners, with nothing of the New England sectary about him; what his fellow-countrymen would nowadays call a regular guy. Boswell had recently met Penn, now one of 'Lonsdale's Ninepins,' at their patron's court. On coming down from Cambridge Penn had spent some time idling on the Continent and in London before his uncle Thomas appointed him, in 1771, Lieutenant-Governor of the family preserve, only to supersede him by his brother John two years later. Somewhat aggrieved, for his governorship had been sound and popular, Richard Penn decided, after returning to London in 1775 to lay before the House of Lords that petition from Congress which, as Boswell says, was 'obstinately and unwisely rejected', to live in England henceforth. In 1784 Lord Lonsdale, into whose orbit he had come, made him M.P. for Appleby in succession to Pitt. The amiable Penn loved his bottle, had no political ambitions, endured Lonsdale with equanimity, and continued to sit in Parliament—Appleby, Haslemere, Lancaster, and Haslemere again—till his death in 1811. Boswell and he took to each other greatly, and they will dine and drain many a bumper of claret together during the next four years.

Entertaining is less frequently possible, alas, for Boswell nowadays, as he laments to Temple; but Malone, who is comfortably off—'£800 a year to spend', as Farington, R.A., put it—gives dinners 'without number' over the way in Queen Anne Street East, now Langham Street, and Boswell is always among his guests. He has now decided to keep his house on a little longer, partly because the Inner Temple scheme fell through, partly because living a stone's-throw from Malone is so convenient for the Great Work, now nearly ready for the press. In February 1790 he estimates the number of words already written as 401,600. 'Does this not frighten you?' he asks Temple gaily. The type to be chosen is *pica*, which will make some 800 pages of 'what, I think, will be, without exception, the most entertaining book you ever read.'

This buoyancy continues a week later.

I cannot account for my healthful mind at this time . . . I have no better prospect of gratifying my ambition, or of increasing my fortune. The irreparable loss of my valuable wife, the helpless state of my daughters . . . is still as it was, but my spirits are vigorous and elastic. I dine in a different company almost every day . . . I drink with Lord Lonsdale one day; the next I am quiet in Malone's elegant study revising my Life of Johnson, of which I have high expectations, both as to fame and profit. The Lord Chancellor told me he had read every word of my Hebridean Journal; he could not help it.

Can it be that even the tiger Lonsdale has succumbed to the Boswellian charm? We may observe that he exacts attentions from Boswell like any Roman patron in Horace's satires, and that 'my attendance at Lord Lonsdale's' during November 1789 is one of the reasons the *Life* is not progressing as it should. Boswell had to be regularly present with the rest of the court at Lonsdale's levees when he was in London. His own social gifts explain the private audiences, no doubt; his prattle over the claret would be a refreshing change for the Bashaw. But the aspirant to Parliamentary honours was not to drink wine with his patron much longer.

6

Dinner at Paoli's in Portman Square on Friday, January 8, 1790, brought Boswell an unexpected grief. That evening the kind General he loved and admired, who had helped him so much with counsel and example, and, on at least one occasion, with a substantial money loan, broke to him the news that he was about to return to Corsica almost immediately as Governor under the French Crown. The Christian Garibaldi, the ardent patriot, paladin of liberty, and hero of his countrymen had faced and accepted the inevitable with Latin realism. There was no hope of expelling the French, even had their rule been obnoxious to the islanders, which it was not. In its last agonies the Old Régime was behaving with perfect tact. The National Assembly had recently granted the Corsicans all the rights and privileges of French citizenship. Mirabeau, lately in England, had approached the illustrious exile and begged his powerful co-operation, and Paoli, who loved Corsica next to his God, had consented.

To a romantic creature like Boswell this could not but be a sad anti-climax to a tremendous epic. More depressing still was the prospect of a London without Paoli, Johnson's successor as his spiritual prop and stay.

Since Johnson's death Boswell had leaned on Paoli more, perhaps, than he knew. That calm beneficent noble presence, that strong unwavering Catholic piety, that warm affection and hospitality which had been extended of late years to all the Boswell family, was now to be removed, perhaps for ever. One sees Boswell twirling his wine-glass in the candlelight with a moody frown. A faint sense of personal injury increased his gloom, doubtless. He, Boswell, had done a great deal for Corsica in his time, and what was once-glorious Corsica henceforth but a suburb of France, nevermore to be mentioned in history? A thin, sallow, twenty-one-year-old lieutenant of French artillery named Buonaparte, one of Paoli's many godsons, billeted at Auxonne, may have been thinking the same at this moment. Strange odious things are happening in France, moreover. What a crown for a Paoli to serve, menaced by a set of ruffians—as Boswell expressed it to Temple a little time ago—who are planning to destroy all order, religious and civil, and have just forced their King to abolish all titles of nobility! ... Well, there is no help for it.

On March 22 Boswell gave his farewell dinner for Paoli. His other guests were the Portuguese and Sardinian Ministers, Lord Macartney, Sir Joseph Banks, President of the Royal Society, Cooks' fellow-explorer, and Richard Cosway, R.A. A week later General Pasquale Paoli sailed for Corsica. He and Boswell were not to meet again in this world.

One grievous blow. Another was imminent. One day in May, as Boswell was dining with Lord Lonsdale and his entourage at

Laleham, his patron suddenly became abusive, as often happened; but now, for the first time, the heat was turned on Boswell himself, whom Lonsdale accused of frequenting 'strange company'. Asked what he meant, he mentioned the name of Reynolds; at which Boswell, astonished, and not without dignity, assured his patron that he was extremely proud of Sir Joshua's friendship. Lonsdale abruptly changed the subject, but a flash of lightning had illuminated Boswell's simple mind. He regarded the incident as a warning and privately determined, he says, to try and get away from this man as soon as possible. He had not long to wait for the finale, and the initiative was not to be his. Writing to Temple a month later from the Bush Inn, Carlisle, in utter anguish, Boswell announces that he and Lord Lonsdale have just parted after nearly fighting a duel.

It would seem that Lonsdale had now tired of his plaything and was disposed to smash it. A little time after the incident at Laleham, Colonel Lowther, who seems to have had a liking for Boswell, warned him that Lonsdale had recently remarked to some of his satellites that if he ever put Boswell into Parliament he, Boswell, would only get drunk and talk foolishly. This destroyed Boswell's final illusion. He wrote to Lonsdale asking to be excused from accompanying him to Carlisle on Thursday, June 17, for pending election-business, on the grounds of pressing private affairs. Undoubtedly he was sick at heart; moreover Temple had come to London specially to see him, and he was also desperately anxious to get on with the *Life*. His request gave Lonsdale his opportunity.

Arriving at Grosvenor Square on the morning of the 17th and being kept waiting two hours, Boswell left the house to call on Malone, returning to find Lonsdale at breakfast, attended by a manservant and a dependant named Jackson, and in surly mood. On being admitted to the presence, Boswell began to explain how difficult the journey to Carlisle was for him at the moment. Lonsdale glared and cut him short. 'You have some sinister motive!' He followed this with an insult. 'What have you done for your salary? I suppose you think we are fond of your company? I suppose you thought I was to bring you into Parliament? I never had any such intention.' The violence of the attack, in the presence of two menials, took Boswell's breath away. He left the house shortly afterwards to see Temple, but Temple was not at home. On returning to Grosvenor Square he was kept waiting again till Lonsdale was ready. It was now afternoon. They walked together towards Hanover Square, where Lonsdale's coach was waiting, and Lonsdale, taking his arm, began an unpleasant monologue on the evils of drinking and talking too freely of one's liberal and independent views. Boswell refrained from reply, perceiving the tyrant to be 'provoked.' They got into the coach and set out for the Great North Road. In due course Lonsdale, heedless of the presence of his man Jackson, resumed the attack. Clearly he was bent on savagery. Before long Boswell was goaded into a retort which lashed Lonsdale's fury into madness. As they approached the village of Barnet, the first stage, he became dangerous.

'You have kept low company all your life! What are *you*, Sir?'

'A gentleman, my Lord, and a man of honour; and I hope to show myself such.'

'You will be settled', Lonsdale snarled, 'when you have a bullet in your belly.'

As soon as they got into the inn at Barnet Boswell took up the challenge, as he was bound to. Lonsdale roughly refused to lend him one of his pistols. There was no regiment in the neighbourhood from whom a pistol might be borrowed. Boswell offered to return to town and arrange a meeting in the proper form. Lonsdale rejected this. Dinner was then served, and the tyrant began to cool down, insisting that Boswell had begun the quarrel. This Boswell denied, offering at the same time to apologise for his own loss of temper. Finally Lonsdale stuck out a hand. 'Boswell, forget all that is past.' They shook hands and got into the coach again, but too much had been said. 'The rest of the journey', Boswell writes to Temple, 'was barely tolerable; we got to Lancaster on Saturday night, and there I left him to the turmoil of a desperate attempt in electioneering . . . I am alone at an inn, in as wretched spirits, ashamed and sunk on account of the disappointment of hopes which led me to endure such grievances. I deserve all I suffer.' And imploring Temple to comfort him and to divulge this degrading humiliation to nobody, he adds: 'As I now resign my recordership, I shall gradually get rid of all communication with this brutal fellow.' And in a miserable postscript: 'Never was a poor ambitious projector more mortified. I am suffering without any prospects of reward, and only from my own folly.' He wrote somewhat similarly to Malone, without going into details.

For lack of a pistol he had probably escaped his first and last duel, unless Lonsdale's berserk fury affected his aim ('I looked on him as a madman'). But even more than the cruelty, even more than the humiliation, the bursting of that gorgeously-tinted bubble he had blown so big and cherished so long sank his spirits to the nadir of despair. He took it, so to speak, on the chin, and we may imagine him humped for hours in a chair, stunned beyond all consolation, staring dully into space. In his diary at this time he turns on himself bitterly, accusing himself of being a bad father, which was not true, and of indulging in middle-age in 'the wild conduct of licentious youth', which was. One faint glimmer of light pierced his darkness, like a farthing dip. There was now nothing to prevent his resigning his recorder-ship, escaping for ever from Lonsdale's baleful orbit, and returning to London to heal his hurt in the sympathy of good friends.

However, to resign, which he did formally on July 1, was easier than to escape. He had been furiously reminded during the late rumpus of having solicited his office, and Lonsdale was going to exact his final drachm of flesh. Arriving in Carlisle on July 3, he breakfasted politely enough with Boswell at the inn. Two days later he was raging over Mr. Recorder's handling of the swearing-in of the freeholders and accusing him of caring for nothing but getting back to London, which was perfectly true. On July 9 another storm arose on the same topic. A cessation of hostilities next day, owing to Lonsdale's absence, was barely noticeable, for a mob arrived to attack 'the Tyrant's garrison', and Boswell, signalling them to desist, escaped a stoning only by retiring with dignity into the inn, 'taking care to appear undismayed'. Returning on July 14, Lonsdale made another scene, accusing Boswell of having babbled of forth-coming Parliamentary favours, which Boswell, backed by his good friend Richard Penn, vigorously denied. At once Lonsdale switched the attack and rated him for throwing up his recorder-ship in 'an unhandsome manner'. Evidently the mere sight of him now was getting on the tyrant's nerves.

All things, as the Oracle of the Bottle remarked to Panurge, move towards their end. Twenty-four hours later Boswell was able to break away at last, sign his final papers, and take his seat in a southbound chaise with his daughter Euphemia, who had come from Auchinleck to keep him company. Two days later he was in London again, sore but thankful. He dined on the evening of his arrival with the ever-kind Malone, who supplied the *fin mot* on the whole unfortunate business. For, as Malone pointed out, if Boswell had been deceived, so had Lonsdale. Boswell had falsely imagined that this mogul would be pleased to promote him; Lonsdale had falsely imagined that a man who had warmly praised him, a procedure to which he was unaccustomed, would think it an honour to be his serf. This was salve, to some extent, for a raw wound. Boswell's recovery was materially assisted the same week by spending a day, with his two daughters, at Reynolds's house in Leicester Fields, where affection and esteem were in the very air. Feeling much better, he writes to Temple a day or two later to this effect, thanking him for a kind and soothing letter, moralising on the vanity of human wishes and the hope of a compensatory state, and confessing that he does not sufficiently try his ways, in the Psalmist's words. He is almost inclined for the moment to agree with Temple, always a lukewarm and sometimes a peevishly critical Johnsonian, that 'my great Oracle did attach too much credit to good principles, without good practice'. Temple, like Boswell, had not so firm a grasp of the merciful doctrine of Intention as the Doctor.

The letter ends with a last grimace in the direction of Lonsdale.

I parted from the northern tyrant in a strange, equivocal state, for he was half irritated, half reconciled; but I promise you I shall keep myself quite independent of him.

Colonel Lowther had recently agreed with Boswell that Lonsdale was slightly insane. The tyrant's mixed moods at parting may have been due to some extent to unwilling respect for a slave who had stood up to him, which very few did. In reasonable moments Boswell could certainly congratulate himself on

his escape. As one of Lonsdale's Ninepins his existence would
have been chaotic, odious, and possibly brief.

He consoled himself finally by weaving into an autobiographical sketch which he published in *The European Magazine* a
little later, a passage of grave, lofty, delicious fantasy:

> It was generally supposed that Mr. Boswell would have had a seat
> in Parliament; and indeed his not being amongst the Representatives
> of the Commons is one of those strange things which occasionally
> happen in the complex operations of our mixed Government. That
> he has not been *brought into Parliament* by some great man is not
> to be wondered at when we peruse his publick declarations.

But although he must have known in his inmost soul that
since Lonsdale had finished with him his political dreams were
over, he continued valiantly to chase the will-o'-the-wisp in
other directions. In his piece for *The European Magazine* he
reveals with unusually childlike candour, even for him, a new
approach this year to the great Pitt, and a characteristic one.
Pitt was the guest of honour at the Lord Mayor's Banquet for
1790, where Boswell, as usual, was also present. It is impossible
to imagine such Arcadian happenings at a Guildhall banquet
nowadays, but at the dessert, it appears, Mr. Boswell was persuaded to rise and sing, 'in praise of Mr. Pitt's conduct in the
dispute with Spain', a ballad of his own composition called *The
Grocer of London,* to the tune of Mr. Dibdin's *Poor Jack* ('There's
a sweet little Cherub . . .'). Prefaced by an adulatory address,
Mr. Boswell's vocal performance was encored six times, and
amid the applause the stern, cold features of the Minister himself
were seen to relax in a smile.[1]

One is reminded inevitably of *Cyrano de Bergerac*:

> . . . Se changer en bouffon,
> Dans l'espoir vil de voir, aux lèvres d'un ministre,
> Naître un sourire, enfin, qui ne soit pas sinistre?
> Non, merci!

[1] Thus the generally received account. Another account in the *Edinburgh
Advertizer* says that Pitt had left table before the ballad was sung. But in
that case Boswell would hardly have regarded the occasion as the triumph
he did?

But our Boswell was no Cyrano, and the ballad of *The Grocer of London,* deriving its title from Pitt's recently-conferred honorary membership of the Worshipful Company of Grocers, achieved print as an anonymous broadsheet and was hawked about the streets, apart from being roared by Boswell and friends on their way home. As the chorus reveals, it is of the most artless Boswellian confection:

> There's a Grocer of London,
>     A Grocer of London,
>     A Grocer of London
> Who watches our trade,
> And takes care of th' Estate of JOHN BULL!

The event thus celebrated is the peace-treaty forced by Pitt in November 1790 on Floridablanca, that notable patron of the Arts who poses in such imperious splendour in an early Goya portrait, surrounded by every luxurious accessory of statecraft, with the painter himself before him, modestly submitting a canvas. Francisco Antonio Monino, Conde de Floridablanca, is incidentally one of the few contemporary potentates who managed to pay Goya with a statesmanlike formula supposed by historians to be the invention, just over a century later, of Mr. Asquith.

The memory of Pitt's wintry smile (we must assume he was present) would be most encouraging. The Prime Minister had not been disposed to take any notice of Mr. Boswell hitherto, and had indeed, since formally acknowledging the *Letter* of 1785, ignored one or two subsequent letters suggesting that Mr. Boswell might wait on him; but he could hardly ignore the Guildhall tribute. In the meantime Boswell, striking while the iron seemed hot, wrote to Dundas, Secretary of State, reminding him of his promise of political support in 1784. A freezing reply from his old college-mate observed that Mr. Boswell had a lively fancy; to which Mr. Boswell retorted with equal iciness by an early post that he was not, at any rate, blessed with 'an accommodating memory, which can recollect or invent facts as it may suit self-interest'. And declaring to Temple his resolution to persevere on the next vacancy', Boswell decided wisely to concentrate for the time being on forthcoming literary fame.

He did so, accordingly, and for the remainder of 1790 he i
working daily on the final sheets of the *Life,* dining out as usual

There is another reminder this September of the kind hear
this fellow constantly possessed. 'My old friend Ross, the player'
he writes to Temple, 'died suddenly yesterday morning. I wa:
sent for, as his most particular friend, and have been so busy
arranging his funeral, at which I am to be chief mourner, that
I have left myself very little time—only about ten minutes.
To busy himself thus over the obsequies of a minor actor—Ros:
had recited a prologue by Boswell at the opening of the Canon
gate theatre, Edinburgh, in 1767—in the midst of his increasing
worries and setbacks is typical Boswell.

For the beginning of the year 1791, the year of his supreme
triumph, found him in the lowest of spirits, with all his old
melancholia and forebodings gaining on him; 'total distaste of
life', 'a kind of mental fever'. In February he dined for the
second time in a month with Jack Wilkes, and was enviously
amazed once more at his evergreen gaiety. In March he wa:
the guest in the City, with Wilkes, of Mr. Deputy Nichols, one
of the directors of *The Gentleman's Magazine.* During dinner
a Common-Councilman named Symms thrilled and cheered him
for a brief moment by suggesting (I guess with a hiccup) that
he, Boswell, should one day be Common Serjeant of London
But this is one transitory gleam of sunshine over the waste of
gloomy waters. He notes in February that he has been 'dismal
ever since moving a month previously to No. 47 Great Portland
Street,[1] and is irritated by his daughters and wishes them
elsewhere.

On April 2 he writes to Temple in pure misery:

I get bad rest in the night, and then I brood over all my complaints,—the sickly mind, which I have had from my early years,—
the disappointment of my hopes of success in life,—the irrevocable
separation between me and that excellent woman, who was my
cousin, my friend, and my wife,—the embarrassment of my affairs,—
the disadvantage to my children in having so wretched a father,—

[1] Now No. 122, as mentioned earlier, and described by Boswell to Temple
as 'a good house'. He would not recognise it to-day, but from still-existent
Georgian houses at the back of Great Portland Street, now a slum, one may
judge what No. 47 looked like.

nay, the want of absolute certainty of being happy after death, the *sure prospect* of which is frightful. No more of this!

It is an unconscious echo of Johnson. 'No more of this!' He brushes away the terrible shadow, shuddering, and having written so far, flings down his pen and can bear to stay indoors no longer. He tried forthwith to get into Drury Lane Theatre for *The Siege of Belgrade*, a new opera, but the house was full. It occurred to him then, in his desperate need for distraction and gaiety, to call on old Charles Macklin, the actor and playwright, at his house round the corner in Bow Street. This almost incredible patriarch, now aged 101 (not, as Boswell estimates, 92 or 93), hale, merry, active, having just put the final polish on another five-act comedy, was one of the seven wonders of London. An earlier generation of wits, Templars, and men-about-town still remembered the exclusive tavern and 'three-shilling Ordinary', described by Fielding somewhere as 'a Temple of Luxury', which the fashionable actor opened in the Grand Piazza, Covent Garden, next door to the theatre, in 1754; the excellence of the fare (*vin compris*), the impressive performance of Macklin as host, and his bankruptcy nine months later for an imposing sum. He paid twenty shillings in the pound, returned to the stage, wrote more comedies, and gave his farewell performance at Covent Garden Theatre in 1789, playing Shylock at the age of 99. It is true that in his emotion on this occasion Macklin was unable to do more than mutter a few lines and leave the rest to his understudy, and his curtain-speech was a tremulous mumble, 'My age! My age!' But age had not withered him. A few months later he opened an art-gallery and exhibition which pleased even Horace Walpole, and in private life he continued a jaunty raconteur, with an endless flow of amusing anecdote.[1]

However, the venerable Macklin's prattle this April night of the London stage of his youth and the gay days of Queen Anne and George I merely increased Boswell's melancholy. It re-

---

[1] Macklin died in July 1797 and is buried in St. Paul's, Covent Garden. The age given on his memorial-tablet on the south wall is 107. The verse-inscription hails him 'Father of the modern Stage', whose years 'a Century and longer ran'.

minded him for some reason of his own youth in Edinburgh ('Would it not torture you to be again at Professor Hunter's, eating *jeel*?'), and he returned glumly home to a sleepless bed.

Not even the near completion of the *Life* can relieve him at this moment, he groans to Temple four days later. His book may be a failure! It may bring him enemies and quarrels! If, on the other hand, it is a success after all, he will live in his Temple chambers, keep resolute hours there, and attend Westminster Hall daily. His spirits are beginning to rise a little already. He is dining next day, he says, with Sir William Scott, King's Advocate at Doctors' Commons, one of Johnson's executors and a member of the Club; a quiet family dinner. Lady Scott has a sister, a Miss Bagnall, worth six or seven hundred a year. She is about 27 years old, lively and gay—'a Ranelagh girl'—but of excellent and devout principles, Sir William tells him. And the old Boswell breaks out and dances a jig.

'Let me see such a woman,' cried I; and accordingly I am to see her. She has refused young and fine gentlemen. 'Bravo!' cried I; 'we see then what her taste is!'

Half in earnest, he cries to Temple: 'A scheme—an adventure seizes my fancy!' Shall he go on with it? 'As I am conscious of my distempered mind, could I *honestly* persuade her to unite her fate with mine?' . . . Are we back in the flighty 1760's? Temple might well ask himself, rubbing his eyes. Is he cracked again? This illusion was probably strengthened by Boswell's publication in April, one month before the *Life*, of an absurd doggerel poem in quarto, at one and sixpence, entitled *No Abolition of Slavery, or the Universal Empire of Love*, dedicated to 'Miss B——'; evidently the Miss Bagnall of his present pre-occupations.

It was a topical piece. In May 1788, acting on a solemn promise to Wilberforce, Pitt, backed by Burke and Fox, had prevailed on the House to take the slave-trade into consideration during its next session and even to pass a Bill in due course for its provisional regulation. In 1789 Wilberforce was pressing eloquently for more vigorous measures, only to see a Bill for abolition thrown out in April 1791 by a huge majority. 'Commerce chinked its purse', said Horace Walpole in disgust. Boswell's sudden impulse to rush into poetry at this moment in the West Indian planters' behalf was timely, for the admired poet Mrs. Letitia Barbauld was demonstrating ardently for the Abolitionists.

As a feudal high Tory, Boswell was naturally on the side of vested interests, and he held the African Negro to be happier and safer enslaved than free, which was sometimes the case. Such views invited a mauling from Johnson, who once shocked a party of Oxford dons by giving the jovial toast 'Here's to the next insurrection of the negroes in the West Indies!' But Boswell seems to have escaped, either by unusual tact or good luck.[1] Without sharing his views in any degree, one cannot but admire the nobly selective indignation of those champions of liberty, contemporary and modern, who would tear Boswell to pieces for wishing to keep the Negro enslaved but have no single word of horror for the long martyrdom of the Catholic Irish. Moreover, if Boswell was a contemptible lunatic on the slavery question, he was not the only one. Greater men than he had admitted the principle. Mosaic Law recognised it, like the laws of ancient Greece and Rome, and when the Catholic Church took over from the Roman Empire and began to abolish slavery she was compelled to do so by degrees, lest the entire social structure should collapse and millions of unfortunates, incapable of fending for themselves, be thrown on the world to starve. In Great Britain considerable business interests were now involved. The slave-traffic begun by the Elizabethans had developed into such a major industry that in the 1790's it employed a fleet of some 130 ships, handling some 40,000 slaves a year; on this traffic was founded the prosperity of the proud port and city of Bristol. Even in the new Republic of the West, recognised by the French philosophers as the home of all the primal virtues, the great Washington could write casually to a friend about this time asking him to trade an unruly slave named Tom for a hogshead of rum, a barrel of limes, and other punch-ingredients.[2]

[1] His arguments, such as they are, are given in the *Life*. It may be noted that the Lord President and three other judges of the Court of Session shared his views in a test-case of 1777 involving a Negro's status in Scotland.
[2] H. Warner Allen: *Rum, the Englishman's Spirit*, London, 1931.

Hence Boswell's opening paean:

> Pernicious as th' effect woild be
> T' abolish negro slavery,
> Such partial freedom would be vain
> Since Love's strong empire must remain . . .

did not sound so ridiculous or brutal to most of his contemporaries as it does to us, though they no doubt thought it odd,
as anyone would, to find stanzas about Love mixed up with a
poem backing the West Indian planters. Boswell had of course
no conception of conditions in the slave-traffic. His kindness
would inevitably have mitigated his feudalism had he ever
peeped under hatches, and the hideous reality of the words
'slave' and 'chain' and 'torment' might have cured him of conventional poetic love-clichés. However, the poem at least gave
him one more opportunity of assuring high quarters of his
readiness for any post they might have in mind for him:

> An ancient baron of the land,
> I by my King shall ever stand!

He was backing the wrong horse. A year hence, after an all-
night sitting, Pitt was to make his famous, his tremendous, his
epoch-making speech on the dawn of civilisation over an Africa
freed from slavery, assisted by the first beams of the rising sun
striking through the dusty Commons windows at exactly the
right moment of his peroration, and providing Pitt with the
perfect Virgilian climax.

> Nosque ubi primus equis Oriens afflavit anhelis,
> Illic sera rubens accendit lumina Vesper.[1]

Fifteen years later the slave-trade was abolished (47 Geo.
III, c.36).

With the Negroes and Miss Bagnall off his mind—he met his
new flame at Sir William Scott's on April 7, decided that she
was 'a fine girl enough, but did not please me much', and dismissed her from his mind forthwith—Boswell turned to more
immediately urgent matters. Apart from hopes of literary glory,

---

[1] And, when on us she [*Aurora*] breathes the living Light,
   Red *Vesper* kindles there the Tapers of the Night. (Dryden, Georgics, I.)

he was looking to the *Life of Johnson* to ease his financial situation, which had become, as he says, 'very disagreeable'. I have not traced all his present liabilities, but a few may be noted. In addition to the £500 a year earmarked for his children's benefit, he had recently speculated £2,500 on a small Ayrshire estate called Knockaroon, belonging to a younger Boswell branch, raising £1,500 on a mortgage, with the remainder still to find. He had lent a cousin, Bruce Boswell, £100 in 1777 and £500 in 1781, still owing when he died. In 1787, having to repay a £500 loan, with three years' interest, to another cousin, Captain Robert Preston, he borrowed £300 from his publisher, Dilly, and £200 from his printer, Henry Baldwin, for that purpose. He owed £200 to Temple and £100 to Wilkes, both repaid in due course, and there were other debts, some due to generosity, some to fecklessness. Against all these liabilities could be set his income from Auchinleck, now above £1,600 a year— £850 net—and rising,[1] and some £1,000 due to him from the estates of his late wife's nephews, but not yet payable; together with whatever small profits were still coming in from the Corsican and Hebrides journals, and whatever the *Life* might make. Little wonder therefore that in his need for ready money at this moment we find Boswell thinking seriously of selling the copyright of the *Life* in advance for £1,000, through Malone, to a speculator named Robinson. The odd thing is that both Malone and Dilly seem to have approved this madness.

Before finally making up his mind Boswell bought a State lottery-ticket and at once began winning the £5,000 first prize in his dreams. British Governments had not yet decided that gambling is immoral, except for Cabinet Ministers and the rich, and regular State lotteries with big prizes afforded the British masses, a proverb all over dice-mad Europe throughout this century as frenetic gamblers, the same thrills as their betters experienced nightly at White's and Boodle's and the Cocoa-Tree.[2] In No. 181 of *The Rambler* (1752) Dr. Johnson deals

[1] It is to be noted that though almost perpetually in straightened circumstances Boswell managed the family estate so well that he could tell Temple in 1789 that Sandie would inherit nearly £3,000 a year.

[2] It is interesting to note that Reynolds was a passionate gambler, though he kept himself strictly within bounds. Lord Inchiquin, who married Reynolds's niece and once won £34,000 at a single sitting, was another.

sonorously with the effect of the prevailing lottery-fever on a respectable young London tradesman whose wild alternate hopes and despairs end at last in the wreck of his business and a nervous breakdown. I cannot avoid quoting, from the end of this essay, the advice given to the distressed gambler by Eumathes, a clergyman. Nobody writes like this nowadays.

There are (said Eumathes) few minds sufficiently firm to be trusted in the hands of chance. Whoever finds himself inclined to anticipate futurity, and exalt possibility to certainty, should avoid every kind of casual adventure, since his grief must always be proportionate to his hope . . . You are now fretting away your life in repentance of an act against which repentance can give no caution but to avoid the occasion of committing it. Rouse from this lazy dream of fortuitous riches, which if obtained, you could scarcely have enjoyed, because they could confer no consciousness of desert; return to rational and manly industry, and consider the mere gift of luck as below the care of a wise man.

The splendid rhetoric! The noble sermon! It converted nobody, least of all his Grace of Canterbury, who in the year following became one of the managers of the national lottery, set up by Act of Parliament, which founded the British Museum. On drawing a blank in due course forty years later Boswell may well have turned up this *Rambler* essay and consoled himself with his old master's wisdom once more. Fortunately, as it happened, he was not compelled after all to the disastrous step of selling his copyright for less than half of what the *Life* ultimately brought him. At the last moment he borrowed another £400 jointly from Dilly and Baldwin, to be repaid out of the first profits, and conveyed his thanks in a jubilant ode of no great attraction in *The Gentleman's Magazine*:

> My cordial Friend,
> Still prompt to lend
> Your cash when I have need on't . . .

The last corrections to the last sheets of the *Life* were made in April of this year, 1791. He tells Dempster this month that though he is feeling the pinch financially, *'they are so good to me here* that I have a full share of the metropolitan advantages.'

The italics are mine. 'They' are his friends, who, one gathers from a modern authority, had with the single exception of Langton now dropped him.

On April 19 Boswell writes to Dempster:

My *magnum opus*, the Life of Dr. Johnson, in two volumes quarto, is to be published on Monday, 16th May . . . I really think it will be the most entertaining collection that has appeared in this age . . .

## 7

If *The Life of Samuel Johnson, LL.D.*, was not received with a unanimous chorus of what Boswell claims to be 'extraordinary approbation', it captured the cultivated public to the extent of selling 1,200 copies in the first four months, a comfortable success.[1] It was a book which was to conquer the English-speaking world quietly, to grow in reputation and magic with the years and blossom in edition after edition, of which the monumental six-volume work of Birkbeck Hill in the 1880's is the greatest, though by no means the latest. A small gaggle of critics instantly attacked it, as they had done the *Journal of a Tour to the Hebrides*, for indiscretion, impertinence, folly, extravagance, exhibitionism, bad taste, violation of propriety and confidence, and even libel. Certain pontiffs had a violent long-standing prejudice against Boswell and an equal one against Johnson, whose addiction to the Christian religion had offended the progressive gentlemen of the *Monthly Review*, for example, in the days of the Hebrides journal, when they charged the Doctor with bigotry and dogmatism, two quaint words of accusation in any hack-critic's mouth. But then as now no inept snarlings could kill a great work, and the public bought and enjoyed steadily.[2] The most diverting of Boswell's critics was

[1] Joseph Farington, R.A., the landscape water-colourist and diarist, one of Boswell's later intimates, says the first (quarto) edition yielded him £1,550, 'which sum is to be made up £2,000 on acct. of the octavo edition.'

[2] Naturally there were good notices, now and especially later. The *Quarterly Review* considered the *Life* 'the richest dictionary of wit and wisdom any language can boast'. The *Edinburgh Review* called it 'a great, a very great work, one of the best books in the world'. Burke told Sir James Mackintosh he thought Johnson appeared more great in Boswell's

perhaps his distant relative, George III, whose mind, upset by
recent brainstorms, was completely bemused by great stretches
of the *Life*. Fanny Burney shows his Majesty trotting into the
Queen's dressing-room nightly in the summer of 1791 and inter-
rupting her toilette by holding endless puzzled discourse with
Fanny on the subject. What? What? What? Eh? Who? Who?
Queen Charlotte herself 'frequently condescended to read over
passages which perplexed or offended her', and Fanny hastened
to explain and justify. She was glad afterwards to think she had
vindicated her dear old Doctor to his sovereigns, but she had
no hesitation in throwing Mr. Boswell to the wolves, demurely
confessing to the King that she was glad she had so seldom met
the gentleman, 'as I knew there was no other security against
all manner of risks in his relations'. In other words, Mr. Boswell,
according to Miss Burney, was a danger to his confidants; which,
in a way, was quite true. *Caveat narrator*. Most of Boswell's
confidants were perfectly aware of this.

To the modern lover of the *Life* Boswell's contemporary critics
are of no more importance than flies, for if he had not written
precisely as he did he would not be Johnson's Boswell. But one
must agree that he was wrong, for example, to set down in print,
during the lifetime of a charming lady, the widow of one of
Johnson's closest friends, a passage which has been always
singled out for condemnation.

While we were alone I endeavored as well as I could to apologise
for a lady who had been divorced from her husband by Act of
Parliament. I said, that he had used her very ill, had behaved brutally
to her, and that she could not continue to live with him without having
her delicacy contaminated; that all affection for him was thus
destroyed; that the essence of conjugal union being gone, there remained only a cold form, a mere civil obligation; that she was in the
prime of life, with qualities to produce happiness; that these ought
not to be lost; and that the gentleman on whose account she was
divorced had gained her heart while thus unhappily situated. Seduced,
perhaps, by the charms of the lady in question, I thus attempted to

---

work than in his (Johnson's) own, which some have twisted into an accusation. Boswell's first champion against his detractors generally was Croker,
editor of the *Life* (eleventh edition) in 1831, whose defence I quote
elsewhere.

# THE
# LIFE
OF
# SAMUEL JOHNSON, LL.D.

COMPREHENDING

## AN ACCOUNT OF HIS STUDIES
## AND NUMEROUS WORKS,
IN CHRONOLOGICAL ORDER;

### A SERIES OF HIS EPISTOLARY CORRESPONDENCE
### AND CONVERSATIONS WITH MANY EMINENT PERSONS;

AND

### VARIOUS ORIGINAL PIECES OF HIS COMPOSITION,
### NEVER BEFORE PUBLISHED:

### THE WHOLE EXHIBITING A VIEW OF LITERATURE AND
### LITERARY MEN IN GREAT-BRITAIN, FOR NEAR
### HALF A CENTURY, DURING WHICH
### HE FLOURISHED.

## BY *JAMES BOSWELL*, ESQ.

———— *Quò fit ut* OMNIS
*Votiva pateat veluti descripta tabella*
VITA SENIS.————
HORAT.

THE THIRD EDITION, REVISED AND AUGMENTED,
IN FOUR VOLUMES.

LONDON:
PRINTED BY H. BALDWIN & SON,
FOR CHARLES DILLY, IN THE POULTRY.

MDCCXCIX.

palliate what I was sensible could not be justified; for when I had finished my harangue, my venerable friend gave me a proper check: 'My dear Sir, never accustom your mind to mingle virtue and vice. The woman's a whore, and there's an end on't.'

Shoals of Boswell's readers, headed by Horace Walpole, could have had no difficulty in identifying the 'whore' immediately as Lady Diana Beauclerk, *née* Spencer. A daughter of Charles, second Duke of Marlborough, she married Viscount Bolingbroke in 1757 at the age of 23, and was divorced from him in 1768 to marry her lover, Topham Beauclerk, at St. George's, Hanover Square.[1] Her grace, beauty, and artistic talent were considerable, and the Doctor, who had loved Beauclerk dearly, was obviously not talking at that moment for publication; nor should Boswell, a gentleman and one of Lady Diana's admirers, have printed what was a hasty remark, and technically inaccurate.

Undoubtedly it is a pity the conversation was printed (though it seems a trifle comic to find the censorious carrying on about Boswell's breach of good manners 150 years afterwards as though they were Lady Diana's family solicitors), and all the more a pity because, as we learn from Hawkins, Lady Diana, who added a warm charity to her other gifts, was the means, with Langton, of helping one or two of Johnson's needy relations after his death. Boswell should have discovered and made a note of this, one cannot help thinking.

Curiously enough, no one has ever thought of indicting Malone for this and a few minor lapses on Boswell's part. Seeing he read the proofs for the press and was well aware of Boswell's slapdash habits, surely the sedate barrister is not a little to blame? Every London newspaper keeps a lawyer or two on its staff to comb the proofs nightly for hidden libels; should one slip through and result in an action, the newspaper loses money and the lawyers their job. In law the newspaper and its printers are solely responsible, I believe; does that affect the responsibility of the legal experts on whose skill they then must depend? Everybody who knew Boswell knew, like Fanny Burney, that

---

[1] An unhappy step, Horace Walpole told Farington; for apart from being dirty and verminous, Beauclerk drank laudanum heavily and was 'the worst-tempered man I ever knew'.

he was a risky fellow to confide anything delicate to, not because he ever acted in deliberate malice, but because he could not help babbling and scribbling without discrimination. It seems to me that Malone should have been more careful.

There is one more passage on which critics contemporary and modern have always fastened with loud denunciations; the one in which Boswell hints, without any evidence, that during Johnson's early days in London his relations with the chance women he occasionally liked to converse with in the streets at night on his way home were sometimes of a sexual nature. To rebut this we have the evidence of Johnson's sterling moral character and rigid control of strong passions, together with that angelic pity for the unfortunate which characterised him. Johnson was especially moved by the misery of London prostitutes, and was once known to carry a sick drab home to his own house and have her properly tended. Hawkins mentions this charitable eccentricity without any of Boswell's implications, and tells one of his rare good stories as well.

At the club in Ivy Lane, our usual hour of departure was eleven, and when that approached he [Johnson] was frequently tempted to wander the streets, and join in the conversation of those miserable females who were there to be met with. Of these he was very inquisitive as to their course of life, the history of their seduction, and the chances of reclaiming them. The first question he generally asked was, if they could read. Of one who was very handsome he asked, for what she thought God had given her so much beauty: she answered—'To please gentlemen.'

I think that on this topic Boswell was indulging in what modern jargon calls 'wishful thinking', and was a little too eager to impute to Johnson his own kind of failing. That he ever betrayed a friend in malice is, one must repeat, a monstrous charge. He was a Mr. Tattle, not a Mr. Snake. In a notably spiteful age his amiability, indeed, is almost abnormal.

There is no need to indulge oneself at this time of day in a panegyric of the *Life*. Even Macaulay confesses its golden spell. It is a book one can never tire of. Poor students of the University of Paris in the Middle Ages were permitted in extreme need to ell all their books, except the Bible and the works of St. Thomas Aquinas, *Biblia dumtaxat & fratis Thomae operibus exceptis.* To hese essential volumes anyone about to be cast away for life on the traditional desert island who added Boswell's would never lack all the printed nourishment and entertainment for oul and spirit a man can need.

If there is anything about the *Life* which has not already been ufficiently extolled, I think it is the delicious occasional etchings of minor figures, such as Mr. Twalmley, the British housewife's riend.

Boswell, you often vaunt so much as to provoke ridicule. You put me in mind of a man who was standing in the kitchen of an inn with his back to the fire, and thus accosted the person next him, 'Do you know, Sir, who I am?' 'No, Sir, (said the other), I have not that advantage.' 'Sir, (said he), I am the *great* TWALMLEY, who invented he New Flood-gate Iron.'

That is taken down from Johnson, but here is one of Boswell's own—the sketch, like a Rowlandson cartoon, of the unnamed clerical poet who submitted his muse one day to Johnson's criticism.

A printed *Ode to the Warlike Genius of Britain* came next in eview; the bard was a lank bony figure, with short black hair; he was writhing himself in agitation while Johnson read, and shewing his teeth in a grin of earnestness, exclaimed in broken sentences, and in a keen sharp tone, 'Is that poetry, Sir? Is it *Pindar*?' JOHNSON. 'Why, Sir, there is here a great deal of what is called poetry.' Then, turning to me, the poet cried, 'My muse has not been long upon the town, and (pointing to the *Ode*) it trembles under the hand of the great critick.' Johnson, in a tone of displeasure, asked him, 'Why do you praise Anson?' I did not trouble him by asking his reason for this question. He proceeded, 'Here is an error, Sir; you have made Genius feminine.' 'Palpable, Sir; (cried the enthusiast), I know it. But (in a lower tone), it was to pay a compliment to the Duchess of Devonshire, with which her Grace was pleased. She is walking across Coxheath, in the military uniform, and I suppose her to be the Genius of Britain.' JOHNSON 'Sir, you are giving a reason for it; but that will not make it right. You may have a reason why two and two should make five; but they will still make but four.'

In this demurely satiric sketch there is all that essential eighteenth century we find equally in the incident at Mrs Garrick's party in Adelphi Terrace in 1781, 'one of the happiest days that I remember to have enjoyed in the whole course of my life.'

Talking of a very respectable author, he [Johnson] told us a curious circumstance in his life, which was, that he had married a printer's devil. REYNOLDS. 'A printer's devil, Sir! Why, I thought a printer's devil was a creature with a black face and in rags.' JOHNSON. 'Yes Sir. But, I suppose, he had her face washed, and put clean clothes on her. (Then looking very serious, and very earnest.) And she did not disgrace him; the woman had a bottom of good sense.' The word *bottom* thus introduced was so ludicrous, when contrasted with his gravity, that most of us could not forbear tittering and laughing though I recollect that the Bishop of Killaloe kept his countenance with perfect steadiness, while Miss Hannah More slyly hid her face behind a lady's back who sat on the same settee with her. His pride could not bear that any expression of his should excite ridicule, when he did not intend it; he therefore resolved to assume and exercise despotick power, glanced sternly around, and called out in a strong tone, 'Where's the merriment?' Then collecting himself, and looking aweful, to make us feel how he could impose restraint, and as it were searching his mind for a still more ludicrous word, he slowly pronounced, 'I say the *woman* was *fundamentally* sensible'; as if he had said, hear this now, and laugh if you dare. We all sat composed as at a funeral.

One needs to know something about Hannah More, that illustrious bluestocking, now in her virginal late thirties, to enjoy this scene thoroughly. The rather forbidding canvas in the National Portrait Gallery does not do her full justice, though I admit that to me Miss More, if a minor character in the Boswellian scene, is at all times more tremendous than any lawnsleeved, periwigged prelate of the Georgian Establishment. She dined constantly at Lambeth Palace and occupied for life, as it were, a *strapontin* attached to the Episcopal Bench. Her philanthropy was practical and sincere, if sometimes injudicious (the ingratitude of Mrs. Yearsley, the poetic milkwoman of Bristol, is a celebrated case in point), and her didactic verse, prose, and even drama had a considerable contemporary vogue

This success, combined with shrewdness, vivacity, and marked conversational gifts—

> Enlighten'd spirits! you who know
> What charms from polish'd converse flow,
> Speak, for you can, the pure delight
> When kindling sympathies unite! [1]

—to which may be added that talent for flattering the eminent which so bored Dr. Johnson, and an agreeable benevolence, which she lost to some extent in middle-age, when she soured into a sabbatarian and a bitter No-Popery bigot, made Miss Hannah More a familiar guest in the best clerical, literary, and even patrician circles. Moreover her decorous flirtation with Horace Walpole, now Lord Orford, who was not so averse to trowel-laid flattery as some, produced a sequence of epistles to 'Saint Hannah' and 'My holy Hannah' in which the old gentleman chirps almost as charmingly in his seventies as in his brilliant heyday.

To picture Miss Hannah More, then, overcome with a fit of giggles at the word 'bottom' and hiding girlishly behind another lady is to picture something rather tremendous. And how the scene lives! Up to the destruction of Adelphi Terrace by Big Business a dozen years ago it was possible to touch these eminent and friendly ghosts often on the elbow, for Garrick's house, No. 5, was unaltered inside or out, and one could stand by Johnson and Boswell the moment after they took their leave.

He and I walked away together; we stopped a little while by the rails of the Adelphi, looking on the Thames, and I said to him with some emotion that I was now thinking of two friends we had lost, who once lived in the buildings behind us, Beauclerk and Garrick. 'Ay, Sir, (said he, tenderly,) and two such friends as cannot be supplied.'

Many have stood on that spot opposite Garrick's house since that day, re-creating this moment. The Adelphi railings in Johnson's day were much higher and the Thames ran immediately beneath, as Pastorini's print shows, save for a narrow wharf; but the scene was otherwise unchanged, and one might easily see the gigantic rolling figure staring dim-eyed over the

[1] *The Bas Bleu*, by Hannah More, 1784.

busy river, and Boswell by his side. Yahoodom has much to answer for.

Mr. Oliver Edwards, the little lawyer of Stevenage, we have already met. He fills a masterly couple of pages of quiet, ironic comedy without one false note. There is another oddly attractive 'super' at Dr. Taylor's house at Ashbourne in Derbyshire.

In the evening our gentleman-farmer, and two others, entertained themselves and the company with a great number of tunes on the fiddle. Johnson desired to have 'Let Ambition fire thy mind' played over again, and appeared to give a patient attention to it; though he owned to me that he was very insensible to the power of musick.

This scene lives perpetually, like the others; the candlelight in Taylor's parlour, the simple old tunes, Johnson's abstracted frown, the very grimaces of the gentleman-farmer and his fellow-performers as they scrape away, their faces glistening with concentration. In the *Life* Boswell does not bother to name this gentleman-farmer. Turning to the diaries, so rich in unused material, we perceive him to be a Mr. Fieldhouse from Staffordshire, staying a few days with Dr. Taylor, who was tutoring his son. 'A brisk, obliging little man, quite upon springs', is Boswell's report, adding that Mr. Fieldhouse was very fond of poetry. Evidently, then, no ordinary gentleman-farmer of the eighteenth century, as that addiction to fiddling, practised chiefly by gypsies, Italians, dancing-masters, vagabonds, and village choir-masters, may perhaps indicate. The day was yet to come when gentlemen-farmers hung their walls with costly colour-prints, read Proust, played the lute, and collected old jade.

Little Mr. Fieldhouse seems, when roused, to have been an assertive and even a combative type, a thruster, a hard man to hounds. A sharp exchange had taken place, the night before the chamber-music, between him and the Doctor, also a product of Staffordshire. The argument arose over the ethics of the case of Mungo Campbell, who shot Alexander, Earl of Eglintoun, in a brawl. As voices and tempers rise, my imagination persists in equipping the little gentleman-farmer with obstinate china-blue eyes and a scratch-wig. He is not the least afraid of the Great Cham. I hear his voice, dogmatic, with a burr and a rasp, applying the closure.

'A poor man has as much honour as a rich man, and Campbell had *that* to defend!'

Perceiving the fellow to be a 'humourist', the Doctor warns him off with the well-known ominous rumble, head down, like a Miura bull about to charge.

'A poor man has no honour.'

But the little matador stands firm, ignores all danger-signals, and makes one more defiant pass with the red cape.

'Lord Eglintoun was a damned fool to run on upon Campbell after being warned that Campbell would shoot him if he did!'

Which spells his doom. The Doctor permitted no swearing in his presence. A furious scowl and a loud, angry repetition of *damned* some half-dozen times finished Mr. Fieldhouse, apparently, for the evening. However, like the Doctor, he bore no malice, as that rustic version of the Giorgione *Concert* the following evening shows. His fellow-fiddlers may well have been the parish clerk and the school-master. The Rev. Dr. John Taylor, prebendary of Westminster, was no snob, for all his wealth and vesty pomp and power as a local magnate and stock-breeder, his opulent coach-and-four, and his magnificent purple-clad butler. At his house Boswell met some mixed company, jotted down in his diary as Derbyshire curiosities in passing: two neighbouring squires, for example, one intelligent and spruce, the other oafish as Squire Western; the ex-landlord of the Black-moor's Head, Ashbourne, a shrewd sedate personage in plain brown and a cut-bob wig, and the landlord of 'the large inn at Buxton'; a rich, shrivelled, skittish little old spinster, a great one for persiflage and a playmate of Johnson's; another spinster, a fat one; an ugly widow, two 'eminent tanners', and other local fauna, who might have provided a fascinating Boswellian page or two had the *Life* been twice or thrice its size, as it should have been. Mr. Fieldhouse, the gentleman-farmer, is a character who somehow detains one. Max Beerbohm should have done for him what he so brilliantly did for the unfortunate clergyman, unnamed alike in the *Life* and the diaries, who rushed to destruction one day at the Thrales' by asking Johnson, at the end of a sonorous review of the best English sermon-writers of the period, whether Dr. Dodd's sermons were 'not addressed to the passions'. Max's exquisite essay on the probable history and subsequent fate of this mild victim would have delighted Boswell, I think

Then, again, there is the genteel but business-like hostess o
the Green Man, Ashbourne, 'a very good inn, the mistress o
which, a mighty civil gentlewoman, curtseying very low, pre
sented me with an engraving of the sign of her house; to whicl
she had subjoined, in her own handwriting, an address in sucl
singular simplicity of style, that I have preserved it pasted upor
one of the boards of my original Journal at this time, and shal
here insert it for the amusement of my readers:

'M. KILLINGLEY'S *duty waits upon Mr. Boswell, is exceedingly*
*obliged to him for this favour; whenever he comes this way, hopes for*
*a continuance of the same. Would Mr. Boswell name the house to his*
*extensive acquaintance, it would be a singular favour conferr'd on one*
*who has it not in her power to make any other return but her mos*
*grateful thanks, and sincerest prayers for his happiness in time, and ir*
*a blessed eternity.—Tuesday morn.*'

At the inn at Edensor, near Chatsworth, where Boswell wen
out of his way on this same journey north to look at the duca
palace, there was another fascinating type, a very jolly landlorc
'whose name, I think, was Malton.'

He happened to mention that 'the celebrated Dr. Johnson had been
in his house.' I inquired *who* this Dr. Johnson was, that I might hear
mine host's notion of him. 'Sir, (said he), Johnson, the great writer;
*Oddity*, as they call him. He's the greatest writer in England; he writes
for the ministry; he has a correspondence abroad, and lets them know
what's going on.'

On hearing this Johnson laughed a good deal, wishing pos
sibly, as we do, that Boswell had been able to spend a little
more time at Edensor. The race of jolly English innkeepers ha
died out long since, with the good claret and burgundy of their
cellars. It may be deduced incidentally, I think, that Boswel
was a popular client at inns along the Great North Road; ar
easy, genial, talkative gentleman for whom the pick of the larder
and the cream of the cellar were good enough, who spent his
money freely and did not put on airs or keep his inferiors at
arms' length. Whether this has any connection with the fact tha
his post-chaise was never held up on the road during his many

urneys north and south would be a fascinating topic for
eculation. Country innkeepers in this age were suspected,
metimes not without reason, of collaboration with the high-
ayman refreshing himself by the kitchen fire; a bond confirmed
' the evidence of that postboy's skeleton and empty saddlebags
und some years ago in the wall of an inn being demolished
ar London, among other testimony. It may be that jolly Mr.
alton of Edensor sped some of his parting guests quite
fferently.

Magnificent as are many of the full-dress conversation-pieces
 the *Life*, delightful as it is to hear the voices of Johnson and
arrick, Reynolds and Burke, Beauclerk and Goldsmith at their
aret, these little sketches of Boswell's made outside the
armed circle are fascinating as the grotesques in an illuminated
ook of Hours. Many more of them would have embellished the
*fe*, doubtless, had Boswell's idea of a romp coincided with
hnson's. The only nocturnal spree of the Doctor's recorded by
oswell is innocence itself, though it did take place partly in
ovent Garden. In an often-quoted passage, Boswell relates how
eauclerk and Langton, after supping at a tavern till three in the
orning, knocked up Johnson in his Temple chambers, for fun;
ow he came to the door in nightshirt and wig, with a poker
ady for action; how on recognising his visitors he cried 'What,
 it you, you dogs? I'll have a frisk with you!'; how all three
llied out to Covent Garden and Johnson tried his clumsy hand
 helping the market-men; how he soon gave this up and joined
s young friends over a smoking bowl at an adjacent tavern;
ow they then went on the river down to Billingsgate, and spent
e rest of the day in harmless dissipation, a word of more
eanings than one.

A merry scene; yet I personally prefer the great enigmatic
ght-piece of Johnson's Joke. Boswell, though he himself does
ot understand it, tells the story in a masterly manner.

On the evening of May 10, 1773, Johnson was taken ill at
nner at Paoli's and had to leave the table. Meeting Boswell
ter by appointment at Chambers's apartments in the Temple,
 grew better and began to talk. Before long something struck
m as irresistibly comic about a will just drawn up by Chambers
r Bennet Langton in favour of Langton's three 'dowdy' sisters.

He suddenly began to laugh immoderately at his own ve
obscure running comment, amid the uncomprehending stares
Chambers and Boswell. He kept on laughing, and Chambers,
lawyer who did not relish mirth at his own expense, 'seem
impatient till he got rid of us'. They got into Inner Temple Lar
and we come to the climax.

Johnson could not stop his merriment, but continued it all the w
until he got without the Temple gate. He then burst into such a fit
laughter that he appeared to be almost in a convulsion; and, in ord
to support himself, laid hold of one of the posts at the side of t
foot-pavement and sent forth peals so loud that in the silence of t
night his voice seemed to resound from Temple Bar to Fleet Dit

Echoes of that huge laughter, as Max Beerbohm has sa
come ringing down the ages. The reason for it will never
known, and Boswell stood by in silence, wondering, and let t
great, the melancholy, the sick old man have his laugh o
'The amazing end of this amazing story', says Christopher Holl
'comes on us so suddenly and so quietly as almost to take o
breath away. "I accompanied him to his door", writes Boswe
"where he gave me his blessing." What an extraordinary ta
It takes less than half a page in Boswell. Has there been sin
his day any other writer of English, except Dickens, who cou
make such a scene live so vividly before us? ... The world 1
once was absent, when there roared out under the stars th
enormous laughter at the joke of Bennet Langton's will whi
Johnson shared alone with God.' [1]
This is the loudest, but by no means the only, burst
Johnson's laughter we hear in the *Life*. Peevish dons, Les
Stephen among them, have alleged that Boswell's picture
Johnson is one-sided and incomplete, and that Murphy a
Hawkins and Mrs. Thrale and Fanny Burney and Hannah Mc
and others give aspects of him, and especially light-heart
aspects, which Boswell never knew. I cannot conceive whe
the Samurai get this theory. Compared with Boswell's Johns
the others are completely trivial. It is painful to find the gre
Sir Walter Raleigh in this galley, wickedly asserting that '

[1] *Dr. Johnson*. London, 1928.

come to closer quarters with Johnson in the best pages of
*The Rambler* than in the most brilliant of the conversations
recalled by Boswell'; as if any essayist ever born revealed himself
to his public as he does to his intimates. The Johnson of *The
Rambler* is the preacher in freshly-starched canonicals, fully
conscious of his mission. The Johnson of much of the *Life* is
Johnson in dressing-gown and slippers, relaxed and easy and
natural, exhibiting moods and quirks and fancies and weaknesses
he could never have dared to print.

A more or less rooted contempt for humanity is at the bottom
of all such donnish whimsies, I fear. I turn to John Wilson
Croker's edition (1831), for the first fair critical judgment of the
Boswell self-displayed in the *Life*. It may stand equally today.

His vanity was inoffensive—his curiosity was commonly directed
towards laudable objects—when he meddled he did so, generally,
from good-natured motives—and his giddiness was only an exuberant
gaiety, which never failed in the respect and reverence due to literature,
morals, and religion; and Posterity gratefully acknowledges the taste,
temper, and talents with which he selected, enjoyed, and described
that polished and intellectual society which still lives in his work,
and without his work had perished.

So much for *MM. les assassins.*

To salute Boswell's achievement, before passing on, as The
Biography is no exaggeration. Oscar Wilde rightly ranked him in
his field above Plato. His secret, whether he knew it or not,
and despite his groans over his hard labour, can be expressed,
I think, in a single word: ecstasy, ἔκστασις; a standing-out-of-
oneself, a gift of God. His *Life* towers over everything else
of the kind like Bourges Cathedral or Montserrat seen from the
plain, even over what, in its absence, would have been the
principal English biography, J. T. Smith's richly vivacious
*Nollekens and his Times*; even over M. Jean-Jacques Brousson's
deliciously amusing and cynical *exposé*, published a few years
ago, of the private life and conversation of Anatole France.
Smith and Brousson being men with a considerable grievance
against their eminent subjects, their work has an astringency

which, pleasing to begin with, tends to pall. What would preserve Boswell's book from putrefaction, as the Doctor would
have said, is the love and admiration in it.

This never declines into hero-worship. 'I will not cut off his
claws and make my tiger a cat to please anyone', Boswell had
retorted to Hannah More's plea, while the *Life* was in the press,
to mitigate Johnson's asperities. Nor does he hesitate to allow
the dear great man to make an exhibition of himself on occasion.
'For anything I see, foreigners are fools' is a typical Johnsonian
absurdity, part of that five per cent pure nonsense which leaven
the majestic reason of Johnson's pronouncements and reminds u
that he, too, is human. Boswell need not have printed this. He
preserved it, I think, with demure amusement, as a pendant to
an equally fascinating remark on the topic of foreigners in the
Hebrides journal. 'I'll carry a Frenchman', booms the Doctor
'to St. Paul's Churchyard and I'll tell him, "By our law you may
walk half round the church, but if you walk round the whole
you'll be punished capitally"; and he will believe me at once
Now, no Englishman', etc., etc., etc. Boswell played up gravely
by suggesting that such imbecile credulity is due to the implicit
submission to which every Frenchman is accustomed, whereas
'every Englishman reasons upon the laws of his country'.
Johnson apparently grunted approval. Did he really believe such
things? In a paper written for *The Adventurer* in 1753 I find
him challenging the pleasing implication of Sir William Temple,
Swift's bland tyrant, that the English alone are free men in a
world of slaves. 'Where is the government to be found', asks
Johnson sensibly, being unable to foresee Bolshevist Russia,
Nazi Germany, or Great Britain in the forthcoming State Utopia,
'that superintends individuals with such vigilance, as not to
leave their private conduct without restraint? Can it enter into a
reasonable mind to imagine, that men of every other nation are
not equally masters of their own time or houses with ourselves,
and equally at liberty to be parcimonious or profuse, frolick or
sullen, abstinent or luxurious? . . . Such liberty is to be found
alike under the government of the many or the few, in mon-
archies or in commonwealths.'

If there is self-contradiction here, I feel the explanation is
fairly simple. When lounging at ease there were curious moments

when the Doctor left off being a scholar, an intellectual, and a London literary lion, and reverted to 'reet Staffordsheer', becoming the typical Midland or Arnold Bennett provincial, with all the naive dogmatic self-sufficiency of the type (and we may remember that Johnson was out of Great Britain only once, for eight weeks, when the Thrales took him to France in 1775). Why the cosmopolite Boswell chose to show him turning 'reet Staffordsheer' on the question of foreigners—and after all ninety per cent of the Island Race would see nothing in Johnson's dictum but obvious gospel, even today—was simply, I make bold to assert again, that he was enjoying a small, private, Puckish joke which harmed nobody and was not incompatible with admiring affection for a very great man talking for once through his beaver.

But one could discuss the myriad facets of the *Life* for ever. One thing remains to be said, perhaps. There are those who have gone through Boswell's pages with a fine-toothed comb, eagerly noting examples of what they believe to be the fellow's private malice. *Haec est altissima et ultissima lectio: sui ipsius cognitio et despectio.*[1]

---

[1] *De Imit. Chr.*, Lib. I, Cap. 2. 'This is the highest and most profitable lesson—the true knowledge and despising of one's own self.'

# Chapter Seven

## VRAYE FOY

### 1

It is both legitimate and agreeable to accompany Mr. James Boswell, author of a work of which the whole town is talking, in a hackney-coach to his publisher's in the City one summer morning a month or two after the publication of *The Life of Samuel Johnson, LL.D.*; an imaginary journey, actually not an infrequent one.

No trace remains today of the wealthy publishing-house of the brothers Charles and Edward Dilly—Edward the loquacious died in 1779, having practically talked himself to death, as somebody said—at No. 22 in the Poultry. Their resemblance to the Brothers Cheeryble is obvious and marked. Though they were Dissenters, carrying on a profitable export-trade to America of sectarian works, their hospitality, like that of most publishers, was epicurean, lavish, and warm-hearted, both in town and at their country-house at Southill, Bedfordshire. At the table of 'my worthy friends and booksellers, Messieurs Dilly in the Poultry', Boswell met a greater number of literary men than at any other, except Sir Joshua Reynolds's. The Dillys possessed admirable discernment in food and wine and no bigotries of any kind. To the end of his life Boswell will be a welcome guest in the Poultry.

How the Dillys carried on business is not altogether clear. Eighteenth-century publishing technique is wrapped in vagueness. Dodsley, for example, kept a shop in Pall Mall and sold his own and presumably other publishers' books over the counter, whereas the Dillys had no shop, and their premises in the

Poultry were a publishing and wholesale department attached to their house, one of those typical tall-windowed four-storey brick City houses of the late seventeenth or early eighteenth century, built when the Poultry arose again, minus half its inns, from the ashes of the Great Fire. Here, in the manner of wealthy London tradesmen almost mid-way into the Victorian Era, the Dillys lived with their business, separated from it by a small courtyard. The printer engaged by Charles Dilly for the *Life of Johnson*, as we know already, was Henry Baldwin, 'now', says Boswell's preface to the Second Edition, 'Master of the Worshipful Company of Stationers, whom I have long known as a worthy and an obliging friend'. Baldwin's chief compositor was Manning, whose pardon Dr. Johnson so humbly begged after flying into a too-hasty rage over a proof-sheet of his *Lives of the Poets*.

Craning his neck as his coach rattled eastwards along the Strand, Boswell may have seen his work displayed in the bookshops of Andrew Millar and Tonson, behind bow-windows of thick, greenish glass. New brown calf and a gilt-lettered red label make no unattractive show, despite Austin Dobson's curious implication that the gaudy cloth bindings of the 1890's spelt progress. Like every good eighteenth-century book, a Dilly production has a sober dignity, together with its only drawback, which is, so far as I can discover, that it will never lie flat when opened.

Mr. Charles Dilly would be seated this summer morning in his private room in the publishing-office, across the cobbled courtyard; a plump, natty, rosy man, closely-shaven, bob-wigged, horn-spectacled, well but soberly dressed in nut-brown or plum-coloured broadcloth, with discreet fresh linen at neck and wrists, poring over costs and returns and refreshing himself at intervals, doubtless, with a pinch from a silver box of Scholten's best Rappee, plain St. Domingo, Kendal Brown, or scented Maccabaw, all suitable to a wealthy publisher's nose. Beamings and exclamations of pleasure as Mr. Boswell is announced by a clerk would be reciprocal, for Mr. Boswell is not only an old friend but a highly profitable author. Their business duly discussed—what more easy or delightful than any interview between a best-seller and his smiling patron?—a bottle of claret would naturally follow their adjournment to the parlour, or perhaps to that dusky, comfortable, pine-panelled drawing-room up the wide, shallow staircase, on the first floor overlooking the street. And I doubt strongly if Boswell could ever enter this room now without seeing once more that memorable gathering of Wednesday, May 15, 1776, and once more hearing the Doctor, as he peered shortsightedly round, address those stage-whispers to Edward Dilly before dinner.

'Who is that gentleman, Sir?'

'Mr. Arthur Lee, Sir.'

'Too, too, too.

But even more embarrassing and productive of cluckings than a rebel like Mr. Lee, later American Ambassador to Spain, is a conspicuous figure laughing with Dr. Lettsom in a corner.

'Who is the gentleman in lace?'

'Mr. Wilkes, Sir.'

And once again Boswell, grinning at his thoughts, would see the Doctor, thoroughly flustered, picking up a book and retiring to a window-seat to compose himself. Why the impact of Wilkes, whom he had come purposely to meet, should so upset the Sage, Boswell does not explain. Perhaps Johnson realised for the first time, as his myopic eyes recognised that amused, notorious, satanic visage a few feet away, what he had let himself in for. It may be noted that in accordance with the awkward custom of the period, no introductions were made.

So Mr. Boswell takes a genial leave of his publisher at length and returns to Great Portland Street; if the day is fine, doubtless on foot. The City of London was still a warm-blooded human place to walk through in the 1790's. Men and women were born and lived and died in it, its countless taverns and clubs flourished day and night, many of its Wren churches had congregations; it was not yet a mere lair or bolting-hutch of Mammon, a kind of financial Sodom from which the inhabitants fled nightly in a body, as from the wrath of God, to the suburbs. Nor had Letters deserted the City yet. Grub (today Milton) Street, Cripplegate, if its heyday as a wasps'-nest of starving poets and pamphleteers was over, could still produce a stinging broadsheet or two; in the Poultry itself was to be born a few years hence the indefatigable Tom Hood; and if the Boar's Head in Eastcheap was not the veritable tavern of Falstaff and Prince Hal, it had occupied the same site since the Fire and was sufficiently Shakesperean to inspire Goldsmith's *Reverie*. Vestiges of the City Boswell knew remain here and there today in little forgotten courts and tangled alleys and byways like Amen Court, and even more in that almost unspoilt backwater, Ely Place, Holborn, where the watchman still patrols at night, crying 'Past twelve!' within locked gates, where the iron bar across the narrow passage leading to the Mitre tavern still foils any highwayman on horse-back who may gallop that way, and where that thirteenth-century English Gothic jewel, the chapel of the Bishops of Ely, in Boswell's day defiled and degraded by plasterwork, now stands restored to its former delicate beauty, with the Mass said in it once more; an example of 'Gothick' continuity which would have pleased him, I think.

The plump, strutting figure in the snuff-coloured suit passes down Ludgate Hill into Fleet Street and is lost in the crowd. From George Dance's crayon profile of 1793 we perceive that Boswell has become a trifle more chinny and jowly than when Reynolds painted him in 1785. To one of his modern critics, indeed, the poor fellow's face is quite repulsive. Unafflicted by such excessive sensibility, I can only say that though Boswell in the last years of his life is admittedly no Apollo Belvedere, the sight of his pursy, homely features gives me no unease, and I would personally rather dine with their owner than with most of the ornaments of current Letters. A few of the pernicketty may have disliked Boswell during his life, but he remained to the end of his days, or nights, one of London's most indefatigable diners-out and mingled to the end with men of intelligence and breeding. They liked him. So do I.

2

Having seen the first edition of the *Life* successfully launched in May 1791, Boswell went immediately on the Home Circuit, which covered Hertfordshire, Essex, Kent, and Surrey, and found his learned brethren there much more congenial than those of the Northern. 'Though I did not get a single brief', he writes valiantly to Temple from London on August 22, on the eve of setting out for Scotland to join Sandie in a little grouse-shooting, 'I do not repent of the expense, as I am showing myself desirous of business and imbibing legal knowledge.' Had he forgotten that in May he acted as one of a number of juniors to Spencer Perceval, that 'honest little fellow', later Prime Minister and victim of a madman's pistol, in a suit concerning land-enclosure in Hampshire? Quite likely. It was not very important.

Early this summer he had found time to gratify curiosity and do an old friend a service by taking a flying trip to Portsmouth to view the Grand Fleet at anchor and to spend a day and night aboard the frigate commanded by his late wife's cousin, Captain Macbride. His purpose, apart from indulging in a new experience, which always charmed him, was to make inquiries on behalf of Temple's eldest son Francis, a midshipman, in whose interests Temple was begging him to approach Dundas. Boswell reports to Temple, before doing so, that the most difficult step in the Navy is from midshipman to lieutenant, which was strictly accurate. Although by the 1790's conditions in the floating hells of H.M. Navy, with which every reader of Smollett is shudderingly familiar, had vastly improved, the life was still hard and, for junior officers, chancy. Midshipmen, whose pay ranged from £1 4s. to £2 5s. a month, had to complete six years' sea-service before attaining commissioned rank, and might then have to wait a dozen years or so for a ship; grey-haired midshipmen were not unknown as late as Dickens's day. Like Nelson, Francis Temple had already made a voyage to the tropics to improve his knowledge and prospects. Evidently Captain Macbride, later Admiral, made it clear that unless strings could be pulled a long wait faced him.

The Navy failed to allure Boswell in his fifties as the Army had done in his twenties. Perhaps Dr. Johnson's well-known fulminations had infected him. 'A sea-life must seem very unnatural to you', he remarks to Temple. 'I am sure it does so to me.' Yet a period of distinct naval glamour had set in by the 1790's, as the Smollett Era gave place to the Dibdin Era and the virtue, comeliness, invincibility, devotion to duty, and steadfastness in true love of typical ratings like Poor Jack and Tom Bowling became familiar to Covent Garden audiences.

His form was of the manliest beauty,
His heart was kind and soft,
Faithful below he did his duty,
And now he's gone aloft.[1]

The jolly Marryat Era was still to come, and I imagine Captain
Marryat would have won Boswell as easily as he does most boys.
What the British Navy owes to Marryat, like the infinite deal more
it owes to James II, has not yet, I think, been properly estimated.

A cheery flash of the old scatterbrain Boswell ends the letter
to Temple we have been reading:

> *You must know I have had several matrimonial schemes of late.*
> I shall amuse you with them from Auchinleck. One was with Miss
> Milles, daughter of the late Dean of Exeter, a most agreeable woman
> *d'un certain age*, and with a fortune of £10,000; she has left town
> for the summer . . .
>
> My *magnum opus* sells wonderfully; twelve hundred are now gone,
> and we hope the whole seventeen hundred may be gone before
> Christmas.

Gaiety—enhanced by delight at his appointment this July as
Secretary for Foreign Correspondence to the Royal Academy,
an office formerly held by Baretti, and carrying a life-member-
ship—did not take long to evaporate. Auchinleck, he tells Temple
in November, on his return to London, was deserted and melancholy, and he missed his wife badly. 'My London spirits were
soon exhausted; I sank into languor and gloom.' Visiting the
neighbouring gentry was of little avail, since he could not escape
from himself. An anxious letter recently from young Francis
Temple had not cheered Boswell to any extent, nor his most
recent visits to his old and dear friend Reynolds.

> My spirits have been still more sunk by seeing Sir Joshua Reynolds
> almost as low as myself. He has, for more than two months past, had
> a pain in his blind eye, the effect of which has been to occasion a
> weakness in the other, and he broods over the dismal apprehension
> of becoming quite blind.

---

[1] It is hardly necessary to add that a recognised authority on sea-songs,
the late Admiral Sir Cyprian Bridge, takes a poor view of Dibdin, a Covent
Garden sailor, and says his songs rarely came to the notice of the Navy's
forecastles and were never popular. As for Garrick's——!

The first President of the Royal Academy was in his seventieth year; wealthy, world-famous, kind, hospitable, deaf, half-blind, and rapidly approaching the tomb. 'He used to be looked upon as perhaps the most happy man in the world', adds Boswell sadly; and indeed not even the great Dr. Mead had lived in the broad sunshine of life, to use Johnson's phrase, more continuously than the King of British Art, who could take his incessant snuff from an opulently-bediamonded gold box sent him, with a flattering autograph-note, by his admirer Catherine the Great, and whose model's throne—that easy chair now preserved reverently under glass in the Diploma Gallery at Burlington House [1]—held most of the famous and the fair of the England of his time. Inevitably, though nobody of intelligence nowadays echoes the youthful Pre-Raphaelites' breezy cry 'Sir Sloshua!', a little of Reynolds's contemporary splendour has faded with the years, like some of his colours, which he did not wield with medieval and Renaissance skill, though he is reputed to have skinned and rubbed down not a few Old Masters, authentic and doubtful, in his vain pursuit of their secret. I am informed by the eminent portraitist, Mr. James Gunn, that many canvasses of that period when Reynolds got his colour by glazing and 'scumbling' have now returned, with the restorers' help, to their basic monochrome. But even the most restless and irritable modern art-critics, apt to ejaculate the loathly word 'academic' with a peculiar grating and hooting emphasis, concede that Reynolds is a great, and in his own fashion, a creative portrait-painter.

Now he was plainly breaking up. 'I force myself to be a great deal with him', Boswell tells Temple, 'and to do what is in my power to amuse him.' To be amusing is not very easy at the moment. 'I attend in Westminster Hall, but there is not the least prospect of my having business. . . . This is a desponding, querulous letter.'

I pause to remark that no one has yet given Boswell credit for the admirable courage with which he fought his losing battle with the English Law over nearly ten years; daily plunging into the arena, daily seeing all the briefs going to other men,

[1] Though the Royal Academy did not lift a finger to prevent the destruction of Sir Joshua's house in Leicester Square in the 1930's.

daily becoming more aware of defeat (despite Malone's comforting remark that ill-success at the Bar should not make him
unhappy, since he had chosen 'a wide and varied course of life'),
and resuming the struggle doggedly. No wonder he dined out
as much as he could, and often drank too much. Whether, as a
recent authority affirms, he was now drinking himself to death
we shall pleasurably examine in due course.

Reynolds died, almost stone-blind, on February 23 in the
following year. The manuscript of Burke's well-known panegyric,
written in a room adjoining that in which his friend's body lay,
is preserved somewhere, I believe, with the marks of Burke's
tears still visible on it. As for Boswell, another great gap had
been torn in his existence. In August he notes sombrely in his
diary how London has changed for him of late. 'No General
Paoli—no Sir Joshua Reynolds—no Sir John Pringle—no General
Oglethorpe!' It sounds dismal enough. Need we pity him too
much? He has plenty of friends left in London. Among the old
ones there is Wilkes, to begin with, whose company in increasing
age is still gay and bawdy and bracing, and whose dinners in
Grosvenor Square, or at his Prince's Gate establishment, where
Mrs. Arnold is still enthroned, are always pleasant. There is
Malone, whose affections, like Langton's, never falters, however often Boswell's turbulent high spirits may ruffle his
rather old-maidish composure. There is John Courtenay, M.P.,
who franks all his letters and entertains him frequently, and
Windham of Norfolk, and the ever-hospitable Dilly, all intimates.
There are his fellow-members of the Royal Academy Club and
the Literary Club, with all of whom, since Hawkins resigned,
he is on cordial and equal terms, with the single exception of
'that ugly, affected, disgusting fellow Gibbon, who poisons our
Club to me', as he once remarked to Temple. Between Boswell
and the stout, sneering historian of the Roman Empire, as
between Boswell and Baretti, there was always an impassable
gulf, unusual in the life of this friendliest of creatures. And there
is the great Burke, who, despite their acute differences on political questions—especially in the matter of Warren Hastings, for
whom Boswell is a frenetic and often tactless partisan—and
despite his overpowering mental equipment and lecturing habit,
which always make Boswell, like most people, feel small, and

despite his firm, kind, maddening refusal to take Boswell's extra-literary ambitions seriously, has certainly a considerable liking for him, even if it is sometimes tinged with irritation and subject to coolnesses on both sides. How can Boswell be said to lack friends? He lost a few throughout the years, like every other human being, but he could make them, whenever he chose, among men of worth, intellect, and standing. It was not every man in London who would shortly receive the Earl of Pembroke's 'compliments and ten thousand thanks to Mr. Boswell' in reply to the suggestion of a forthcoming visit to Wilton.

I find I have overlooked four of his closest intimates. Boswell is on excellent terms nowadays with his two schoolboy sons, Sandie and Jamie, and his two elder daughters, Veronica and Euphemia; also little Betsy, though Betsy is too young to share most of their amusements. Grouse-shooting in the holidays with Sandie the Etonian, whose congratulatory Latin verses on the *Life* gratified his father more, perhaps, than any other tributes, bouts of 'drafts' with Jamie, a much better player, and tea and card-parties with the girls are current examples of their comradeship. At home, as Euphemia Boswell told Farington, R.A., in 1801, he was the same pleasant, good-humoured companion as abroad, and his fits of low spirits passed off in an hour.

We need not picture the two elder Boswell girls, incidentally, as milk-and-water misses, all curls, curtseys, and deference. Like any other girls they frequently provoke their father to extreme annoyance by contradicting and lecturing him.[1] He complains testily to Sandie in a letter of August 1792 that they have been spoiled by living in London and associating with people who 'cajole' them, and says their want of reserve and respect towards him frequently distresses him. But, he adds, they have good hearts; as well they might, considering what they owe him. Apart from his allotting the greater part of his income to his children's benefit, the Isham papers show that ever since their infancy this rackety fellow has been as fond a father as Steele, whom he so often recalls; keenly interested in his children, romping and reading with them, and—a point his

[1] 'They are exceedingly advanced for their years ... nor have I almost any authority over them. My only hold is their *affection*.'—Boswell to Temple, November 28, 1789.

critics have glided over unanimously in tactful silence—seeing
to their religious instruction with particular care. On more wet
Sunday evenings than one, surrounded by his offspring and
reading with them from some devotional work like Dr. Ogden's
*Sermons*, or the Book of Common Prayer, Boswell compares not
unfavourably with Mr. Fairchild of *The Fairchild Family*; or
perhaps favourably, since he would never have subjected his
children to that celebrated sadistic ordeal of the gibbet. Now
they are grown up he accompanies his daughters regularly to
Portland Chapel, now St. Paul's, Great Portland Street, or some
other Anglican church. One finds it difficult to reconcile these
things with the stock picture of the selfish loafer and reprobate
drinking himself to death and reeling down the road to ruin.

Pondering which strange discrepancy, we hear a rumble of
wheels and perceive a two-horse travelling chaise pulling up at
a quarter to eight one bright August morning of this year 1792
outside No. 47 Great Portland Street. Into it, after the baggage
has been stowed by a manservant, step the Misses Veronica
and Euphemia Boswell, followed by James Boswell, Esq. In the
highest of spirits they settle into their seats. The coachman cracks
his whip, and the chaise rolls away down Oxford Street towards
the Great West Road, its occupants exulting in the fresh blue-
and-gold of the early summer morning, *le bel, le vierge, le vivace
aujourd'hui*. The Boswells are on the way to a holiday in
Cornwall.

### 3

Even today, despite the hordes of kindly artists who infest her
shores and interpret her every mood, and despite the civilising
influence of the Great Western Railway, Cornwall wears a
foreign and even (to the mild Anglo-Saxon eye) a sinister air,
due to the savage beauty of her coasts and the haunted desola-
tion of her inland wastes, but chiefly to her dark and secret
Hispano-Celt aboriginals. In 1792, though the ancient Cornish
tongue had died a few years before with old Dolly Pentreath,
Cornwall stood infinitely more aloof. O happy age, rich in
emotions, when Horace Walpole could shudder, amid a thousand
perils, at wild faces jabbering a language unknown, and discover
the country to be Sussex.

Boswell's impressions of Cornwall may be noted here and now. The inland scenery reminds him of the bad parts of Lowland Scotland. The blackavised natives, short, fierce, hairy, inscrutable, side-glancing, inaccessible, barefooted like 'Skye boys', remind him of Swift's Yahoos. The Cornish climate—it rained lavishly during the four weeks the Boswells were there—brings on at length one of his blackest attacks of melancholia. Falmouth Bay he admires, the dizzy steeps of Land's End he labels 'horrid', and the stench of Marazion poisons all St. Michael's Mount. He apparently saw nothing of the beautiful places we admire year by year in every modern Royal Academy Exhibition—Lamorna Cove, Kynance, Kennack, Tintagel, St. Ives (fishing-boats), Carbis Bay (sunset); nor did he experience the terrifying magic of huge Atlantic seas crashing on Gunwalloe Sands in a south-west gale. Smugglers and wreckers, though both were flourishing marvellously in the 1790's, are as absent from his diary as the giant Tregeagle and other mystical local fauna. Nevertheless Mr. James and the Misses Boswell enjoyed their month in Cornwall.

They had gone down to visit the Reverend William Johnston Temple at his rectory of St. Gluvias, opposite Penrhyn, where Boswell's oldest friend and mild unwearied confidant had a comfortable living, with a drab and peevish wife and a pleasant grown-up family. The Boswells received a deal of hospitality on their way down. The first call out of London had been at Bagshot, where Boswell's youngest daughter Betsy was staying with the Williamses, the family of a school-friend. Here Boswell records a comic moment of embarrassment. Fourteen-year-old Miss Williams, Betsy's friend, had stayed with Betsy at Great Portland Street, and it seems that one evening Mr. Boswell, flushed with wine, had permitted himself to embrace the agreeable young creature with slightly more than paternal fondness. This memory made him a little 'remorseful'—more accurately, perhaps, self-conscious—on meeting her hospitable parents, but the feeling soon passed off. The next evening he and his daughters dined at the palace at Salisbury with his old friend the Bishop, Dr. Douglas, and played whist. Two evenings later they were at Wilton, that noble seat of the Sidneys,

> ... *Pembroke's* princely dome, where mimick Art
> Decks with a magick hand the dazzling bow'rs,
> Its living hues where the warm pencil pours,
> And breathing forms from the rude marble start ...[1]

Lord Pembroke's charming, flattering welcome made Boswell regret, as the Earl strolled with him round those historic parterres before dinner, arm-in-arm, discussing the golden days of Johnson and Paoli, that he and Pembroke had met so little during the past few years. On August 21 the Boswells reached Exeter and encountered an hospitable relative, Major Hamilton. Two days later they crossed the Devon border and came by way of Bodmin and Truro to pleasant St. Gluvias.

Amid Boswell's notes of Cornish hospitality there are two arresting episodes. On August 29, when he and his daughters dined with Sir William Lemon, M.P., at Carclew, there was some general badinage at table on the subject of Mr. Boswell's gallantry towards one of the ladies present. A certain uneasiness under the mirth did not escape him. 'I observed at dinner a kind of apprehension that I might make a *Book* of my Tour', he notes. After dinner Lady Lemon, saying half-laughingly, half-nervously, 'Pray don't insert this!' ('I laughed and said "No, no" ') showed that this preoccupation was more than momentary. The same thing had occurred in London a few weeks previously. Some friends of Sir William Scott, asked to meet Boswell at dinner, had expressed the same trepidation, whereupon Boswell promptly declined the invitation. Such annoying suspicions could probably be traced to Mrs. Thrale and her spiteful anecdotes. Evidently eighteenth-century hostesses were more shy of being 'put into a book' than hostesses are today.

The second Cornish episode affords us another glimpse of the old essential Boswell, apart from an interesting vignette of a third-rate provincial theatre. Rain fell so heavily on September 3 at St. Gluvias that Boswell and Temple spent most of the day sorting and arranging Boswell's correspondence with his friend over thirty years, and sentimentalising over lost youth. Boswell had this day picked up and glanced through the first volume of Rousseau's recently-published *Confessions*, which may have in-

---

[1] Rev. Thos. Warton, Poet Laureate.

spired this mood. In the evening the weather cleared, and the Boswells and the younger Temples went into Falmouth to the play. The theatre was two public rooms at 'a low inn'; the orchestra was two fiddlers, one a Negro; the triple playbill was *Which is the Man?*, *The Wapping Landlady*, and *The Padlock*. Boswell says nothing about the performance, and for a very good reason. Glancing at one of the rustic boxes on the opposite side of the pit, he perceived in the company of three foreign gentlemen, 'a little french Mademoiselle I knew for some time in London, by the name of Divry'. He affected not to know the lady, and she, recognising him equally, did the same; but his ever-susceptible heart began to flutter, and the ranting of the players could not drown the lilt of a suddenly-remembered old French song of his Grand Tour:

> Je reconnois les atteintes
> Qui m'ont autrefois charmés . . .

With an effort he put an end to these twinges of the flesh at length by reflecting what a 'base and mercenary creature' the little charmer actually was, and the encounter had no sequel. One could wish this glimpse of romantic mystery, very fitting to a novel by 'Q', had been longer and more revealing. What could an attractive London cocotte and her escort of three foreign gentlemen possibly be doing in a place like Falmouth? Bourbon *émigrés*? Jacobin agents? Russian spies, about to probe or even damage at Plymouth or Falmouth some of that three million pounds'-worth of naval preparation which had assisted Pitt to force his recent peace-treaty on Spain? (The growing imperialist aggressiveness of Russia under Catherine the Great, as today, was one of the Cabinet's major preoccupations.) Was the little Mademoiselle connected in some way with the money Danton was said to be drawing from the British Government? Enigma; but the possibilities are enchanting.

Only once during this holiday did Boswell really drink too much. This was at Lord Falmouth's seat at Tregothnan, where he became so 'noisy and rattling' that Temple was visibly uneasy, though to be sure Lord Falmouth himself was equally drunk. Lady Falmouth took no notice and showed most polite attention to Veronica and Euphemia, whose next-day comments on Papa's exhibition are not recorded.[1] At Lord Camelford's two days later Boswell dined with studious moderation, though extremely interested in a White Hermitage he had never met before. At Lord Eliot's on the following day there were seven kinds of wine at dinner, apart from cider and beer; but Boswell records, looking somewhat down his nose, that neither Eliot nor his son buzzed the bottle very handsomely.

Returning to London by the end of September, Boswell at once joined the Home Circuit at Chelmsford in a fit of deep depression; partly, no doubt, reaction from a holiday, partly due to what coroners call 'natural causes'. In November he dined with Wilkes in Grosvenor Square and recorded again with envy how pleasant it was to see his old gay friend 'enjoying life as I have seen him do in Italy, six and twenty years ago'. He dined out constantly this winter, drank, as usual, too much at intervals, and frequented the Essex Head Club in Essex Street, Strand, with the remnants of the Johnsonian foundation-members of that assembly; the Italian tutor Sastres, whose poor opinion of Boswell I have quoted in an early page, and the dilettante-naturalist Daines Barrington were among them. Fortunately a new interest had come into Boswell's life since the summer of this year; a noble and absorbing and unselfish interest, dictated entirely by that good heart of his, which, if the reader is not tired of hearing about such things, was to provide him with some months of unprofitable labour cheerfully performed.

Friday, August 17, 1792, the day the Boswells left London for Cornwall, was a day later than they had intended. Boswell had delayed departure at the last moment on account of an appointment granted, at his own urgent request, at the Whitehall office of the Rt. Hon. Henry Dundas, Secretary of State, at one o'clock on the 16th. This appointment the overbearing Dundas, who had little time for Boswell (though he had been 'frank and good-humoured' enough when asked to dinner in 1787) and probably expected a foolish application for some place, did not keep.[2]

---

[1] They may have provoked the testy letter to Sandie, p. 242 *ante*.

[2] Boswell had no illusions about Dundas now. 'My first letter to Dundas, concerning your son, was repeating my words to you, that I was afraid he did not like me (or something to that effect) but that I believed him to

Dundas was mistaken. Boswell was not concerned for his own interests this time. On returning home he wrote Dundas a coldly polite note, asking the favour of 'two lines directed *Penrhyn, Cornwall,* assuring me that nothing harsh shall be done to the unfortunate adventurers from New South Wales, for whom I interest myself . . .'

Once more, as in the case of John Reid the sheep-stealer and two or three or four more miserable abandoned wretches who awakened his benevolence in his Scotch Bar days, Boswell was to forget his troubles temporarily in the alleviation of those of others. A provincial Jenny Diver named Mary Bryant, *née* Broad, is the principal character in the episode to follow.

Mary Broad, aged 22, sentenced for life at Exeter Assizes for a street robbery at Plymouth, was among the first batch of 750 convicts of both sexes to be sent to the new penal colony of Port Jackson, Botany Bay, in May 1787, the secession of the American Colonies having forced the British Government to find another dumping-ground for these waste-products of its civilisation, who were packing all the gaols. The convoy took eight months to reach Australia. No preparations had been made at Port Jackson to receive the convicts. There were no houses, no crops, no proper agricultural implements, and little food. By 1790 actual starvation loomed. At the end of that year Mary Broad, who had married a fellow-convict, a Cornish fisherman-smuggler named William Bryant, transported for seven years for fighting His Majesty's revenue officers, decided that escape could be no worse than continuous misery. Bryant at length contrived to buy stores unperceived from a visiting Dutch ship, with two old muskets and some powder. On the night of March 28, 1791, taking his wife, their two children—one aged three, the other a baby at the breast—and seven male fellow-convicts, he commandeered the Governor's sailing-cutter, foiled the alarm, and put to sea, making for the Dutch island of Timor, more than 3,000 miles away to the north-west, half-way round Australia.

The hardships of the fugitives, which included several murder-

---

be a generous fellow', etc., etc.—Boswell to Temple, August 22, 1791. Dundas, though he repelled Temple by his coarseness, apparently did what Boswell asked of him on young Temple's behalf in due course.

ous attacks from natives by land and sea, were frightful. On June 5 nevertheless they made Kupang in Timor, like Bligh of the *Bounty* two years previously, and were charitably received by the Governor, passing themselves off as survivors from the wreck of an English vessel. Inevitably, before long, one of Bryant's mates got drunk and blabbed, and the irate Governor, clapping them all in chains except the babies, packed them off to England in the next Dutch East India Company frigate. By the time Mary Bryant got to London in July 1792, to be charged at Bow Street and committed to Newgate pending trial as a returned transportee, she had lost husband and both children by fever on the high seas and was a pitiable object indeed. It is here that James Boswell, reading about her and her four fellow-survivors in the *London Chronicle* and being moved by pure compassion, comes into her story.

He hurried down to Newgate immediately and saw all five prisoners, who were lying there waiting their turn to appear at Old Bailey. No one had taken any interest in them, they had no legal help, and the penalty they faced was death. Swallowing his private feelings against Mr. Secretary Dundas, who held their fate in his hands, Boswell began at once to besiege him vigorously in their behalf. Ten months later his unremitting labours bore fruit. Mary Bryant, who had been returned with the others to Newgate without trial to work out their sentences—the Government was in merciful mood—was released by Royal clemency, extended six months later, after further hard work by Boswell, to her fellow-convicts as well.

His endeavours for Mary Bryant were not finished yet. On being discharged from Newgate in May 1793 she took a respectable lodging in Little Titchfield Street, and Boswell, setting about raising funds to help her, called on Lord Chancellor Thurlow for this purpose one morning at breakfast-time in his house on the corner of King Street and St. James's Square. The great man received him amiably and rang for more coffee, tea, and hot buttered toast, and Boswell, after accepting a compliment on his speech in a recent Lords' appeal, opened his case for Mary Bryant. Thurlow, who had been so sympathetic over Dr. Johnson's Italian holiday, refused to excite himself over the affairs of an obscure female convict. 'Damn her blood, let her go to a day's work,' growled Lord Thurlow, munching his toast. After listening a little longer he owned that Boswell was a persuasive advocate, promised a donation, and finally asked Boswell and Miss Veronica to dinner to meet the eldest of his daughters; an invitation which Boswell, who had strong feudal principles on the social aspects of bastardy and thought Chancellors of England should marry their mistresses, tactfully sidestepped.

To conclude this affair we may skip five months more and come to October 1793. Boswell has arranged at last that Mary Bryant shall return to Fowey, her Cornish home; her respectable parents, who have lately inherited some money, have agreed to receive her back kindly. After dinner on October 12, accordingly, Boswell and his schoolboy son Jamie take a hackney-coach to Titchfield Street. Later, while Jamie goes on to Dilly's, his father takes Mary down to the Southwark wharf from which her vessel, the *Ann and Elizabeth*, is due to sail for Cornwall early next morning. Over a farewell bowl of punch at a public-house on the wharf Boswell makes the last arrangements, assuring her of a regular ten pounds a year as long as she behaves herself, 'being resolved', he says in his diary, 'to make it up to her myself in so far as subscriptions should fail.'

Having taken her aboard, bidden her goodbye with 'sincere good will', and paid the captain her passage-money, Boswell returned home. He never saw Mary Bryant again, and there is no more news of her. A year later, as a letter of his from Auchinleck to his brother David in London reveals, he was already paying the whole of her annuity himself. Six months after that he was dead.

The case of Mary Bryant demonstrates to what heights of practical Franciscan pity Boswell could rise towards the end of a life intermittently clouded by disappointment and despondency. That he had no ulterior motive is clear. Whether a poor jailbird like Mary Bryant possessed any looks or not after her ordeals and her recent ten months in Newgate, she was certainly not Boswell's mistress; if she had been, he would have noted it automatically in his diary with his other passing amours, and, even more conclusively, he would never have dreamed of taking his fifteen-year-old son, the Westminster boy, to call on her. His most suspicious critics have to admit that his behaviour in this

case is pure altruism, or, as the civilised would say, pure
Christian charity (*caritas*). Perhaps—who knows?—the Good
Samaritan himself drank too much at times.

## 4

We return to the beginning of 1793.

Forlorn as Auchinleck seemed to its laird nowadays, dank
and cold and melancholy as the Palladian family manor was
with its many shuttered windows and its dust-sheets and its
memories, the estate had a call on him this year which gave
him a moment of pride and feudal pleasure. Old Mr. John Dunn,
the parish minister, his first tutor, to whom Lord Auchinleck
had given the family living, had died in the previous October.
It was Boswell's duty and privilege as laird to appoint or at
least confirm the successor to a pastor he had known all his
life and had, to some extent, sympathised with on that dread
occasion when Jove's thunderbolt ('Sir, you know no more of
our Church than a Hottentot!') crashed on Mr. Dunn's unfortunate wig.

Informing Temple on February 26 that he is just about to
start north by the Carlisle coach, Boswell spreads his wings with
serio-comic pomp.

It is quite right that I should now go down. The choice of a minister
to a worthy parish is a matter of very great importance, and I cannot
be sure of the real wishes of the people without being present. Only
think, Temple, how serious a duty I am about to discharge! I, *James
Boswell, Esq.*—you know what vanity that name includes!—I have
promised to come down on purpose, and his Honour's goodness is
gratefully acknowledged. Besides, I have several matters of consequence to my estate to adjust . . .

He much dislikes the prospect of being alone, except for his
housekeeper, Mrs. Bruce, in 'that house where once I was so
happy', and he intends, he says, to stay at Auchinleck only about
three weeks, having to appear in a Lords' appeal-case in April,
when, in addition, the Second Edition of the *Life* is due for
publication, continuing some valuable additional matter. Boswell's qualifications for appointing a Presbyterian parish minister

are not obvious. It would seem that his duty was merely to approve the choice of the kirk-session from the rival candidates who, as in *Auld Licht Idylls*, would each give the elders and congregation a sample of pulpit-oratory in turn. Boswell himself, though he would readily join in Presbyterian family prayers out of courtesy to a Hebridean host, and though he dutifully attended the parish kirk with his father when he and Dr. Johnson were at Auchinleck, deprecating Johnson's refusal to countenance sectarian assemblies and advancing the theory that the Thirty-Nine Articles and the Westminister Confession are identical in doctrine (which must have infuriated some of his more implacable Scottish readers), had no love for Calvinism and noticeably left it behind, like 'jeel', every time he recrossed the Border. Evidently he was nothing more than a figurehead during the election of his new parish minister, and the portentous flourish of his announcement to Temple is what his age called 'flam', and intended for nothing else, though some people insist on taking Boswell seriously at all times.

With this letter he sent his old friend a packet of books and pamphlets which is such a typical cross-section of the average eighteenth-century English library that I cannot forbear setting down the list. It includes Brumoy's *Théâtre des Grecs*, a set of Thornton's *Plautus* ('I forget the price—they are above £4 4s.'), a printed sermon by the Bishop of St. David's, Hay's poems *The Village* and *The Library*, a *Letter to Charles James Fox* ('reckoned the best pamphlet that has appeared for some time'), two recent numbers of *The European Magazine* (containing 'your friend's' autobiographical sketch, already noted), and 'an excellent little tract on *Contentment*, by Dr. Paley.' One might encounter almost this identical bundle, dusty, foxed, battered, tied with string, in any country town junk-shop today, jostling a corroded brass warming-pan, a riveted 'Seve' teapot, a pair of rusty horse-pistols, a bootjack, and a faded colour-print of the Hero of Culloden.

Boswell himself was not reading much at home in the evenings nowadays. This excellent habit would have saved him a nasty experience in the coming June.

Despite the cold and dreary weather, breakfast in the Blue Room overlooking the river at Strawberry Hill on June 12, 1793, must have been enlivened to some extent for the aged Lord Orford, as we should henceforth style Horace Walpole, by perusal of the previous night's *London Chronicle*, if his tyrannical Swiss valet, Colomb, had seen fit to bring it in with the tea-equipage. Raising to his lips a teacup of 'fine old white embossed Japanese china', Lord Orford may have replaced it a moment with unsteady, chalkstoned fingers in order to study one particular news-item again more carefully.

Last Wednesday night [said the *Chronicle*] as James Boswell, Esq., was returning home from the City, he was attacked in Titchfield-street, knocked down, robbed, and left lying in the street quite stunned, so that the villain got clear off. A gentleman happening to pass that way, with the assistance of the watchman and patrole, conducted him safe to his house in Great Portland-street, when it was found he had received a severe cut on the back part of his head, and a contusion on both his arms; he has ever since been almost constantly confined to his bed, with a considerable degree of pain and fever.

Well, well, well, his lordship may have reflected, stroking his Disraeli-like profile and sipping his China tea by the fire. Johnson's zany in trouble at last, and not to be wondered at, indeed, considering his habits! Perhaps this accident will increase the sales of his absurd and tedious book—who knows? The public is so *saugrenu!*

Walpole's most recent contact with Boswell, so far as I know, is mentioned in a letter to Miss Berry in May 1791.

After the Doctor's death Burke, Sir Joshua Reynolds, and Boswell sent an ambling circular-letter to me, begging subscriptions to a monument for him—the two last, I think, impertinently; as they could not but know my opinion, and could not suppose I would contribute to a monument for one who had endeavoured, poor soul! to degrade my friend's [Gray's] superlative poetry. I would not deign to write an answer; but sent down word by my footman, as I would have done to parish-officers with a brief, that I would not subscribe.

I take the haughty Walpole to represent contemporary anti-Boswellism at its highest, for Baretti and Gibbon, more open enemies, had not the same itch for scribbling their likes and dislikes in letters to half the world. Not that Walpole's and

Gibbon's would be the only eyebrows raised in scorn or merriment at Boswell's misadventure. *The London Chronicle* was a twopenny evening paper published thrice weekly, with a circulation of some 2,500 to 3,000.[1] It appeared at most of the fashionable tea-tables, and I do not doubt that a few marked copies of the June 8-11 issue arrived in Ayrshire within a post or two. We may take it that Boswell had once more achieved that publicity he loved, though perhaps not exactly as he liked it.

The mishap reported by the *Chronicle* had been a bad shaking for the victim, who, one fears, was a little drunk at the time. He betook himself to his old confessor as usual a fortnight later.

My dear Temple,—Behold my *hand!* The robbery is only of a few shillings, but the cut on my head and the bruises on my arms were sad things, and confined me to bed, in pain and fever and helplessness, as a child, many days. By means of Surgeon Earle and Apothecary Devaynes, I am now, thank God, pretty well. This however shall be a crisis in my life: I trust I shall henceforth be a sober, regular man. Indeed, my indulgence in wine has, of late years especially, been excessive . . .

The old refrain. But he has really had a fright.

Your suggestion as to my being carried off in a state of intoxication is awful. I thank you for it, my dear friend. It impressed me much, I assure you.

Temple's hint that his friend might die a sudden death while drunk was certainly an appalling thought, and by no means fantasy. The London night was full of menace, as we have perceived. Footpads fractured a gentleman's skull in Soho in the same week that Boswell was held up. Everything was heavily against the victim of prowling thugs: the rare, dim oil lamps, the twisting alleys, the dark arches and byways, the few and generally far-off constables, who might be asleep, or drunk, or bad characters themselves, the absurd elderly night-watchmen hobbling along with lantern, staff and rattle. Safe in bed in

[1] Dr. Johnson's favourite newspaper. He wrote the front page 'leader', or manifesto of policy, for its first number, January 1, 1757. Boswell gives the *Chronicle* a puff in the *Life* for 'good sense, accuracy, moderation, and delicacy', and says it was more read on the Continent than any other British journal.

Great Portland Street and recovering from his shock, Boswell
doubtless realised what may have been a lucky escape, for his
assailant might easily have cut his throat in a rage at his small
takings, and got away undetected. Unlike Popish thugs, they
would never give you time to say a prayer.

Boswell's firm intention this time to lead a more creditable
life lasted as long as the others. Other hopes continued to flicker
also, indomitably if intermittently. Had he ever liked Goldsmith's
verse he might have remembered, without pleasure, some lines
from *The Captivity* which well fitted his case.

> To the last moment of his breath
> On Hope the wretch relies,
> And even the pang preceding death
> Bids Expectation rise . . .

Writing in July to thank James Abercrombie of Philadelphia,
an ardent admirer of the *Life,* for copies of two letters from
Dr. Johnson to American friends, Boswell expresses a great desire
to visit the United States, now ten years old. 'I once flattered
myself', he adds wistfully, 'that I should be sent thither in a
station of some importance', reminding us that we have somehow
overlooked one more than usually exciting 'rise of expectation'.
It was a brief but dazzling one. Returning with Boswell from
Lord Lonsdale's house in a hackney-coach one December night
four years before, Governor Richard Penn mentioned the possibility of an appointment, already urged in his behalf by Lonsdale
on Pitt, as Ambassador to the United States. Hardly were the
words out of his mouth before Boswell jovially remarked that his
Excellency would need a good First Secretary. Certainly, agreed
the genial Penn. Well, in that case——? Why, of course! Sure!
As the coach rumbled up Bond Street they shook hands delightedly on it, and that night Boswell confided to his diary:
'*This was an opening for me into the New World.*' How many
weeks this new dream lasted I cannot discover. The ambassador-
ship failed to materialise. There will be an even more enticing
dream to dazzle the diplomat Boswell before long.

Meanwhile, bored by yet another briefless circuit and looking
round for diversion, he toyed for a time, as we learn from a
letter to his friend Andrew Gibb, with the possibility of visiting

the front in Flanders, where a British army under the Duke of
York was attacking the French in conjunction with an Austrian
army under the Prince of Coburg. Early this year Pitt's desperate
efforts to keep the peace had broken down and he had become,
in the mouth of every Jacobin, *l'ennemi du genre humain*. The
year 1793 had started ominously for the Republic with
Dumouriez' defeat and desertion at Neerwinden, followed swiftly
by the fall of the strong-points of Condé, Mayence, and Valenciennes, with their garrisons. By July British G.H.Q. was at
Valenciennes, and it was here that Boswell proposed to visit
the victorious army, for in those easy days such visits, given
the necessary influence, were a matter of course. While he was
still considering which strings to pull a more immediate and
practicable military diversion presented itself. As a sort of
prelude he made Bennet Langton, a major in the Royal North
Lincolnshire Militia, now undergoing annual training, invite him
to Warley Camp, as he had invited Dr. Johnson in 1778 and
1783.

It is tempting but unfair to dismiss Pitt's Militia, viewed
through contemporary eyes, as a comic predecessor of the Home
Guard of 1939-44. If the Trained Bands of London were a traditional joke to the Cockney—there is a passage in *The London
Spy* making robustious play with a company on parade in Westminster Palace Yard and the antics of 'so many *Greasie Cooks,
Tun-bellied Lick-Spiggots*, and *fat wheezing Butchers*, sweating
in their Buff Doublets, under the Command of some *Fiery-fac'd
Brewer*, whose *Gudgel-Gut* was hoop'd in with a Golden Sash' [1]—
there is plenty of evidence that the military value of Pitt's
Militia many years later was far from negligible, though it
varied, as with the late Home Guard, according to the keenness
and efficiency of battalion and company commanders.

Like Captain Edward Gibbon (retired), Major Langton took
his soldiering seriously, and the annual training at Warley seems
not to have been chiefly an excuse for banquets like the one
given by the wealthy officers of the Sussex Militia at the Old
Ship tavern, Brighton, in 1779, at which Mrs. Thrale, Fanny

[1] Johnson was drawn by ballot for the Trained Bands *circa* 1757 and
provided himself with musket and sword, though never called on to serve

Burney, Arthur Murphy, and the Bishop of Peterborough were
guests. Like Gibbon, also, Langton specialised in musketry, and
Johnson's remark in 1778 that 'the men indeed do load their
muskets and fire with wonderful celerity' may have been em-
bodied in more official language. The obvious difficulty with
Pitt's Militia was the enforcement of discipline. Drunken,
slovenly, and stupid files on parade, lack of proper care of arms
and equipment, routine duties shirked or badly performed, a
tendency to steal poultry and waste ammunition, and occasional
insubordination were among the problems most commanding
officers had to face.

Had the Militia ever been called upon to repel invasion it
would doubtless have acquitted itself as valorously as the raw
French levies at Wattignies. Meanwhile, like the Home Guard,
it rendered invaluable assistance to the Army by releasing
regular troops for operations abroad, and the three years' service
for which militiamen were drawn by ballot, with every trick the
ballot can imply, did the rank-and-file no harm. As for their
officers, what many of them lacked in efficiency and zeal was
more than compensated by the bright scarlet and gold lace of
the uniform, the kneeboots, laced hat, sash, and sword, which
made the amateur indistinguishable at a distance from the real
article. Mr. Pitt's gentlemen did great execution, if contemporary
caricatures are any guide, among Britain's admiring fair, and
occasionally conducted affairs of honour with quite professional
spirit. I find in *The Gentleman's Magazine* for May 1760 the
report of a candlelight duel in Manchester, of all places, which
is the essence of every stage-duel in romantic comedy. A Major
Glover of the Lancashire Militia, finding himself smacked jovially
on the back by a Mr. Jackson, an apothecary, in the playhouse,
retorted in kind with such vigour that they adjourned forthwith
to an adjacent tavern, ordered lights and a bottle in an upper
room, and fell to with their swords. Within five minutes Mr.
Jackson was run through and died, taking the blame and for-
giving the Major. One cannot help feeling that such a correct
and brisk affair, reflecting honour on the whole corps of *Herren
Offiziere* of Pitt's Militia, may have infused an extra touch of
swagger into their general deportment.

It seems that Warley Camp in the fickle July of 1793 was a disappointment. Susceptible as any Kaffir or Belfast Orangeman to the heady drug of screaming pipes and well-banged drums, Boswell was perhaps too old now to feel that impulse, once confessed to Johnson, to rush into the fray when the military music started and lay down his life for the House of Hanover. He also caught a cold. Whatever the reason, he tired of the tented field within a couple of weeks and dashed back to London, as a gaily apologetic letter to Langton dated July 24 reveals. Its peroration is pure triple-extract of Boswell. 'O London! London! there let me be; there let me see my friends; there a fair chance is given of pleasing and being pleased!' And he adds vaguely, 'I hesitate as to Valenciennes.' Perhaps the scarlet magic which had so excited him in the 1760's had faded; perhaps it was turning out difficult to pull those strings.

He need not regret the Valenciennes project unduly. The year still held plenty of opportunity of 'pleasing and being pleased'.

5

Mark this year how the inspissated gloom (according to the rhetors) of Boswell's decline is lit up ever and anon by the twinkling, fitful coloured lamps of hope and respite, like every other human existence.

We have just seen him flying in boredom from Warley Camp back to London. He is due immediately, one would say, for one of those familiar black spells of melancholia, brooding over his briefless desk in Chambers, brooding in Court, brooding at table, brooding over the newspapers, brooding in bed. Is he? Within a week we find him at Eton, jaunty, welcome, basking in appreciation, thrilled with childlike and pardonable satisfaction at his conquest of England's leading public school and the *cachet* of Eton's approval, and complacently presenting his friends the Provost, the Head Master, and the Under Master with copies of the Second Edition of the *Life* ('which', he remarks with gusto to Sandie, 'goes off wonderfully well'.) He will later make the same present, in Jamie's behalf, to the Head and Under Master of Westminster, but with less of a glow. *Floreat Etona* is engraved on Boswell's heart long since.

One or two more interesting lights and darks may be noted
s the year 1793 wanes. In September he enjoyed for a few days,
nd for the last time, the company of his dear Temple, who had
ome up to take his son John James to Eton, and on the 19th
e gave a dinner-party for his host of Paris days, Father Alex-
nder Gordon, Rector of the Scots College, whom he had not
een for many years. Father Gordon was now an *émigré*, the
cots College having been suppressed, with every other
eminary, religious house, oratory, and church in Paris, by the
acobins and turned into a prison.[1] His conversation seems to
ave charmed Temple, who was also present, equally with Sir
Christopher Hawkins, one of Boswell's recent Cornish acquain-
ances, for all three travelled down to the West together a week
ater.

Early in October, as the glow of conducting Mary Bryant's
ase to a successful conclusion faded, news of the suicide of
Andrew Erskine, Lord Kellie's son, that ebullient companion and
orrespondent of his youth, gave Boswell a painful shock; but
his sorrow passed, like any other. At Covent Garden one
vening about a week later, seated close to the orchestra and
lelighting as ever in the gaieties of another revival of *The
Beggar's Opera,* he found the ancestral Charles Macklin by his
ide, remarking between the acts that he, Macklin, had played
n Gay's piece 'when it first came out'; a remark Boswell records
vith polite dubiety. No doubt at the age of 103 the old gentle-
nan's memory was not what it had been. I do not find his name
vith that of Walker (Macheath) and Lavinia Fenton (Polly)
n the original cast of 1729, when Macklin was 39.

Not long afterwards Boswell himself was playing juvenile lead
n a traditional romantic comedy-scene ('. . . Don Juan, by Mr.
Boswell. Act i, Sc. i, a Church in Seville') with all his youthful
rio. Although he certainly never went to church, like the Don,
imply to quiz chance-encountered beauties,

> . . . las damas,
> Las que van guapas y frescas,

[1] Saint-Just was imprisoned here for a few hours during Thermidor. In
800 the College was given back to the Scots priesthood. Under Louis-
Philippe, its function having come to an end, it became an *institution libre,*
nd it has since served as an orphanage.

he was as susceptible as any Pepys to charms which migh
impinge there on his frequently-wandering eye. So having re
marked, during High Mass at the Spanish Embassy Chapel on
Sunday morning, November 10, a strikingly attractive *devot*
who looked to him like a foreign actress or an Opera dancer
behold Don Jaime Boswell after Mass pacing discreetly behind
the fair unknown and her duenna all the way from Spanish Plac
to Thornhaugh, now Huntley, Street, Bloomsbury, noting th
house, No. 5, into which they vanished, and resolving to mak
inquiries in the neighborhood. He never did so, but I thinl
he tripped homewards after this episode humming a tune, witl
his foolish head full of moonlight and guitars.

Such coloured interludes do not brighten every day, naturally
Melancholy and restlessness oppress this mercurial fellow, a
winter closes in, for longer periods than they used. 'Much altered
for the worse', noted his friend Farington in October. Hi
evenings at home, however infrequent, are becoming tedious
he is dreading middle-aged solitude and needing more congenia
company at table than that of two loved but often irritating
daughters. A half-comic, half-pathetic diary-note of late Septem
ber records that he had just dined with the Earl of Inchiquin
later Marquis of Thomond, and his handsome Countess, *né*
Mary Palmer—niece and heiress to Sir Joshua Reynolds, wh
left her £40,000 (there is a fine Downman portrait of her in a
private collection)—after encountering their chariot that day by
chance. Being engaged to go to the play after dinner, his hos
and hostess left their unhappy guest dithering vaguely in th
street, 'just warmed with wine', with nowhere to go. Boswel
solved this particular evening's problem by going home to bed
at 6.45 in disgust. 'Strange kind of Life', he reflects, recording it

There is another slice of almost similar pathos a little later
with a happier ending. He describes himself standing dejectedly
on a December afternoon in the courtyard of St. James's Palace
staring into the chilly gathering dusk, listening to the grea
clock striking half-past four, utterly desolate. He had walked
slowly from Great Portland Street, hoping to meet a dinner
companion on the way. As he returned dismally up St. James'
Street, knowing it was now too late, a friendly voice hailed him
It was the voice of Lord Eardley. Boswell was saved.

Sampson, first and last Baron Eardley in the peerage of
eland, now in his fifties, is an interesting figure. His father, the
miable and powerful Sampson Gideon, king of the Money
larket, a Portuguese Jew, had financed a couple of Prime
linisters and raised a million-pound loan to get the Government
ver the Jacobite scare of 1745. Though the elder Gideon never
hanged his faith, he married a Protestant and had his children
rought up in that religion. His only son Sampson, created a
aronet at the age of eleven for his father's services and raised
o the peerage in 1789, having married meanwhile the daughter
f Chief Justice Sir John Eardley Wilmot, is, I believe, the first
emi-alien of Jewish blood to achieve a British barony, though
here were numbers of immensely wealthy and eligible Jewish
nanciers, moneylenders, and merchants, German, Spanish, and
ortuguese, in the City at this period, apart from one or two
pulent Jewish physicians like Meyer Schomberg.[1]

Altogether there were some 20,000 Jews in London at this
me. The inky gentlemen who compiled the Newgate Calendar
dulge in rather sour comment on the case of four Jews hanged
t Tyburn in 1771 for robbery and murder, accusing the lower
rders of London Jewry of practising regular perjury for hire
'cheap as Jew bail' was a current saying), circulating base
noney, receiving stolen goods, corrupting servants, and other
aginesque activities, cloaked by the traditional traffic in old
lothes and miscellaneous rubbish. But except for the four
riminals mentioned above, Jews figure in the Calendar hardly
t all, from which one may deduce that, as Johnson said of
teele, they chiefly practised the lighter vices. The influence of
reat money-lenders like Gideon and Isaac Fernandez Silva at
he St. James's, or what Swift calls the hither-end, of town was
f course considerable, as in any age, and they were indispen-
able in the politics of the period, as Wilkes's heavy dealings
ith them reveal. I cannot find any trace of Boswell's ever having
one to the Jews', hard up as he constantly was, and his friend-
hip with Lord Eardley had no mercenary strings. Eardley, a
ighly cultivated and agreeable man, had long since made a

[1] Hawkins (*Life of Johnson*) estimates Schomberg's income at £4,000 a
ear. He discarded the synagogue at the beginning of his career.

position for himself in the arrogant and closely-fenced London
society of the eighteenth century.

A few days after dining with Lord Eardley Boswell enjoyed
himself in a vastly different world, dining at the hospitable table
in Red Lion Square, Bloomsbury, of Charles Butler, the leading
English Catholic layman of his time. Boswell had met Butler
recently at Dilly's, with the banker-poet Samuel Rogers. A little
nervous at first of 'so well-informed and shrewd a man', he felt
quickly under the spell of a debonair and somewhat imperious
personality. Butler, a connoisseur of poetry and a devout Johnsonian, was nephew to Dr. Alban Butler the hagiologist and a
lawyer of some erudition, with a notable work on Coke-upon-
Littleton, one or two other legal treatises, and a biography of
Erasmus to his pen. Like every other lawyer of his religion,
race, and period he had been forced, after leaving the English
College at Douay, to practise 'under the Bar', till the Act of
1791 enabled him to be called at the age of 41; the first call for
a Catholic lawyer since 1688.[1] He is notable for his achievement
as secretary to the Committee formed by a group of nobility and
gentry in 1782 'to manage the publick affairs of the Catholicks
of this Kingdom'. With vigorous efficiency and urbane shrewdness Butler combined strong unobtrusive piety and a bull-headed
Anglo-Saxon, or perhaps Gallican, capacity for opposition to his
co-leader, Bishop Milner of the Midland District, during that
difficult period of disagreement on policy when two commanding
independent minds clashed like rapiers.

Boswell, who stayed on for a family supper, reports good wine,
food, and talk at Butler's dinner-table, where the eminent lawyer
Serjeant Marshall was present. Later in the evening the *émigré*
Bishop of Périgord, 'a lively little Frenchman', joined them. One
could wish, for Boswell's sake and our own, that it had been his
brilliant and wayward lordship of Autun instead; but Talleyrand-
Périgord, who had already apostasized and been excommuni-
cated by Pius VI, and did not return to his religion till he lay
dying nearly half a century later, would be no guest of Charles
Butler's during his brief London period as the Republic's envoy.
Of that very small proportion of the French clergy who managed
to emigrate to England from the Terror, Boswell seems to have

[1] He became a King's Counsel in 1832.

nown and helped at least one priest existing by giving French
essons. The majority of the *émigrés* in Holy Orders taught Latin
r French, lived on Catholic charity, or discreetly starved. A
ew were able to serve the new Catholic parishes, chiefly in
.ondon. In that still unharmed late-eighteenth-century back-
vater, Holly Place, Hampstead, a little church with a façade
f unaltered simplicity and grace remembers one of these exiles,
ie Abbé Morel.

So 1793 unrolled to its end, leaving Boswell no more unhappy
r happy on balance than any of its predecessors. The *Life* was
till selling briskly, the Mary Bryant affair had afforded him
uuch benevolent activity and gratification, and he had had a
ong, enjoyable quarrel in print with Miss Anna Seward, the
oetess, known to her admirers as the Swan of Lichfield. A foot-
ote in Malone's third edition of the *Life* refers any reader
ungry for details to *The Gentleman's Magazine,* Vols. LIII-
IV. A summary may amuse.

The squabble centred round *Verses to a Lady, on receiving
om her a Sprig of Myrtle,* composed by Johnson at Lichfield in
is youth. Miss Seward, a typically self-sufficient and overbear-
ig literary spinster, described by Miss Mitford as 'a sort of Dr.
)arwin in petticoats', had informed Boswell, while he was col-
ecting material concerning Johnson's early Lichfield days, that
ie knew the exact circumstances. Her written assurance was
mphatic enough to convince anyone.

*I know* those verses were addressed to Lucy Porter, when he
[ohnson] was enamoured of her in his boyish days, two or three years
efore he had seen her mother, his future wife. He wrote them at my
randfather's, and gave them to Lucy in the presence of my mother . . .
ie used to repeat them to me . . . We all know honest Lucy Porter
• have been incapable of the mean vanity of applying to herself a
ompliment *not intended* for her.

Boswell duly printed Miss Seward's information, which flatly
ontradicted the version given by Mrs. Thrale in her *Anecdotes,*
ccording to which Johnson told Mrs. Thrale that he wrote the
erses in five minutes for his friend Edmund Hector to give
omeone else for 'a girl he courted'. For once Mrs. Thrale turned
ut to be accurate. Hector himself confirmed this to Boswell in

January 1794, having discovered the original manuscript of th
verses by accident. They had been given by him, Hector, to
Mr. Morgan Graves for his lady-love in 1731, Johnson being
complete stranger to the Porter family at the time. Summing u
*The Gentleman's Magazine* controversy, Mr. Hector had
parting shot for Miss Seward.

If you intend to convince this obstinate woman, and to exhibit t
the publick the truth of your narrative, you are at liberty to make wha
use you please of this statement.

This annoyed the Swan of Lichfield considerably. She had
been sufficiently furious with Mr. Boswell already, for a footnot
in the *Life* treated with polite irony her 'beautifully imagined
reflections on a story of the infant Johnson's composing a four
line poem on a dead duck at the age of three, a fantasy derive
from Lucy Porter. Miss Seward's prophetic variations on th
dead duck theme, in flowing high-souled prose, had afforded he
considerable satisfaction, and her resentment was acrid. I woul
not recommend anyone desirous of entertainment to disturb th
dusty files of *The Gentleman's Magazine* on her account. A
Max Beerbohm has truly said, an author with a grievance is o
all God's creatures the most tedious, and Miss Seward, who wa
far from attractive, one gathers, in her most pleasing mood
had a very big grievance indeed, having supplied Mr. Boswel
with 'several sheets of paper' containing what she considere
to be priceless information. Boswell's retorts affect a strain o
heavily polite waggery almost as tiresome as the Swan o
Lichfield's song.

He was also engaged over the later half of this year in pre
paring the Third Edition of the *Life*, with further valuable nev
matter. In the preface to the Second Edition, which had com
out on July 1, he uttered that famous boast which was relativel
true: 'I have *Johnsonised* the land; and I trust they will not onl
*talk*, but *think*, Johnson.' A list of *Corrections and Additions* t
the First Edition was published simultaneously with the Second
The *Life* was recognised already as a master-work. I find i
impossible to believe that in his darkest depths of depressio
henceforth Boswell could forget this entirely.

He saw 1793 out at last, most enjoyably, at a great Roya

Academy banquet held on New Year's Eve to celebrate the
twenty-fifth anniversary of its foundation. George III was actively
interested, there was considerable fuss over the preparations, and
Boswell, as Secretary for Foreign Correspondence, took a full
share in the debates and made (says Farington) at least one very
good speech. The company was brilliant and the dinner, which
included woodcock, asparagus, and champagne, admirable. The
only flaw in the evening's entertainment, from the Boswellian
standpoint, was due to the musical enthusiasm of Benjamin West,
the reigning President and the only American, so far, to hold
that office. After the loyal toasts a harpsichord was dragged into
the middle of the banqueting-hall, forcing several of the company to give up their seats, and a regular recital began with
a concerto by three of the leading musical artists of the day,
Cramer, Shield, and Borghi, stopping all conversation and up-
setting Boswell and the other three-bottle men, 'the Grenadiers',
as a merry R.A. called them, considerably. However, after the
musicians and the fashionables had departed Boswell stayed on
to supper with an intimate half-dozen and welcomed in 1794
with bumpers, getting home none the worse (he says).

And so we come to the last full year of James Boswell's life.


6


There is, or was, a Borgia Legend. Owing to the amiable habit
of historians of copying from each other, it has taken some 400
years to explode. Funck-Brentano cleared the name of poor little
golden Lucrezia, perhaps the most slandered figure in history,
with impeccable evidence a few years ago, Alexander VI has
quite recently undergone scientific and surprising rehabilitation
at the hands of a free-thinking Italian scholar, Oreste Ferrara,
and bullnecked Cesare's turn is doubtless coming. Today it is
plain that the anti-Borgia libels of contemporary pamphleteers
and penny-a-liners, on which the consecrated Borgia Legend
was built, are almost pure fiction.

Though the Boswell Legend, with which we are now firmly
familiar, is not quite so rococo, its climax is likewise fantasy to
a large extent. Strong and upright men judging a weak, deplorable character have allowed the inexorable sanctions of Greek

drama to sway them imperceptibly, I think. For forty years Boswell drinks too much, is too fond of women, is mentally unstable, notoriously given to hypochondria, and a relative failure. He should therefore justly decline into a huddled alcoholic wreck brooding over a wasted life, hopeless, despised, diseased, a warning to all. I myself was tempted, *insanientis dum sapientiae consultus erro,* to accept this appropriate finale until I consulted the Isham documents for a more intimate view of inevitable deliquescence. Disconcertingly enough Boswell reveals himself, to the final entry in his diary, as the Boswell we have known all along; gay and gloomy, resolving and backsliding, drunk and sober, occasionally—though very rarely nowadays—slipping into lechery, groping desperately after better things, haunting church and tavern alike, hoping and dreaming; ridden, perhaps, a trifle oftener nowadays by the old black mental nightmare, but still able to shake it off; and—which is notable—dining out almost nightly, generally with the kind of hosts who would never have tolerated the Boswell of the legend.

His sprightly social versatility in these last fifteen months of his life continues, in fact, to be remarkable. To be the welcome guest within a few days of a Jewish peer and a Catholic leader argues at least that one's easy good-breeding and conversational gifts have not waned to any extent. Nor is Boswell any less of a public figure, in his own way. Sharing a hackney-coach with Benjamin West, P.R.A., on the way to dine at the Royal Academy Club in Gerrard Street one evening this January, he was delighted to hear that the King had put a finger on one of the signatures to the recent loyal anniversary address from the Academy, with the laughing remark, 'Boswell writes a very good hand for a Scotchman!' I do not know if this document is preserved. Is it possible that the signature was shaky, like a certain example in the Literary Club's attendance-book? Or was the Royal laugh called forth simply by that liking for the quaint Scots chatterbox which so many of George III's subjects shared?

There is further evidence of Boswell's continuing social status in his presence in March of this year, 1794, at the table of Dr. Beilby Porteus, Bishop of London, that courteous prelate of whom Thackeray remarks that his tears over George II's grave won him George III's lawn.

Dr. Porteus' other guests at Lambeth Palace that evening were Bennet Langton, Jacob Bryant, the antiquary, and the Rev. Clayton Cracherode, the classical scholar, bibliophile, and collector of rare editions of the classics, who left a library valued at £40,000 to the British Museum, of which he was a trustee. Boswell had met Dr. Porteus, then Bishop of Chester, at Langton's table as far back as 1778, and had been his guest once or twice already. There is no hint in his brief diary-note that anything resembling an orgy took place on this present occasion. It was the kind of dinner-party a wealthy bishop usually gives. One may picture a background of dignified opulence: lawnsleeved portraits against dark oak panelling; soft candlelight gleaming on massy silver candelabra, plate, and cutlery; sober-liveried menservants gliding over thick carpets under the eye of an impressive majordomo in black or purple with a huge cauliflower periwig, like Mr. Peters, butler to the Rev. Dr. Taylor; an even flow of mellow conversation. Bryant was noted for a quiet humour, Cracherode was the mildest of scholars, Langton the least turbulent of men, Porteus the most polished of prelates, even when expressing his antagonism to Catholic emancipation. The talk at the Bishop's table, unperturbed by whoopings, noisy jests, or song, and undefiled by lewdness, would be the exact antithesis of that Boswell had enjoyed two evenings previously at the table of Jack Wilkes, where some jolly fellows, including the head keeper of the wild animals at the Tower, the predecessor of the London Zoo, were present, and Boswell got very drunk.

He does not describe the dinner at Lambeth. If he had fallen backwards off his chair, or talked too loudly, or spilled wine from a shaking glass, or disgraced himself in any way, he would have recorded it, as he always did. I deduce that his behaviour was perfect and that he kept his end up, as we say nowadays, faultlessly; for if he was no great scholar he loved letters deeply and was an amusing talker and an admirable listener. My conclusion from this dinner-party, among so much other evidence, is that the Boswell of the coloured lantern-slides, the broken wreck drinking himself to death, is pure imagination. Mental and physical ravages of the kind he is credited with in some quarters during these two closing years could not be disguised, and one cannot see Langton taking a kind of Mr. Dolls [1] to dine at Lambeth.

This point conceded, I trust, we may note without undue surprise that the very next evening afterwards, at the Free-masons' Tavern in Great Queen Street, Boswell dined and wined copiously—his own word—in the jovial company of Richard Penn, Sir John Honeywood, a couple of Guardees, and some other good fellows. That this revel was a reaction from the strain of episcopal guesthood I do not doubt; but the fact still remains that Boswell was suitable, to the very end, to any kind of company, and that, like Bismarck, he drank but was not a drunkard.

The year 1794 had opened agreeably enough. Attending Chelms-ford Sessions the third week in January and supping with the Bar, Boswell went on to visit Langton, whose Militia regiment was exercising in the neighbourhood. Having watched manœuvres and dined with Langton he returned to town for a very special engagement, which I cannot view unmoved, so evocative is it of the long-vanished golden age of the English Inn. With Richard Penn and a few other hand-picked guests Boswell dined on February 4 at the London Tavern, Bishopsgate, with its celebrated landlord, Mr. Bleaden, once a waiter at White's. The London Tavern has long since been replaced by the less hospitable Royal Bank of Scotland. It was an imposing building, erected in 1768 on the site of an earlier tavern from the designs of Richard Jupp; in its basement West Indian turtles swam in tanks of sea-water, awaiting their green and glutinous destiny in the mutinous paunches of the City Livery companies, most of whom feasted there. Its kitchens and cellar had a reputation far beyond the City.

From a bill of fare to make a modern gourmet cry with frustration Mr. Bleaden's guests selected 'exquisite beefsteaks', game, an 'Omlet', and pastry, washed down with Madeira, sherry, old hock, burgundy, champagne, and port. Long before the end of an evening of song and merriment Boswell had passed out, in the modern idiom, waking next morning from 'total oblivion' to find himself in bed at Great Portland Street.

This same week his kind heart set him a tedious task once

[1] Vide *Our Mutual Friend*.

more. Three *émigrés* dined with him and his brother David on February 6; the Abbé Esnard, whom Boswell was helping apparently to obtain French lessons, a Vicomte d'Alzon, and a Chevalier de Fieulieux. Two days later a message imploring help came to Boswell from the Vicomte and the Chevalier. They had both been arrested, wrongfully, as it turned out, for debt at a tailor's suit and carried off to a sponging-house, helpless in a strange land. After a deal of trouble Boswell was able to get them released. 'Much satisfied with my benevolent exertions', he advised the Vicomte, for the honour of British Law, to bring an action for false imprisonment.

Another gratification eased his troubles this month. Confiding his ever-looming *tædium vitæ* to his benevolent, authoritative friend Joseph Farington, R.A., the landscape-painter, known as the Dictator of the Academy, after a 'joyous social day', he was greatly cheered to be told he had no real reason to complain and that his sacrifices for his children's sake were most laudable, as indeed they were. In a moment of critical self-examination afterwards he set down in his diary his chief cause for repining, which was plainly his thwarted hopes of attaining to consequence and wealth for his family's sake. On the other hand, he notes, he could soothe himself with 'my fame as a Writer' and with hopes in due course by careful management to pay off his debts and enlarge the Auchinleck estates. To indulge such hopes while living for preference more than four hundred miles away may seem curious, but Auchinleck was well managed, and Boswell never relaxed control. By the time the estate came to Sandie its income had, in fact, nearly doubled.

He penetrated into another fascinating new world this March, when Richard Penn gave a large, practically all-American dinner-party for the United States Minister, Thomas Pinckney. Pinckney, ex-Governor of South Carolina and a typical Southern aristocrat, was among those leaders of the American Revolution who had close British ties, a cosmopolitan culture, and a strong distaste for democracy. A sound Greek scholar of Westminster School and Christ Church, Oxford, he had been called to the English Bar before going to France to study strategy and tactics at the Royal Military Academy, Caen. Returning home to fight for the Revolution, he was severely wounded and taken prisoner by the British at Camden, New Jersey. His appointment by Washington as Minister to the Court of St. James's in 1792 was therefore almost inevitable. One feels it would have done Dr. Johnson a world of good to have been among Penn's guests that evening, for the Doctor, though officially an impossible jingo on the American question, was not implacable. His ritual roarings of 'traitors' and 'rebel dogs' had changed to gratified purrs on at least one occasion, when the Americans returned good for evil by printing *Rasselas*, and his letters to American admirers are politeness itself.

This same month a dinner at the Literary Club provoked Boswell, not for the first time in recent years, to yawns. The other members present were the Duke of Leeds, Lord Spencer, Lord Lucan, Dr. Burney, and Windham. 'It was not as in the days of Johnson. I drank liberally.' Three serious peers at table with no Johnson to inspire and rule the conversation may have been a trifle oppressive, and Boswell seems to have left most of the talk to the others. He had another House of Lords appeal on his mind. Perhaps he was mentally rehearsing the speech he delivered in Stewart v. Newnham, 'sufficiently well', in the week following. A little afterwards, quite suddenly, ambition leaped and flamed wildly. He perceived Corsica to be in need of him again, and we can sympathise with him. His great opportunity seemed to have come at last.

Much had happened in Corsica since the national hero's return in 1790, amid the affectionate enthusiasm of his fellow-countrymen, as Governor and Lieutenant-General under the French Monarchy. Following the triumph of the Terror and the execution of Louis XVI, Paoli had come up sharply against the fanatic island Jacobins, whose militant atheism and windy bragging and bloodlust he naturally could not endure. The majority of Corsicans shared their Governor's antagonism, and clashes became frequent. In May 1793 Paoli was denounced to the Convention in Paris and ordered to appear at its bar forthwith. He at once summoned the island Cortes and proclaimed Corsica in rebellion, not against France, but against the dominant terrorist clique. The Convention replied a month later by placing him *hors la loi*, and civil war immediately broke out in the island, with the turbulent and powerful Buonaparte clan, following the example of its most celebrated member, on the Jacobin side. In the next year Paoli, newly elected President and hard pressed, appealed, after expelling a number of Buonapartes, to London. A strong British force was despatched, Corsica was reduced and occupied, and the President and Cortes offered the island to the British Crown.

It is at this point that Mr. Boswell of Auchinleck, scanning the newspapers excitedly and hearing that a British administration for Corsica is to be set up, writes eagerly to Dundas, Secretary of State, on March 17 recalling his, Boswell's, long and intimate friendship with President Paoli and his well-known connection with Corsica and leading Corsicans in the past, and offering the Government his services as British Minister or Commissioner.[1]

Dundas' long Scotch upper lip curled, doubtless, as he flipped this communication aside. (That gomeral again!) The ensuing appointment of Sir Gilbert Elliot, first Earl of Minto, as Viceroy of Corsica inflicted a slight not only on Boswell, which was not very important, but on Paoli, which was; for Elliot on arrival selected Pozzo di Borgo as his principal adviser, and Paoli's position became difficult. The British Government solved this problem in due course by inviting Paoli to return to England as its guest; and though the news caused immediate riots all over the island, Paoli, now in his seventieth year, weary with age, inhibited by courtesy and patriotism alike from any desire to make trouble, acquiesced with dignity. Arriving in England shortly after Boswell's death, he resumed his Government pension and his place in London society and died, full of years and honour, in 1807, one of the noble figures of history, as his adversary Napoleon admitted. It is not unnatural that in his native island Paoli's memory is overshadowed today by the Napoleon-Cultus, more profitable to the tourist industry.[2]

The Corsican impulse was Boswell's final flutter. At long last

[1] He showed the letter beforehand to Sir John Dick, who approved it.
[2] In 1795 Napoleon retook Corsica, and after a brief re-occupation by British troops in 1814 it was restored to France a year later. Paoli's remains were exhumed from the old Catholic cemetery of St. Pancras in 1889 and returned. There is a cenotaph, with a Flaxman bust, in the south aisle of Westminster Abbey.

he seems to have realised that neither Dundas, nor Pitt, nor Burke, nor anyone in high places had the least intention of helping him to any public career whatsoever. Whether he realised equally his entire unfitness for such things, who can say? The traditional comedian who yearns to dazzle the world as Hamlet is perennial. Boswell may have imposed on himself so long that he died believing himself hardly used by the politicians. If he did not, if in a last clairvoyant moment he grasped this final truth about James Boswell, it remains a secret shared by Boswell with God alone.

This crowning disappointment was undoubtedly severe, and deprived life of its savour for some weeks. Boswell notes this spring with listless melancholy that he has lost the faculty of recording conversations—'or perhaps I have seen and heard so much now that no conversation impresses me'; which is quite likely, since he had been satiated with the most brilliant talk in London for the past thirty years. But his spirits revive before long, and life goes on as usual. He dines frequently with his learned brethren at Old Bailey, and has begun to attend Portland Chapel regularly. His old friend Dr. Douglas, Bishop of Salisbury, is in town—his lordship of the suave manner and the 'sly glistening look' was frequently in town—and he dines with him, with Sir Grey Cowper, with Malone, with Sir Joseph Banks, President of the Royal Society, and with Daines Barrington, part of whose long correspondence with White of Selborne has lately been merged into the notable English classic he is said to have inspired.[1]

The Isham Papers break off abruptly, for good, with the entry of Saturday, April 12, 1794, when Boswell dined with Dilly and Miss Dilly and spent a pleasant evening with his friend George Dance, R.A., who had drawn his portrait the year before. News of him for the next few months is relatively scrappy, and derived

---

[1] *The Natural History and Antiquities of Selborne, in the County of Southampton*, containing 44 letters to Thomas Pennant and 66 to Daines Barrington, with engravings, was published by the Rev. Gilbert White in 1789. As readers of Lamb are aware, Barrington in old age tried to bribe the Temple gardener to poison all the Temple sparrows; a peculiar development for White's friend.

mainly from indirect sources. On May 31 he wrote to Temple,
advising him in Dilly's behalf that a sermon and other collected
writings against the Terror in France would not sell, the British
market being at saturation-point. The letter winds to its end with
a refrain, already quoted in part in an early page of this book,
which we could now, like most of Boswell's intimates, recite
by heart.

I thank you sincerely for your friendly admonition on my frailty in
indulging so much in wine. I *do* resolve *anew* to be on my guard, as
I am sensible how very pernicious as well as disreputable such a
habit is. How miserably have I yielded to it in various years! Recollect
what General Paoli said to you,—recollect what happened at Berwick.

What Paoli said, what happened at Berwick, are not known,
but may be easily conjectured. 'His intemperance for some
months before he died', wrote Farington rather priggishly in
1796, 'I imputed to a species of insanity.'

On June 14, with Farington, Boswell attended one of the
current hearings of the Warren Hastings trial, now dragging to
its weary close and long since devoid of those enjoyable sensations of the early days, when Burke and Fox stormed and
thundered, and Sheridan fell backwards with admirable timing
into Burke's arms after a superb four days' performance, and
fine ladies sobbed and screamed, and Mrs. Siddons was carried
out in a swoon and Mrs. Sheridan in a fit. By June 1794 the
fireworks had become few and unexciting. 'Burke very dull and
tedious', notes Farington. 'Abusive without wit or entertainment.'
The 'managers', Burke, Francis, and Windham, were replying
to the defence, tributes to Hastings from India, European and
native, were still coming in, and the acquittal ten months hence
was probably already a foregone conclusion, as Farington hints,
despite what Lord Rosebery calls 'the undying rancour of Francis
['Junius'] and the sleepless humanity of Burke.' [1] Boswell,
scenting his hero's coming triumph, may have rejoiced.

Early in July he went up to Auchinleck again, as a wine-
cellar inventory in his writing reveals. He was still at Auchinleck

[1] An M.P. named Nichols accounted to Farington for Burke's inflexibility
by the fact that Hastings prevented Burke's son 'from being in effect
Rajah of Tanjore'. Lobby gossip, doubtless.

in October, when he wrote to his brother David in Great Titchfield Street a letter steeped in gloom. Although Veronica and Euphemia were with him, and receiving a fair amount of cheerful company, and though he was busily occupied with estate business, he was in the depths of unhappiness and longing for London, as usual. 'How hard it is', he cries to David, 'that I do not enjoy this fine place!' And he complains of being able to expect nowadays 'only temporary alleviation of misery, and some gleams of enjoyment.' Did David Boswell take this wail seriously? He had, like Temple, heard it five hundred times before. It began, as we know, in the 1750's, and had been a recurring *motif* in the Boswellian symphony ever since. It may be noted that the letter to David is chiefly concerned with the payment of Mary Bryant's 'gratuity' out of Boswell's own pocket.

He was back in London early in 1795, and plunged at once into diversion, giving a large dinner-party on March 4, at which the guests were Malone, Lord Delaval, Count Castenau, Farington, Sir William Wolsely, Colonel St. Paul, Captain Lee of the Life Guards, Osborne, ex-British Minister at Dresden, and Major Wynyard, hero of a celebrated psychic experience on which Boswell would naturally be delighted to cross-examine him 'as Johnson taught me.' [1] The two elder Misses Boswell and young Mr. James were also of this party.

We catch another glimpse of their father in a letter of March, gallantly assuring the Countess of Orkney that he will be pleased to wait on her ladyship at Cliefden 'whenever you let me know that I may come', and again in April, when he writes to Malone protesting against the Rev. Dr. Samuel Parr's cool attempt to foist his Latin epitaph for the Johnson Monument on the Memorial Committee of the Literary Club without criticism.

---

[1] While in barracks with their regiment at Halifax, Nova Scotia, in 1785, Major Wynyard and his colonel, Sherbrooke, claimed to have been visited by an apparition of Wynyard's brother John, who died in London that very day and hour. Boswell, ever interested in the supernatural, discussed the case exhaustively with his friends. Reynolds and Malone were sceptical; Courtenay, an agnostic, was inclined to accept the story; Langton suggested a practical joke. Summing up to Temple in March 1789, after discussing the matter with him in two letters, Boswell declares, 'For my part, I have no difficulty in believing the story to be supernaturally true'; which has exposed him to a few more gibes from enemies past and present.

And then, on April 13, an entry in Farington's diary affords us a distinct view of him at last.

Boswell this day attended the Literary Club, and went from thence too ill to walk home. He went out no more.

The end was now approaching. That superb Boswellian constitution which had defied nearly forty intensive years of the bottle was breaking—had broken—down at last. Barring normal reactions from drinking-bouts and some recurring evidence of an indisposition connected with his other favourite pastime (though the mercury-pills he confided in may have been chiefly a prophylactic, for he was intensely nervous on this question, and he could not have gone on drinking as he did if anything serious had befallen him), Boswell had never suffered any illness or been bedridden in his life. His freedom from gout is above all extraordinary. While all around him crippled ex-boon-companions were languishing at home on gruel, or awaking public pity like the bandaged Pitt agonising in the Commons, he ignored this major scourge of every disciple of Anacreon with magnificent aplomb.

A day or two after the collapse at the Club, Temple, himself recovering from shock and injuries in a riding accident, received his last letter from his indefatigable correspondent, confidant, and penitent. The first sentence, written by Boswell himself, is barely legible.

My dear Temple,—I would fain write to you in my own hand, but really cannot. Alas, my friend, what a state is this! My son James is to write for me what remains of this letter, and I am to dictate. The pain which continued for so many weeks was very severe indeed, and when it went off I thought myself quite well; but I soon felt a conviction that I was by no means as I should be—so exceedingly weak, as my miserable attempt to write to you afforded a full proof. All then that can be said is, that I must wait with patience.

But O, my friend! how strange is it that, at this very time of my illness, you and Miss Temple should have been in such a dangerous state. Much occasion for thankfulness is there that it has not been worse with you. Pray write, or make somebody write, frequently. I feel myself a good deal stronger to-day, notwithstanding the scrawl. God bless you, my dear Temple! I ever am your old and affectionate friend, here and I trust hereafter.                    JAMES BOSWELL.

To this Jamie added a private and significant postscript:

Dear Sir,—You will find by the foregoing, the whole (*sic*) of which was dictated by my father, that he is ignorant of the dangerous situation in which he was, and, I am sorry to say, still continues to be. Yesterday and to-day he has been somewhat better, and we trust that the nourishment which he is now able to take, and his strong constitution, will support him through.

I remain, with respect,

JAMES BOSWELL, Jr.

The mysterious 'pain of so many weeks' was due, as will appear, to a growing tumour on the bladder. From the meagre evidence available a Harley Street specialist has diagnosed for me in addition uraemia, or kidney-trouble. Farington reasonably remarks of the Duke of Leeds, who died of the same kind of tumour, that, as with Boswell, his disorder attacked his weakest part.

Almost immediately Jamie reported to Temple that his father was much better. The pain had gone, and the greatest care was being taken of him by his friend, Dr. Warren—Warren of the Literary Club, Physician to the King—assisted by Mr. Earle the surgeon, Mr. Devaynes the apothecary, and Mr. Kingston. A few days later came a relapse, with fever, severe shivering, violent headache, stomach disorder, and vomiting. 'He thinks himself better today, but cannot conjecture when he shall recover. His affection for you remains the same. You will receive a long and full letter from him.'

This letter was never written, though Boswell had recovered sufficiently by April 24, stimulated by a too-optimistic conjecture of Warren's, to dictate a brief note in his old dashing 'spirited' style to Warren Hastings, congratulating him on his acquittal (twenty-three votes to six) by the Lords in Westminster Hall the day before, after a trial spread over seven years and costing Hastings £70,000. 'The moment I am able to go abroad, I will fly to Mr. Hastings and expand my soul in the purest satisfaction.' Alas, ten days later David Boswell had grave news for Temple. 'I am sorry to say my poor brother is in the most imminent danger; a swelling in his bladder has mortified, but he is yet alive, and God Almighty may restore him to us.' Another ten days dragged on and Jamie wrote again, sombrely. His father was considerably worse; much weaker, more vomiting. Feeling better one day, wishing to leave his bed, and being lifted out with the surgeon's consent, he had fainted away. 'Since that he has been in a very bad way indeed, and there are now, I fear, little or no hopes of his recovery.'

> Miserere, Judex meus,
> Mortis in discrimine.

The end had come. Round Boswell's bed hung his brother David, his sons Alexander and James, and his daughters Veronica, on whom the main burden of his nursing had fallen, and Euphemia. His final visitors we do not know, nor what spiritual viaticum he received at the last, and the matter, since it probably decided his fate for all eternity, is naturally of no great interest to modern critics. But we have it on the authority of an obscure Scots friend and admirer, the Rev. Samuel Martin of Monimail, who regarded Boswell with 'affectionate concern and respect', deploring his lifelong strayings from the twin paths of Presbyterianism and Whiggery, that 'at the end prayer was his stay'. It could hardly be otherwise with one who had managed to keep faith alight under a bushel of follies. He died, Malone said, without pain or effort.

On May 19 David Boswell conveyed the last news to Temple, with an aspiration for the departed soul which may have been a memory of his long residence in Spain.

I have now the painful task of informing you that my dear brother expired this morning at two o'clock. We have both lost a kind, affectionate friend, and I shall never have such another. He has suffered a great deal during his illness, which has lasted five weeks, but not much in his last moments. May God Almighty have mercy upon his soul, and receive him into His heavenly kingdom.

He is to be buried at Auchinleck, for which place his two sons will set out in two or three days. They and his two eldest daughters have behaved in a most affectionate, exemplary manner during his confinement; they all desire to be kindly remembered to you, and Miss Temple, and beg your sympathy on this melancholy occasion.

So the mortal part of James Boswell set out on his last and most expensive journey—costing £250—along that Great North

Road he had so often travelled, and his coffin, on its way to the family vault, lay overnight at more than one inn where his roving eye and bustling meddlesome kindliness were well known. His papers, apart from that mass of MSS. locked away in the Kincardine ebony cabinet and acquired 130 years later by Colonel Isham, were left to Malone. They included a bundle of newspaper-clippings, 'probably intended', thinks Farington, 'for some purpose he had schemed.' Whether this scheme was the Life of Reynolds, one of many literary projects toyed with of late years, I cannot tell. His will, nobly feudal, left an estate of more than £2,000 a year to Sandie, the new laird, £150 a year to Jamie, and £100 a year apiece to the three girls, with shares in a £500 bequest to Veronica in addition. Lord Auchinleck's grim widow was left an annuity of £400.

The obituary notice in *The Gentleman's Magazine* was full and generous. 'His enemies', said the anonymous writer, believed to be Chalmers, 'are welcome, if they please, to dwell on his failings. Of these he had not many, and they were injurious to no person. It does not seem to me that he ever did, or could, injure any human being intentionally.' Which is all true enough, and his enemies certainly have dwelt on his failings ever since, with great gusto and exclusivity.

It is to be hoped that the attempt to restore a decent balance in these pages has succeeded sufficiently to make any more comment on this complex, trying, lovable, intensely human character a waste of words. Most men display themselves to the world carefully posed, like a studio-photograph. Boswell carelessly exhibited an X-ray film, and the world cannot forgive this crudeness. It disturbs the rapt self-worship of fools who deny the Fall.

7

Visitors to St. Paul's Cathedral, London, can hardly avoid being instantly impressed by one in particular of those colossal marble statues under the Dome which at a first glance might almost be mistaken for the statues of saints and apostles one finds abroad. The striking monument to Dr. Samuel Johnson, carved by John Bacon, R.A., was erected by public subscription,

under the auspices of the Literary Club, in the early part of
1796, at the considerable cost of eleven hundred guineas, towards
which Mrs. Thrale-Piozzi subscribed two. It represents the
Doctor, curly-haired, half-naked in a Roman toga, a kind of
Orson with enormous muscular thews and a brooding, menacing
expression, leaning against a pillar, one vast elbow propped on
a scroll inscribed in cursive Greek capitals. The whole conveys
a remarkable suggestion, if I may be excused this flippancy, of a
gladiator at the Games who has received disturbing news from
home. One feels strongly that the Memorial Committee would
have been wiser to employ Flaxman, who carved the Reynolds
statue adjacent, or even Nollekens, whose most rococo inspiration
might have done the Doctor more justice. Underneath Bacon's
figure is the Latin epitaph composed at the Memorial Committee's invitation by the Rev. Dr. Samuel Parr, that eminent
Harrovian classic, who was seized with confusion and dismay
(though he later became somewhat stiff and conceited) when
he reflected on 'the confined and difficult species of composition
in which alone they [Johnson's attainments] can be expressed
with propriety upon his monument.' The result seems hardly
to justify the fuss. Better memorial Latin, unless I err, was
written by Jacques Tournebroche for the Abbé Coignard.

There is not the smallest memorial to James Boswell in Westminster Abbey, where so many periwigged mediocrities posture
and gesticulate from their tombs in bronze and marble, tempting
Heaven with their arrogance. I think the Renaissance would
have accorded him at least a votive tablet, if not a *tombeau* of
verse-offerings by friendly hands, though he himself erected a
memorial more enduring. Musing on these things, I have toyed
with the pleasing fancy of venturing to supply the deficiency
with an imaginary Boswell Monument embodying a sonorous
epitaph in the taste of his age, in which any lack of academic
polish should be compensated by strong affection.

The reader is invited, then, to imagine a complicated and
towering funereal confection in marble in the style of Nollekens
or Roubiliac, surmounted by the figures of Britannia and Literature weeping over a large oval medallion of bronze, draped and
laurelled, framing the Boswell profile, somewhat idealised, in
*basso-relievo*. Underneath, on a sarcophagus shaped like a

tea-caddy, is the Boswell crest of the hooded hawk with the motto, *Vraye Foy,* over an epitaph deeply chiselled as follows:

D.O.M.

Siste, viator!
Si humani generis fragilitatis,
Si carnis peccatorum Bacchique orgiorum,
Vel sitis potentiae puerilis,
Vel omnis vanitatis
Unquam misericordia es commotus,
Custodi paululum memoria
JACOBUM BOSWELL, Armigerum,
Dom: Auchinlech: in Comitat: Ayr:
Virum plurimis infirmitatibus,
Quae in homine inveniri possint,
Valde praeditum;
Potatorem, moechum, advocatum; verbo stylique garrulitate
intemperantem,
Animi levitatis tanquam speculi;
Quae omnia tibi, viatori probo,
(Proh pudor!)
Invisa sunt.
His stultitiis addidit per totam vitam
Auream misericordiam,
Bonitatem quae vere absurda saeculo huic videretur,
Simplicitatem atque animi candorem ignobiles,
Fidem obstinatam,
Sanctitatis desiderationem libidine saepius expulsam, tamen
usque recurrentem;
Reliquit Litterarum Reipublicae
Monumentum praeclarissimum.
Morte acerba raptus, eheu!
(Nec defuit vero poenitentia nec Christi spes)
Anno aetatis quinquagesimo quinto,
In patria jacet sepultus.
Cujus animam de morte aeterna libera, Domine!

That is to say:

To the Glory of God.
Stay, traveller!
If thou has ever been moved by pity for human weakness,
For fleshly sins and the lures of Bacchus,

For a childish thirst for preferment,
For vanity of every kind,
        Ponder a moment the memory
                of
        JAMES BOSWELL, Esquire,
Laird of Auchinleck in the County of Ayr,
    A man largely adorned by most of the infirmities
        To be found in human kind;
Bibber, lecher, lawyer; of uncontrolled garrulity alike in word
                and pen,
        A mirror of frivolity:
    All of which things to thee, upright traveller,
        (O, shame!)
        Are anathema.

To these follies he added throughout his life
    A golden charity,
    A kindness which to this age will seem indeed absurd,
    A foolish simplicity and candour,
    A steadfast faith,
A longing for goodness, too often expelled by the flesh, yet ever
                returning;
He bequeathed to the Republic of Letters
    A monument of extreme splendour.
        Rapt away, alas! by inexorable Death
    (Not without penitence, indeed, nor hope in Christ),
        In the 55th year of his age,
        He lies buried in his own land.
Whose soul deliver, O Lord, from eternal doom!

:—:   END   :—:

# Appendix

---

## A NOTE ON HEREDITY

'Heredity', announced Zola in the 1870's, 'has its laws, like gravity.'
On this attractive theory, derived from the latest dogma of Claude
Bernard and other scientific pontiffs of the moment, Zola, a typical
materialist *primaire,* as Léon Daudet said, proceeded to erect the
twelve novels of the Rougon-Marquart cycle, a study of the offspring
of a drunkard and a lunatic and the purest arbitrary rubbish. Science
today admits heredity to be a problem of extreme complexity and
by no means easily comprehensible. One is therefore not unduly
surprised to find the unstable and dissolute Boswell's sons, inbred from
a tubercular mother and deriving from stock with a 'mental' streak in
it, developing into sober, healthy men of substance and distinction,
and only one of his family—Euphemia, the second daughter—manifest-
ing any eccentricity whatsover, and that late, and of the mildest.

I am indebted to Dr. Halliday Sutherland for a diagram showing
the transmission of qualities through the generations. The first sixteen
letters of the alphabet are here deemed to be married in pairs, the
subsequent generations being shown alternatively in 'lower case' and
capital letters, the 'lower case' letters transmitting qualities denoted
by the capitals, and vice-versa.

```
A-B C-D E-F  G-H I-J  K-L M-N O-P    (Great-great-grandparents)
 |   |   |    |   |    |   |   |
ab - cd  ef - gh  ij - kl  mn - op     (Great-grandparents)
     |        |        |        |
ABCD——EFGH        IJKL——MNOP           (Grandparents)
   |                   |
   abcdefgh————————ijklmnop            (Parents)
              |
         ABCDEFGHIJKLMNOP              (Child)
```

'Biologically', explains Dr. Sutherland, 'an individual has no parents, but four grandparents and sixteen great-great-grandparents. This means that a child inherits through its parents the qualities of its grandparents, and through its great-grandparents the qualities of its great-great-grandparents. If you take the last individual on the chart to be Boswell, for example, you might be able to know from which generation any weakness was inherited. But this is not quite so simple as it seems, because if in a family there were two similar taints, then of course each generation would show the same taint. The man who wrote the Book of Exodus knew as much as we do when he said that a taint is transmitted to the third and fourth generation. Thereafter it disappears.'

With this preliminary clearing of the ground we may proceed to glance at Boswell's offspring.

Alexander (Sandie), whom his father had intended for the Bar, via Utrecht and Edinburgh, discarded this plan on becoming Laird of Auchinleck in 1795, travelled a year in Germany, and translated some German verse in such a fashion as to win warm praise from Walter Scott, whose lifelong friend he became after serving as an officer in the same Militia cavalry regiment in 1797. Under Scott's influence Sandie betook himself—thanks to his father's self-sacrifice he could afford such luxuries, apart from 'his carriage and four, his hounds, and his racehorses', as his sister Euphemia told Farington—seriously to poetry, and published a collection of original Scots-dialect verse in the manner of Allan Ramsay and Burns, whom he adored. In 1815 he turned dilettante, antiquary, and typographer, like Horace Walpole, setting up a private press at Auchinleck, the *Officina Typographica Straminia*, and issuing a sequence of late-medieval and Renaissance reprints, many from his grandfather's library, of obscure but interesting Scottish authors. In 1818, having become Laureate of the Harveian Club and a leading member of the Roxburghe, having almost single-handed brought about the erection of the Burns Memorial on the Doon, and having published more original verse, this time in the manner of Scott, Sandie sat in Parliament for Plympton, Devon, till 1820. In 1821 George IV created him a baronet. He married, in the tribal Boswell fashion, one of the Montgomeries of Lainshaw, his mother's clan, and had several children. Scott and Lockhart, among others, speak warmly of Sir Alexander Boswell's culture, literary ardour, high spirits, and frank and jovial charm. In March 1822, following attacks by him and others of Scott's friends on James Stuart of Dunearn in Glasgow journals, Sir Alexander was called out by Stuart. In the ensuing duel, with Lord Queensberry's heir as his second, he was shot through the collarbone and, to the distress of

Walter Scott, who bore some responsibility in the affair, died next day at Balmuto, the ancestral Boswell home. He is buried at Auchinleck. It may be noted that Sandie's physical vigour, like his mental, was well above the average. He was a strapping, muscular figure, devoted to field-sports, as boisterous at times as his father, at times a trifle overbearing. His son James, second and last baronet, continued the Boswell line with a couple of daughters.

James (Jamie), Boswell's second son, a more sedate type, took his M.A. degree at Oxford, was elected a Fellow of Brasenose and called to the Bar, and in 1805 was appointed a Commissioner in Bankruptcy. A promising legal career thus begun, he turned, like Sandie, to literature. Having, while still an undergraduate, contributed the notes signed 'J.B.O.' to Malone's third edition (1799) of Boswell's *Life of Johnson*, Jamie became Malone's and Walter Scott's intimate, edited the sixth edition of his father's work himself, completed the second edition of Malone's great critical Shakespeare after Malone's death, and in 1821 edited the 'Third Variorum' Shakespeare in 21 volumes. He died, unmarried and in debt, in his Temple chambers a few weeks before Sandie's fatal duel. Lockhart awards him considerable Shakespearean scholarship and admirable social gifts. A member of the Roxburghe Club, Jamie inherited, like his brother, the paternal gift for light convivial lyrics, and, also like his brother, none of the bacchic paternal weaknesses which had accompanied it.

Veronica Boswell, infected after birth, like her mother, with tuberculosis, which is not inheritable, died at the age of twenty-three in October 1795, five months after her father, of rapid consumption, accelerated apparently by a strain incurred while helping to lift him in his last illness. I find it difficult to agree with a modern critic weeping over Veronica's tomb that she perished a meek and heart-broken victim to paternal degradation and filial duty, fading out like a 'Keepsake' heroine of the 1840's. Boswell himself has shown us that Veronica was a decidedly aggressive type, apt to defy and domineer, though possessing, like himself, an affectionate heart.

As for Euphemia, she was healthy enough, and the keen eye of Joseph Farington, who called on her in Edinburgh in September 1801, noted no eccentricity of any kind. During a long talk on her father, of whom she spoke with strong affection, her elder brother, whose abilities she admired, and her family generally, Euphemia nevertheless revealed, in a slightly acid remark on the continuance of the Feudal System and 'the sacrifices which custom makes of the younger children, who are educated as gentlemen and gentlewomen, and left with pittances only to support those characters', what was to become an obsession before long. Having cut herself off with her

£ 100 a year from the family at length to write opera (she said), she began addressing financial appeals to her friends and acquaintance, under the delusion that her relations were leaving her in want. She died, unmarried, at the age of sixty.

Elizabeth (Betsy), who was normal enough, followed the Boswell tradition by marrying a cousin, William, in 1799, and died in 1814.

# INDEX